Designer's Guide to

SURFACES AND FINISHES

Designer's Guide to

SURFACES AND FINISHES

Penny Radford

WHITNEY

A QUILL BOOK

Copyright © 1984 Quill Publishing Limited
First published 1984 in the United States by the
Whitney Library of Design
an imprint of Watson-Guptill Publications, a division of Billboard
Publications, Inc., 1515 Broadway, New York, NY 10036

First published in paperback in 1991

ISBN 0-8230-1311-1

This book was designed and produced by
Quill Publishng Limited
6 Blundell Street
London N7 9BH

Art direction and design Nigel Osborne
Editorial director Christopher Fagg
Senior editor Liz Wilhide
Project editor Sabina Goodchild
Editorial assistants Deidre McGarry Michelle Newton
Design assistant Carol McCleeve
Paste-up Elaine Cappi Mick Pacey
Illustrator Ray Brown
Picture research Keith Bernstein
Photography John Heseltine Ian Howes Jon Wyand

Filmset by Leaper & Gard, Bristol
Origination by Hong Kong Graphic Arts Service Centre Limited, Hong Kong
Printed in Hong Kong

In one way this is a very specialist book. In other ways, it's very definitely not. It's specialized in that it focuses on simply one aspect of interior design, what you might call 'the lining of the box'. On the other hand, it does it exhaustively, covering in words and pictures just about every practicable surface or finish you might conceivably want to put on a ceiling, a wall or a floor and how to put them there. The reasoning behind this approach is simple. Whether you're starting from scratch in a brand new first home, taking the treasured collections of a lifetime to a new environment, or simply piling your possessions in the middle of the room where they've already established their territory and redecorating round them, the basic box that you're about to blitz is more than merely a backdrop for the furniture. It is, instead, the scene in which that furniture is set — and there's no question which plays the leading role. Remove all the furniture from a beautifully decorated room and the room would still look beautiful. Indeed, it might look even more so, since most of us tend to over- rather than under-furnish. On the other hand, no amount of splendid, carefully selected, old or new furniture and accessories can rescue a room whose surface treatments are inappropriate or in disrepair.

So, first things first: choosing and using the right surfaces and finishes is what this book is about. This is seldom done in isolation, of course, because you can't disregard the demands made by the colour, style and scale of what you already own. Sometimes, the challenge of finding an acceptable compromise between old and new can be more exciting than having an absolutely free hand, and having some real limitations can even be a relief when, otherwise, the options seem dauntingly limitless. But if you are starting out, or starting over, and there's a battle for the budget between decoration and furniture, forget the furniture — at least for now. It's surprising how little you really need beyond the basics: a stove, fridge, table, bed and bedlinen, one frying pan, saucepan, kitchen knife, wooden spoon and a couple of chairs, plates, cups, knives, forks and spoons will get you a long, long way. This needn't even rule out entertaining if you use disposable or, better still — and cheaper — get guests to bring their own eating equipment and sit them on the floor. But give them a good floor to sit on, make it the best you can afford and frame it with freshly finished walls and woodwork. As for you, the owners, the morale boost you'll get from living with clean, new surfaces will make up a thousand-fold for the temporary absence of the 'extras' and give you the willpower to wait until, with these too, you can have what you really want instead of settling for second best.

However, just as there's a huge difference between furniture that's simply shabby and beautiful or old, cared-for pieces whose age is part of their charm, so there's a difference between showing up and showing off. If a room is to be the setting for its contents, it must also be appropriate to them - and that, too, is what this book is about. New, or newly decorated, surfaces needn't, actually, shouldn't, shout their newness at you with the kind of brittle brightness that's most commonly the result of a couple of coats of cheap emulsion and one of gloss paint. What you're aiming for is a set of surfaces which suit the room and its contents so well that, even *if they were finished yesterday, they look as though they belonged and had always been there; the room's personality feels as though it just grew rather than as if it had had its decorative character disciplined into it. How do you get this effect? I believe it comes from combining quality of workmanship with subtlety of choice: properly prepared finishes that are thickly matt, have a perfect, smooth sheen or whose gloss has the depth that comes from patiently repeated coats of varnish; color so carefully selected and blended that they seem natural companions, even in contrast; surfaces which progress harmoniously through a sequence of textures, whether three-dimensional or merely 'distressed', as in some of the broken-color paint techniques; patterns which are so right for their position and so meticulously applied that, instead of seeming like a superficial addition, they instantly become an integral part of the background. But subtle doesn't mean wishy-washy — it's strength not weakness, courage not cowardice; it is, if you like, assertive not defensive decorating and it leaves room for all sorts of stylistic expressions from elegant understatement to high drama.*

There's no such thing as an ugly room, only one which hasn't yet been allowed — or persuaded — to realize its potential. Rooms, like people, are seldom perfect, but if you have 'eyes to hear', most of them can actually tell you what's wrong with them and how to put it right. Walk round the room, look at it from different angles (and especially from the doorway) and ask yourself: Is the room too long for its width, the ceiling too high or low for its size? Do the windows dominate it because they're too big, too tall or too many, or are there only one or two small windows, inserted like peepholes in a large flank of wall? How symmetrical is their positioning, are they at an awkward height? Which way do they face — do they get cold light from the north, bright, early-morning light from the east, full sunlight from the south or the warm, late-afternoon glow from the west? Ask predominantly the same questions about doors (except, obviously, those concerning light): Is there just one doorway or a scattering of them — and are these positioned symmetrically enough to make a feature of them or would it be better if they 'disappeared' into the wall? Are they attractive in themselves or what could be done to make them so? Then look at the room again as a whole. Are alcoves or extrusions of similar depth and equally balanced or are the wall surfaces a maze of odd planes and angles and how do they affect the proportions of the room? Do any need to be emphasized to help the rooms' depth or minimized by filling them with shelves or closing them off with cupboard doors?

It is, of course, impossible to provide a recipe for an unseen room, but if you examine each of its features in turn you will easily see which of them work in favor of the room as a whole and which work against it. In decorating the room you will want to minimize its less attractive features, make the most of its good points and aim to integrate the various surfaces so that you achieve an overall feeling of balance. Many of the problems you'll come across are illustrated, along with their solutions, on the next few pages and, as you'll see, a 'problem' which is cracked creatively can often become a positive benefit.

INTRODUCTION

We are influenced by what we see and touch just as much as by what we hear, taste or smell, yet most of us are less aware of how and why our surroundings make us feel good or bad than of the way we react to stimuli of our other senses. Decoration is the imagination, the eye and the touch; it is sensual as well as visual expression. If you can create an environment that not only looks good but feels good, there is no doubt that it will do you good, too.

COLOR

Color is what makes a room bright or dark, cheerful or depressing, stark or comfortable, warm or cold, soothing or stimulating, elegant, dramatic or playful. Color is light and mood, ambience and style.

It doesn't surprise me in the slightest that so many people lack confidence in using color — or that so many people get it wrong. It's pretty hard to feel confident about working with a medium when you don't understand what it does or why, so I shall try to make that aspect of color a little clearer. But apart from that, I think the reason for getting it 'wrong' is more often than not the result of trying too hard to get it 'right'. Color is to do with feeling, perception and instinct, qualities we all possess, but which

we have been conditioned into rejecting as reliable bases for decision-making. We're taught, instead, that making sound choices can come only out of logical, analytical and objective thought. I cannot imagine a less sound method of planning a color scheme than to regard it as an intellectual exercise. Of course, there are practical considerations, like how many liters of this and how many rolls of that and will the dog hairs show on the other, and there are aids and accessories to working with color. But, above all, trust your own taste and judgement. What you instinctively react to, positively or negatively, and the way you feel about what you see is not just a good enough reason for making visual decisions, but quite possibly the only good reason for doing so.

Far left Stark in contrast but not stark in atmosphere; white dominates here, making space in a narrow galley kitchen, with bright poppy for some cheerful detailing.

Center Analyze this room and you'll realize that the basic color scheme is a fairly plain white-and-cream, but it's the treatment of the various surfaces which make them, and the room, interesting. Texture plays as important a part as colour — the carpet's sculpted stripes, the louvered panels, the quilted covers — and it takes only the smallest injection of color and pattern in the bold, large-scale, maroon-and-black squiggles to bring the room to life.

Left Muted colors and patterns which are sympathetic in shape and scale make a mellow mixture. This scheme is surprisingly easy on the eye, despite the number of different ingredients, but if you examine each element carefully and in comparison with those around it, you'll find that there are linking factors, in both color and design, between them all.

Above Imagine the fun the designer had with a palette of colors, putting together this collection of co-ordinating fabrics.
Above right Here the drama comes from the difference in tone and intensity of the various adjacent blues, as much as from the designer's courage in taking wavy, horizontal stripes round the walls.

This is not to say simply 'You're on your own', or that there's nothing to learn. Look around you for inspiration in shaping your color sense — there's nothing shameful about borrowing. Most professional decorators' work would be the poorer, as would mine, without other peoples' imaginations to act as sharpening stones for their own. But what we grow to is a style which is individual to us because what we inevitably add — as you will, even if you don't realize it immediately — is a blend, a balance, a flavor which is uniquely our own.

Professionals also have learned knowledge about color and its behavior, both in a pure and an applied sense. For the amateur, the basic principles are easy and quick enough to grasp and are all you really need to achieve what you want from color in home decoration. For example, the 'purity' of a color usually refers to its strength or intensity. The colors of the rainbow, including the three primaries, red, yellow and blue, are all pure colors, undiluted by any other hue (simply another word for color) or by white or black, which would weaken their purity. Strictly speaking, the lightening of a color with white or darkening with black are referred to respectively as 'tints' and 'shades' of the original color, although both these terms have come to be used very loosely, and 'tone', 'tonal value' or 'value' are all used to describe the *level* of lightness or darkness of the color. Tone is probably one of the most useful concepts for the practical side of decorating since it gives us a way of

explaining, for example, that one of the safest ways to combine colors is to use different tones of the same color: a series of blues might range through powder, sky and cornflower to navy; or that to get a balanced blend of different colors, you might want them all to have the same tonal value: the classic ice-cream colors are good examples here — they're all different color but none of them really stand out because they all have a high, equalizing proportion of white pigment — pigment being the raw material of color, which comes in various natural and synthetic forms.

Colors are traditionally arranged in a 'chromatic scale', often in the form of a color wheel and those that are next or fairly close to each other on the wheel are described, and work, as 'harmonious' colors. 'Contrasting' colors are those opposite or nearly opposite to each other; these are sometimes also called 'complementary' colors, because when they're mixed in equal quantities they cancel each other out and produce, rather surprisingly, a neutral gray — try mixing equal quantities of orange and blue or red and turquoise and see what happens. The practical advantages of understanding this are, for example, that you'll know what tinting color to use to get a softer or more sophisticated shade from a rather harsh-colored can of bought paint — that is, by adding a little of its complementary color. When placed next to each other, true contrasts also strengthen and intensify each other, but without changing your perception of their color, whereas

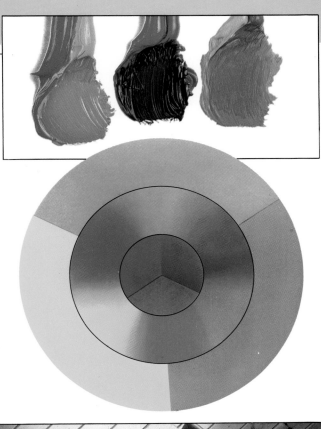

While color theory is an immensely complicated subject, understanding basic color relationships is an important part of interior design. Red, yellow and blue — the painter's primaries (**above right**) can in theory be combined to produce every shade on the color wheel (**right**). The additive primaries — red, green and blue — are so-called because while light is produced when they are combined (**below**). Combinations of any two of the additive primaries produce the complementary color of the third color. These colors known as subtractive primaries (**bottom**). If white light is passed through filters of all three subtractive primaries black is produced.

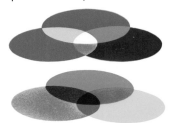

colors slightly closer to each other, but not adjacent, on the color wheel — such as blue and red-purple — each seem to send the other 'off-hue' when they're placed in juxtaposition. These generally make uncomfortable combinations but, by playing around with the proportions in which they're used and adding in one or more shades of the colors between them, they can often be linked into an unusual and successful 'family' of decorating colors. Large, adjacent areas of true contrasts can be equally disturbing, unless each is tinted with a small amount of the other to give them a more sympathetic relationship; but small quantities of one against larger areas of another will often work to provide limited areas of vibrant contrast.

If you like unusual colors and combinations, you might try playing with 'discords'. These are the colors that are produced when the sequence of light and dark colors, as they appear on the color wheel, are thrown off balance by adding as much light to the dark colors and black to the light as will reverse their normal relationship. If you've ever winced at pale blue and chocolate brown, it's not necessarily because of the disparity in tonal value, but because the brown is really a yellow, orange or red 'in disguise' (darkened with black), and the true blue has been lightened with white, so that, their natural tonal relationship has been turned upside down. The safest method to handle discords is to use very small quantities of one with another: a pale blue fabric overprinted with a scattering of tiny brown dots and dashes could look very pretty — the same colors in equal stripes would look awful.

In theory, the three primary colors of red, yellow and blue can between them produce all other colors. In fact, this is not strictly true — or at least they cannot produce pure colors of the same intensity as we're now used to seeing in manufactured ranges of pigments. Certainly, at child's paint-box level, mixing two primaries produces a secondary color: red + yellow = orange, yellow + blue = green, blue + red = purple; and mixing two secondary colors produces a tertiary color, such as the olive produced by mixing purple and green. Further intermixing, with the addition of black and white, obviously expands the range of colors you can achieve, but ultimately will leave you lacking the brilliance of some of the artificially made colors you can now buy.

Nevertheless, the best way to learn about color behavior in its pure sense is to play with a reasonably well-stocked paint-box. It will help you enormously in choosing not only the right paint shades but fabrics, wall and floor coverings, too, because you'll know what you're looking for and why. Once you realize, for example, that there is a real relationship between purple, green and olive you will begin to see how, with a bit of tinkering, modification, intermixing and balancing, they could be applied together in decoration.

Applied color

There are some generally well-known and accepted observations about the way colors perform when they are applied as decoration. These just about bear repeating because they are useful tools for visually adjusting space, proportion, light and mood. You will probably know, for example, that pale colors seem to expand a space, making it lighter and airier, while dark colors contract it, defining and containing the area more closely so that it feels smaller and more intimate. But within light and dark, there's also the distinction between warm and cool. By looking at the color wheel you can not only see these very neatly divided but, even on this scale, get an indication of how they behave: the bright, warm colors — rich yellows, oranges and reds, which will cheer up a cold room and visually 'raise the temperature' — leap out at you and are sometimes called 'advancing' colors because they seem to bring forward the surfaces to which they are applied. The cooler, quieter colors in the blue/green/grey range are, literally, more 'retiring' and, although they can make a calm and undemanding background, they may make some rooms, north- and east-facing especially, feel cold. The shape and symmetry of the room will also affect the way you color it. If the wall surfaces are alive with all sorts of odd angles and alcoves and dotted with doors and windows of different heights and widths, painting the woodwork in a markedly contrasting color will only draw attention to this disturbing variety of detail. In a room like this, integrate woodwork as closely as possible with the walls, and keep all surfaces in as flat a finish as possible. This will produce a much more unified effect, which will still provide interest and contrast, but will be more restful on the eyes.

These 'rules' are worth knowing, if only to prepare you for ways of bending or breaking them; as long as you compensate for natural color behavior, you can use most colors as and where you want. For example, in a north-facing room that is not only cold, but dark and small, a color that is warm, bright and strong would be overwhelming, but a softer shade of one of the warm colors — say, brick-red instead of poppy — would make it lighter and warmer without overpowering it. The blues, greens and greys can be darkened for depth, given warm undertones by choosing shades with a touch of red or yellow in them and their tendency to coldness offset with mellow terracottas, mustards and other warm earth colors. Strong colors can also be used in almost any size of room if they're kept in check with neutrals; some of the 'broken color' techniques are perfect ways of achieving this, but the same can apply to any fabric or wallpaper in which there's a strong color on a fairly neutral background. This method means that you don't need to banish strong colors entirely from any room, just understand how to temper their strength to what the room will tolerate.

Right A fairly simple, tonal scheme, easy on the eye and easy to achieve — it just uses about half-a-dozen different pale-to-mid pinks which work happily together and bring out the warmth in the wood.
Far right A setting which, although similarly subdued in coloring, has an altogether different level of drama. The reason is mostly a case of 'less is more' — fewer colors, fewer objects clutter the view and this allows the important ingredients to stand out, helped by a greater degree of contrast (black and splashes of peacock blue against the terracotta, with white walls throwing them all into relief).
Below A bedroom which relies on white, scattered with simple, child-like primaries, for a mood of lightness and gaiety — a perfect choice for a north- or east-facing room.

PATTERN

Pattern is everywhere — either natural and spontaneous or man-designed and man-made. At an abstract level, the kind of decorative pattern we're concerned with here is simply a two-dimensional arrangement of colors, shapes and symbols. Yet, as a method of expression and communication, human beings have found the making of these marks — figurative or non-figurative — so irresistible that pattern in decoration has come down through the centuries and across all the continents. From the infinite variety of forms, just as cultures, periods, stylistic movements, even individuals can be identified by the patterns they produced as surely as by a fingerprint, so using these patterns in interiors today can evoke the spirit of those different countries, societies and eras. It may seem light years away from the small, stylized flower print on the walls of your living room (although perhaps not so far from the Greek key design on the rug), but if it does nothing more than persuade you to treat pattern with respect, it serves its purpose.

Pattern deserves respect — it's a powerful medium which can make or break a room. In fact, I've considered campaigning to have every bolt of patterned fabric and role of patterned paper labelled with a warning, 'Handle with care', because a little or a lot of the right pattern in the right place can transform a set of surfaces and make the most miraculous relief, whereas the wrong pattern — or even the right pattern — in the wrong place, can be a decorative disaster, costing a lot more than another couple of cans of paint to correct. But don't let that frighten you, because you're in such good commercial hands these days that you need never really venture out on a limb with pattern unless you want to. There are so many excellent ranges of wallpapers, many with matching or coordinating fabrics, some with carpets, too, and in such safe combinations of color and design that the job — or at least one version of it — is practically done for you. By 'safe', I don't mean bland or boring, but the kind of small scale designs — geometrics, abstracts, florals and spatter, sponge or other textural effects — which can look smart or pretty, depending on the colorway, and made to work in almost any room.

This may be the lazy way of using pattern, but there's nothing wrong with that. A lot of skill, thought and time goes into a good, professionally produced pattern and it can be a kind of lifesaver to the amateur decorator; if all else, and especially your confidence, fails you, find a pattern you like and build your color scheme around it. You may only use the pattern itself in the form of a rug, curtains, blinds or a couple of cushions, yet it will pull the whole scheme together because it contains all the color elements in the room. You'll often find, too, that the proportion and distribution of color in a pattern are

reasonably good guides as to how much of each color to use in the room itself, and in what relationship, but this is by no means an infallible method of 'translation'; the dominant color will depend especially on the size of the room and the amount and direction of light, so you'd still be well advised to plan the scheme out properly before going ahead.

Apart from providing an instant color scheme and interest on plain surfaces, pattern can be used to link areas of different coloring if it contains the ingredients of both; it can also link and echo shape and texture as well as color. On the practical side, pattern can often distract the eye from imperfect surfaces and some types will tend to show up dirt rather less than plain surfaces. But of course, there's pattern and pattern. It may simply be a stencilled surround on a wood floor, a border of contrasting color round a plain, tiled area, a single Kelim rug, diagonal stripes on doors, panels picked out in fine lines on walls, or a decorative frieze. Any of these can represent the pattern input in a room, just as much as the full-blown, fabric-and-wallpaper treatment, and may be all the room needs.

Apart from coloring, the two pivotal points for success with pattern are scale and quantity. Small patterns for small rooms, certainly, but that doesn't automatically indicate large patterns for large rooms, only that you may

be able to get away with a bolder approach to pattern in a bigger area. I've seldom seen two large-repeat patterns work well together; small patterns can work echoing a large one in color and design, or echoing each other. If you want to mix a lot of patterns together, keep them all small-scale, mix design styles but keep a strong color theme running through them. Pattern also needs to suit the architectural style of a room. Some rooms are very adaptable in the kind of pattern treatment they'll take, but you'd be as likely to find strict geometrics happily at home in a mullion-windowed, oak-beamed cottage as you would ginghams in, let us say, an Adams-style drawing room. Just bear in mind the atmosphere of the room.

When planning for pattern, don't forget the other kinds of pattern the room itself will generate: books, by objects on shelves, collections of pictures, even by the way the furniture is arranged. You may need to rethink some of these patterns, even plan some of them out — behind cupboard doors or into plain-painted alcoves — in order to plan more pattern in. Pattern can be very demanding on the eye, so try to avoid giving yourself, or anyone else, visual indigestion by using too much or too many. When someone said 'Too much of a good thing can be wonderful', I don't personally believe they meant pattern. So, do be warned about over-stepping the mark on pattern.

Far left Patterns mix most successfully when they share shapes and colors. Compatible in color and stripe, these are sufficiently different in design and scale to make a sparky partnership.
Centre Highly individual pieces of furniture need not limit pattern choice. These two have strong character and color, yet any of the surrounding rugs would suit them.
Top left Color and pattern mixes that please the eye shouldn't shout their logic at you. Just as the leaves of the plants in the center picture almost unnoticeably pick up the pattern and color of the table so, here, the scattering of rust-on-cream dots on a ruched blind echo the texture of the grained window.
Above left Surfaces surrounding a strikingly patterned floor may need to be plain, leaving accessories to pick up the pattern's colors.
Above Pattern can often be more texture than design, like this blue-and-white trellis paper, which provides the perfect foil for white wicker.

Right Where does pattern end and texture begin? Every material has a texture and most have pattern, formal or informal and made by nature or man. The secret in the successful blending of both is to really look at the materials you're using, see where their similarities and differences lie, whether they'll work next to each other or whether they need something between them to make the link. In this way, by moving the various materials around, the most unlikely combinations can often be made to work together in surprising harmony.

TEXTURE

If anything differentiates the amateur decorator from the professional, it's the appreciation and use of texture. This is the magic ingredient, the one which appeals not only to the eye but to the touch and which can most easily and instantly create the greatest feeling of luxury, and not necessarily at any great cost. Texture is the meeting point between plain and pattern; sometimes it can be difficult to decide which is which. Is a herringbone brick floor, texture or pattern — or crunchy cotton lace or thick, embossed Anaglypta wallpaper?   These are one-color materials, but what about porphyry-spattered walls or flecked, oat-meal tweed? In every case you want to remember that texture is really visual just as much as it is sensual and thus should be treated accordingly.

Of course, everything you can touch has a texture — eggshell paint, ceramic tiles and linoleum just as much as linen, velvet or a fluffy Flokati rug. Some have a more

pronounced, three-dimensional texture than others and between them vary from hard to soft, rough to smooth. But mixing textures in an interior doesn't only provide a satisfying variety of sensual experience, it's also a miraculous way of introducing subtle visual variety, which is much easier on the eye than a cascade of different colors or a plethora of pattern. You don't even need to move beyond the range of neutral or earth colors to find variety. Imagine, for example, floors paved with wood blocks or quarry tiles covered with tongue-and-groove boarding and carpeted with coir, Berber or nubbly undyed Indian rugs, walls lined with granular burlap, coarse jute or woven wool. These alone are enough to make your mouth water, but texture is everywhere and in every color, and if you choose by touch as well as by eye and aim for variety you'll quite simply add a different dimension to decorating, which is entirely neglected if you do not take texture into account right from the start.

Above In this white-walled room where colors are mostly muted earth-tones and pattern is restricted to rugs and hangings, texture takes over as the dominant decorative force. Stone, wood, leather, metal, cane, wool — all undemanding yet satisfying natural materials — combine with greenery outside and in to create an environment which has a calm, classic, timeless quality about it and a feeling of both space and security.

Above, right and **far right**
Proper planning will prevent
nasty surprises once your fond
imaginings have become all too real
and, perhaps, irredeemable. Make
sample boards, as the professionals
do, to assess whether colors,
textures and patterns will work
together. This is a remarkably
accurate halfway stage between the
raw beginnings of a room and the
finished article and is an
invaluable aid to ensuring that what
you see in your mind's eye is what
you get.

PLANNING

Whether you're decorating a single room or a whole house,
treat yourself as a professional decorator would a client
and make up a sample board — several if necessary — to
assess how the various possible ingredients of color,
pattern and texture will work together.

Use large sheets of white card and pins or sticky tabs to
fix the samples to it; don't use any kind of permanent fixing
for the samples as you may want to move them around
from board to board. When planning a room, start with the
floor and if you have a variety of possible floor coverings,
fix one to each card; if you're intending to have a wooden
floor, a piece of veneer or wood-grain paper should give
you a reasonably accurate facsimile, but otherwise try to
get actual samples of the materials — tiles, carpets, fabrics
and so on — so that you can assess texture as well as color,
as both will need to blend and contrast well.

Walls will come next, just because of their sheer size
and the degree to which they dominate the room. For paint
colors, cut out samples from commercial shade cards or
make your own by tinting a small amount of white paint,
but again get actual samples of fabrics and wallpapers and,
as other intended or existing furnishings also have to be
taken into account at planning stage, get catalogue
pictures of new furniture and swatches of any proposed
coverings. As you're working on a small-scale version of
the real thing, it can also help to have a photograph of the
room and of any existing furniture or bits and pieces that

need to be planned into it.

Try to get enough of each type of sample to build up a
set of swatches round each floor covering. If this isn't
possible, keep trying the different samples out against
your main swatchcard until you reach a decision. And
although you're working in microcosm at this stage, keep
scale in mind and try to use samples whose sizes are
roughly in ratio to the way the various materials will
eventually be used.

Planning a whole house is merely an extension of the
same method. This time, make tight groups of swatches
representing floor, walls, woodwork and other furnishings for each room and place these groups on the card in a
sequence that reproduces as nearly as possible their
actual, geographical relationship. You might, for example,
arrange the ground floor groups at one end of the board,
set the hall/staircase/landing group in the middle and the
upper floor groups at the other end. In this exercise, the
aim is not only to see that each group works as a separate
entity, but that they relate happily with each other,
bearing in mind particularly the point at doorways where
different wall and floor treatments meet and there is a view
from one room into the next.

It's really worth being as perfectionist as possible with
your planning boards — chopping and changing samples
and adjusting paint shades even by fine degrees until you
get the combination just right. Even at this scale, a
properly prepared sample board is handy.

Instant decorating

Here, to end this section, is a bit of heresy. I'm certainly not suggesting that you ignore all that's gone before, or what follows, either. However, if what you want most at the moment is just to get the job done, here's a simple formula.

Let's assume that color schemes can be divided into five catagories: monochrome — black, white and greys; neutral — all the shades of cream, beige and brown; tonal — different tones of the same color; related — two or three 'harmonious' colors (those adjacent to each other on the color wheel); or contrasting — comprising opposites or near opposites on the color wheel. All you have to do is decide which type of color scheme you like and/or which would best suit the room, find a pattern which incorporates most or all the color elements and build the whole scheme around it, by choosing other surfaces or finishes to match the exact shade of the colors as they're used in the pattern.

From where I stand it's really impossible to advise you on both the exact distribution and proportion of color, pattern and texture for any individual room. Without seeing the style, atmosphere, size and so on it is difficult and wrong to lay down absolute rules. You will have to decide ultimately for yourself, but what I can do, and what I have done, is to set out some basic premises for you to follow and adapt to individual rooms. The table below is a guideline, which summarizes some of the points you are likely to find most helpful.

Do assess carefully just how much of any pattern the room can take, whether you have chosen to base your scheme on a fabric, wallpaper or just the border of a rug.

Do, as a general principle, keep the floor a darker tone than the walls, to 'ground' the room. How dark the walls should be will depend mainly on its size and aspect.

Don't use equal quantities of each color or tone — varying proportions will make the scheme more interesting. Watch, in particular, proportions of contrasts — it takes just a little of one against quite a lot of another to make a scheme lively. In monochrome schemes, small patches of brilliant color can be especially effective, as can small areas of the warmer earth tones — mustard, terracotta, even khaki and olive — in schemes based on neutrals.

Don't forget texture — decoration is in the touch as much as the eye.

Do make up a sample board first, even in 'instant decorating', so that what you see is what you get.

Above 'No-color' rooms, perhaps surprisingly, need planning just as carefully as rooms which overflow with color and pattern. In a room where you're relying on different tones and textures to provide visual variety, the quantity and distribution of each separate element is crucial. And, once these have been accurately represented on your sample board, you should also be able to get a very good idea of exactly what accents of bright color — and these may be minimal — will be needed to break the scheme's monotony.

FINISHES

Paint really deserves a section to itself because, along with its allied media of glazes, stains and varnishes, which are dealt with in the relevant subsections, it is still the cheapest, most versatile and generally the most practical method of both decorating and protecting interior surfaces.

Covering a room in paint is not simply a thing of today. You should remember that as you decorate your own four walls, you are perpetuating a tradition that is known to reach back over at least 30,000 years and believed to extend back much further. The most well-quoted example of early interior decoration is the cave paintings at Altamira in northern Spain, where the exceptional quality of both execution and preservation (the latter assisted by atmospheric conditions) suggest that brushes were being used with natural pigments mixed in animal fat. This was already a considerable refinement on earlier paintings, which were thought to have been finger-painted with different colored local clays, diluted with water.

By the time wall-painting surfaces again in ancient Egypt — or at least the remaining evidence of it — craftsmen had discovered not only how to bind the pigments so that they didn't rub off, by using natural substances such as plant juices, honey, egg and milk (early American settlers were still blending dry pigments in buttermilk for stencilling), but also how to make artificial pigments. Subsequently, as they began to use wood and iron structurally, they discovered the preservative as well as the decorative powers of paint. Other early painting media included the Greek and Roman method of blending pigments into melted beeswax, and a similar medium is used even today by some craftsmen as an antiquing finish for woodwork. I have not included it in the book, however, as I have not yet tried it myself, but for

those who'd like to experiment, the principle is simply to mix dry powder colours in the appropriate shades into the melted beeswax mixture (see page 96, but use bleached wax and increase the quantity of turpentine by about 50 per cent) and let it cool to a paste before dragging or pouncing it on with a lightly loaded brush.

Although there's a historical cloud over the exact, or even vague date when oil began to be used as a painting medium, there is evidence to suggest that the earliest 'oil paints' were probably just natural pigments ground in an oil such as linseed. Refinements were slowly worked on and added over the centuries, often by the artists of the time; these refinements included vegetable drying oils, turpentine and petroleum spirits as solvents for resin 'binders', the preservative properties of white lead (now discontinued in interior paints mainly because of its toxicity) and, eventually, chemical pigments to augment and replace the vegetable and mineral varieties.

Paint today still depends on a classic blend of four main types of ingredient: pigment to provide the color; a 'binder' of natural or synthetic resin, which plays the dual role of carrying the pigment and, when dry, forming the thin, tough, decorative and protective film; a drier to speed up the drying of the resin; and a thinner, often referred to as 'solvent', which dilutes the paint to usable consistency. In addition, paint very often contains an 'extender' such as whiting, kaolin, talc and natural or synthetic silica.

Above Even within the general catagory of 'low-luster', paints vary from make to make in their degree of shine, so it's worth shopping around. Here, a low-sheen variety gives solid colors an expensive, almost imperceptible gleam to sympathize with and set off aluminum and chrome.

Above right Gloss paint is here used deliberately and, in this context, quite daringly to emphasize the natural patterning of tongue-and-groove and reflect light from the sequence of sash windows back into the room with its mirror-like shine. What tempers this scheme is the choice of tone — not a brash brilliant or hard white but a 'broken' off-white, which gives the shiny surfaces an uncharacteristic gentleness.

Far right The absolutely matt finish of flat oil paint provides a serene, undemanding background of cool blue. Good proportions make it safe to emphasize architectural detail so, to save the scheme from monotony and give it 'edge', the arch, architraves and cornice are picked out in white, mid-sheen paint and the door semi-glossed in a light, soft navy.

Paint manufacture is currently a highly technical, specialized and competitive industry involving advanced chemistry and physics, but this, to my mind, is as much as you or I need to know about what today's paints are. What concerns us is what they do and, more specifically, since we're talking about interior decoration rather than, for example, weather-proofing or rust protection, their aesthetic rather than functional performance. Because, although there are literally thousands of custom-made paints for every conceivable purpose, only a tiny proportion of them are of general use to the interior decorator, amateur or professional. Since most people are mainly concerned about the final result, I have classified the paints according to finish. Paint comes, these days, in just about every imaginable finish from flat, 'soft' and chalky to hard, high gloss. However, on both plaster and wood-work, I think plain painted, one-color surfaces tend to look best in the flattest possible, appropriate finish. I have a particular aversion to gloss paint — that brash, unsubtle shine that lies thickly on the surface and shouts at you, showing up every imperfection of angle, line and finish — and I know many professional decorators who agree. Obviously, woodwork surfaces that get handled need the increased degree of protection supplied by an oil-based paint, but they'll generally look best in a low-luster or even a flat finish; in any case, if gloss is what you want, a few coats of gloss varnish will provide a degree of depth and quality of shine that simply isn't achievable with paint. With walls it's a case of what's suitable and the finish will be dictated not only by personal preference, but

PAINT TYPES

FLAT PAINTS

Flat oil paint Without doubt the best, completely flat paint for all interior surfaces in terms of consistency, coverage and finish. Only available in Britain through specialist suppliers.

Undercoat A normally flat, oil-based paint designed to provide a sound, non-porous ground for other, oil-based finishing coats and not as a top coat in itself. However, it's easily available and often used very successfully as a substitute for flat oil paint; it covers more thinly, so you may need an extra coat, and its powdery texture is best protected with matt varnish. It's worth buying one of the better quality brands, especially if you're using it as a ground for subsequent over-decoration, as these dry to a smoother, less-absorbent finish. Colors are limited, but it's easily tinted.

Latex This is the rather loose general term used to describe both the familiar flat latex paint and the newer matt vinyls, used as standard finishes for plasterwork. They are quick, cheap and easy to use, they cover well and have good adhesion; being water-based, they have virtually no smell, they allow the surface to breathe (so can be applied to new plaster — but not to metal, which they will corrode), they dry quickly leaving a washable surface and, as long as it's clean and in good condition, can be re-covered with almost any other finish. Today's latex paints also withstand steamy kitchens and bathrooms. On the minus side, they generally have more sheen than flat oil paint but, perversely, are at the same time much more porous, which makes them unsuitable grounds for most over-decoration (unless sealed first with matt varnish), although they can be thinned for use as washes.

LOW-LUSTER TO GLOSS

Trade eggshell So called because it's generally only available through specialist suppliers to the decorating 'trade'. It is pricy, but with a quality and durability to match. Oil-based, it is smooth and hard with a subdued, expensive looking sheen. It's fine for walls, too, tints easily, covers well and makes the perfect non-porous ground for many of the other decorating techniques. On the minus side, it's slightly harder to work with than the other low-luster finishes mentioned, needing thorough brushing on and careful laying off to get smooth, even coverage with no brush strokes.

Other low-luster finishes These paints are all much of a muchness. The only important distinction to make is between those that are oil- or alkyd-based and those based on water. The oil-/alkyd-based paints can be used in the same way as trade eggshell; they are easier to work with but have less covering power and a heavier finished look. Applying several, well-thinned coats rather than one or two undiluted ones can help their appearance enormously. The water-based versions were designed primarily as fast-drying, soft-sheen finishes for walls. On woodwork they're more durable than flat latex, have increased washability and can be used as ground for some over-decoration, although they're naturally more porous and less hard-wearing than oil-based finishes.

Gloss paints These, too, are all very similar in character, usually based on oil-modified, alkyd media, with generic terms such as semi-gloss, gloss, high or hard gloss describing the increasing levels of shine. The degree of shine is also usually commensurate with the strength of the surface, its water and dirt resistance, and therefore its washability and durability, although it is still prone to chipping.

by the decorative treatment chosen (some will simply look wrong unless they're given the appropriate level of sheen described in the individual paint finishes) and by the condition of the wall itself — the greater the sheen, the more any surface defects will show. As for the contrast of finish between plaster and woodwork, I think generally they should be as similar as possible; but this is a hard generalization to make because it depends so much on the individual room, its proportions and detailing. In the end it is up to you to make the best of what's available.

Thinning

Always thin paint with the compatible diluent. In the case of all the paints mentioned above, this means mineral spirits for oil-based paints, water for water-based. The principle of two thinned coats being better than one thick one applies to just about any finish. The degree to which you thin the paint depends on the purpose — whether, for example, it is a preparation or finishing coat. The first 'mist' coat of latex on new plaster can be thinned up to 50 per cent with water, the first undercoat to a similar extent with mineral spirits, since in both cases you're aiming not for coverage but to satisfy and even out the porosity of the surface and create a binding layer between this and the next coat. Subsequent undercoats may be applied full strength, but sparingly and well brushed out, as what you want to avoid, in this as in all paint coats, is a thick film which may dry on top but remain soft underneath. Thinning finishing coats to a certain degree obviously helps to avoid this problem as well as making it easier to eliminate brush strokes and achieve a fine, smooth finish. Paint consistencies vary so much that it's hard to generalize about proportions, but aim to thin paint to the point where it just holds on the brush. In flat and low-luster paints this consistency should resemble light cream, gloss paints more like tomato catsup. Most manufacturers give their own thinning recommendations and with some paints the makers will have done the job for you so that no thinning will be necessary at all. The non-drip or jelly variety cannot be thinned either — as this involves stirring which would disrupt their constitution — and must be used in their rather thick, sticky, manufactured form, which is one of the reasons why I try to avoid them.

Tinting

Color is an extraordinary thing and I have often found that, despite leafing through dozens of shade cards and hundreds of colors, I still can't find the exact shade I'm looking for. Some paint retailers and specialist decorating suppliers will mix paint to match paper or fabric samples, but you usually pay for this service. In any case, it often happens that the color is only in your mind's eye. However, no-one should be daunted by the prospect of

mixing their own paint colors; it's exciting and enormously satisfying. Pigments come in many different forms, but usually fall into two categories with a couple of exceptions: those which are soluble in water and can therefore be used only to tint water-based paints, and those soluble in mineral spirits, which should be used only for oil-based paint.

Whichever pigment you use, mix it into a liquid with a small amount of the appropriate diluent, then stir the paint in thoroughly, a little at a time, straining it afterwards if you suspect there may be any undissolved particles of

Below Luck may lead you to a sympathetic set of manufactured paint shades but it can often be simpler to tint your own. Here, home-tinting saved a long search for the precise, palest-of-pinks that would co-ordinate walls with covers. **Right** This delicious cocktail of off-whites was entirely home-concocted and gives the scheme an individual one-off quality to which, quite honestly, bought whites can still not aspire.

SUGGESTED MATERIALS FOR TINTING PAINT TYPES

WATER-BASED PAINTS

Poster colors Rather crude, heavy colors, but inexpensive and easy to mix.

Artists' gouache Tubes of expensive but exciting, concentrated, opaque colors

Artists' acrylics Expensive again and with a more limited color selection than other artists' ranges; best on sharp pastels and soft mid-tones, weak on earth colors and neutrals; exceptionally quick drying, but you can buy a retarder.

OIL-BASED PAINTS

Artists' oils By far the most comprehensive, finely-graduated range, but also far from cheap and relatively slow drying.

OIL- AND WATER-BASED PAINTS

Artists' powder pigment (dissolve in water) Fewer colors than the oil ranges, but good selection of strong, clear shades; they don't dissolve as easily as poster colors, so straining mixed paint is recommended.

Universal stainers (dissolve in water) The decorating trade's tinting medium with different ranges from different manufacturers; there are highly concentrated, clear colors, which are easily soluble. Color ranges lack variety and subtlety, but intermixing helps.

1 Never, never sand bare, new plaster or you'll create scratches which will show through at least two coats of paint. Just go over the new surface lightly with a stripping knife to lift off any nibs left by the plasterer. Once your first paint coat is dry, fill any defects, sand gently with very fine abrasive paper to avoid breaking through the paint film and touch up filled areas with your first paint coat before applying the next.

2 Always dust off any loose material created by filling and sanding before applying a new coat. For high-quality work, use a slightly sticky 'tack-rag' to remove dust and grit. You can buy these in decorating shops but the Basic Preparation section tells you how to make your own.

3 Transfer small amounts of paint from the can into a paint kettle. This will enable you to keep the can covered and so avoid a surface skin forming on the paint, and will minimize wastage if any loose material gets into the kettle. To lessen the chance of this happening, always release excess paint from the brush by pressing the bristles against the inside of the kettle.

4 Work down walls in full-width sections about 18-24in (45-60cm) deep. Lay on enough paint to cover the part of section on which you're working but don't apply it too liberally in the hope that more paint will mean less painting: you'll end up with uneven coverage and although the paint will dry on the surface, the excess may stay soft underneath.

pigment that could cause streaks. A can of basic white paint will give you all the options, especially for paler colors, but for darker shades it's probably more sensible (and may be more economical) to choose one near to the color you want, then make the final adjustments with small amounts of pigment. Use pigments with caution anyway — they are generally highly concentrated and a little goes a remarkably long way — and never add pigment to paint in a greater proportion than 1:8 or the paint, which is already pigmented, may start to set. It's also important to test the result on paper before using it. Paint changes color from wet to dry; manufacturers' shade cards allow for this, but you will probably still need to make your own.

All these pigments can obviously also be used on their own or mixed with different materials for other forms of decoration. Artists' powder pigments and gouache make good stains and washes; the speed with which acrylics dry make them a boon for stencilling and decorative details such as lining (mix with a little emulsion paint/acrylic medium to give it opaque/translucent 'body'); artists' powder pigments and oil colors can be used to tint varnishes. However, decoration with water-soluble

pigments especially will need a protective coating of varnish to prevent them rubbing or washing off. As for varnishing other pigmented finishes — I'd rather be safe than sorry.

EQUIPMENT For plasterwork use broad, 4 or 5in (10 or 12.5cm), flat wall brushes. For woodwork, brushes are usually held by the stock, between thumb and fingers. It's really worth having a 3, 2 and 1in (7.5, 5 and 2.5cm) 'cutting in' brush for fine work, such as going around the puttied areas on windows, finishing baseboards and attacking recesses on moldings. Get the best brushes you can afford — they'll repay you with performance — and look after them. Even new brushes need cleaning; flick dust out of the bristles by pulling them back and then releasing them like a catapult, or twirling the handle between your palms, then rinse in mineral spirits and twirl them dry. Break brushes in by using them for priming and so on, until all the short hairs have worked free. Clean brushes used for oil-based paint first with solvent (mineral spirits), then in soap and lukewarm water before rinsing them and hanging them up to dry. Rinse out brushes used for water-based paint in cold water first, to flush away most of the paint, then wash these, too, in warm, soapy water, rinse and hang to dry. Never leave brushes resting on their tips or the bristles will distort. They can be stored flat when dry. During a prolonged decorating period, oil-paint brushes can be suspended overnight with the bristles immersed in a 1:1 mixture of raw linseed oil and mineral spirits, covering the container to keep dust and air out and then rinsing them with solvent and twirling them dry; emulsion paint brushes can also be kept moist for a limited period by wrapping the bristles in plastic wrap or a plastic bag.

Rollers are very tempting for large scale work, and although some decorators frown upon them, they are such sophisticated pieces of equipment these days that they should not be dismissed. If I have any criticism, it's that they tend to apply the paint more superficially than brushes. Choose a good quality roller in man-made fiber in a width and pile to suit the job — normally short pile for very smooth surfaces, medium pile for all-purpose work and long pile for textured surfaces — and get one with an extension handle for high walls or ceilings. Use a sloping paint-tray and never fill it more than one-third its length with paint or the ribs at the bottom will not be able to work effectively and the roller will get overloaded. Wash new rollers out in the appropriate solvent. After use, remove as much excess paint as possible before rinsing with solvent as above, then wash them in warm, soapy water, rinse and hang to dry. For short breaks they can be kept from drying out, like brushes, in a plastic bag. Rollers can be used for most paint finishes, although I don't personally like

5

6

5 Once you've laid the paint on, work it evenly over and into the surface with crossing brush-strokes to eliminate any initial 'tramlines'. If you find these hard to remove, there may simply be too much paint on the surface and you'll need to extend it quickly over an adjacent bare area.
6. Lay off with a nearly dry brush and feather-light strokes in one direction only. Once you've laid off a section, don't go back over it or you'll spoil the surface, which will have already started to dry.

using them for gloss. I've seen roller-painted gloss peel off in sheets because of insufficient adhesion. If you do want to use them for gloss, make sure the foundation is well toothed for it to cling to; you may also have to lay off lightly with a brush after rolling to lose the orange-peel effect.

Application

The final section of this book takes you through all the stages of preparing the various surfaces. Here, it is worth repeating that flat water-based paints such as latex usually need no undercoat, although on new walls it's best to apply a well-thinned sealing coat of the same paint for a sound base. Undercoat is essential for a good finish with any of the oil-based paints. How many coats depends not only on the porosity of the surface, but the brand of paint you're using and the color you're covering. For bare wood or plaster, some manufacturers recommend a four-coat system of primer, plus two undercoats and one top coat; others, that you use, one undercoat and two top coats, still others, one coat of each. On pre-painted surfaces that are in good condition, one coat of each should be enough unless you're covering a greatly contrasting color, especially dark with light, in which case you may

well need two undercoats and should choose or tint them to match the finishing coat. In addition, since all manufacturers formulate their own primer, undercoat and top coat to be mutually compatible, it's worth buying the same brand to do all these jobs. One of the most important things to remember when building up a painted surface to a good finish is that you are working from hard to soft: that is, the sub-coats should always be less flexible than the top coat — the right paint, not over-applied and brushed out to a thin film. If you work the other way around, the finishing coats may be on too unsolid a base and so strain and crack.

Paint applied with a brush has a certain look, as does paint applied with a roller — small globules of air give it a texture. Another method of applying paint to wall and ceiling, which is becoming increasingly popular in America, is spray painting. The use of a compressor and large commercial spray-gun is widely adopted for applying paint in new apartments and houses. Although it is time consuming to mask windows and other fittings, the actual spraying time is minimal. The paint also dries quickly, cutting down on drying time between coats. A vignetted effect is also made much easier using a paint spray. This is a useful technique to know as it can speed up work.

Above When roller painting, buy a paint tray with a sloping base and only fill it each time to a maximum of one third its length or the ribs at the bottom of the tray will not be able to do their job, which is to spread the paint evenly over the roller, and it will get overloaded.

Right When painting ceilings, even with a roller, it's well worth investing in (or borrowing) an extra step ladder and a scaffold board so that you can walk across the room from one side to the other. For very high ceilings, get a roller with an extension handle.

SEQUENCE The traditional painting sequence is ceiling, walls, woodwork. Ceiling and each flank of wall should be painted in one go as stops and starts will show. When painting a ceiling, start on the window side and work across the room in 2ft (60cm) strips, parallel to the window. Paint these strips in sections approximately 2ft (60cm) square, laying on the paint with strokes parallel to the window, spreading it evenly with broad, half-moon-shaped, crossing brush strokes and laying off towards the light. Try not to let the strips overlap when brushing on, but cross-brush and lay off to blend the two wet edges together.

When painting walls, start at the top right-hand corner (top left if you're left-handed) and work from top to bottom in similar 2ft (60cm) strips, parallel to the ceiling, cross-brushing each strip into the next as you go and laying off with a light, straight, downward stroke. When painting walls or ceilings, always paint in the edges of each section first — that is, where they meet the ceiling or another wall — using the tip of the brush and trying not to overlap onto adjacent flanks.

The sequence for woodwork is windows, picture rail, doors, mantelpiece and baseboards — the idea being that the brush is well worked in and clean by the time you get to the door, baseboards being the place most likely to pick up dust and get messy again. The sequence for painting windows and doors is shown, and for all woodwork the laying off strokes should be in the direction of the grain.

METHOD There are a number of very good reasons for using a 'kettle', tipping in a small amount of paint at a time from the can. It is much lighter to carry for a start; it will also enable you to keep the rest of the paint covered and prevent it from drying, hardening and forming a surface skin; and if any bits of dried paint or other foreign bodies fall into the paint, it lessens the amount of wastage. Professional painters don't immerse the brush up to the stock, either. Dip just the first inch or so into the kettle and press each face of the bristles against the inside of the can to release any excess paint — wiping them across the rim will create a build-up of dried deposits that will eventually fall off into the paint and make it gritty. For the same reason, take off any paint around the inside walls of the kettle with a near-dry brush at regular intervals.

Work methodically, section-by-section, laying on enough paint to cover the section, crossing your brush **strokes to eliminate 'tracks' and then laying off with a** nearly dry brush and long, feather-light, one-directional strokes to get a completely smooth finish. Work quickly enough to keep the wet edges of each section 'alive' until you can lay off the next section into it, but don't go back over a section once you've finished as it will already have started its drying process and you'll spoil the texture. If you need to put the brush down occasionally, always lay it in the same direction across the top of the kettle so that only one side of the rim gets paint-smeared and the brush handle stays clean.

The amount of paint applied varies a little according to the finish, but there are two, old, painters' saws that are worth remembering. 'Use less paint and more painting' doesn't mean 'starving' the surface, but it does mean that it's thorough brushwork, not a splosh-and-spread technique, that produces a good finish. 'Spread the middle and starve the edges' means lay off all corners and angles with a nearly dry brush, otherwise you'll build up a thick edge of paint, which may peel or chip off when knocked.

Treatments for finishes
Apply flat, water-based paint such as *latex* liberaly and don't over-brush them — some painters recommend laying off this type of paint towards the light, as with ceilings, rather than downwards. *Flat oil paints* and *low-luster finishes* also need fairly liberal application, but they should then be brushed out to a thin, even film and laid off carefully. *Gloss paint* should be laid on generously over a small

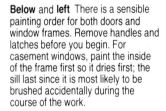

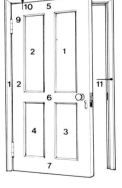

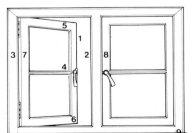

Upper far left If paint has become contaminated with dust, grit or bits of dried-up paint, it's worth going to the trouble of straining it — you can buy paper cones specially made for the job from good decorating shops.

Lower far left Hold flat wall brushes by the handle when you're painting walls and ceilings, but on woodwork you'll have more control of the brush if you hold it between thumb and fingers by the stock.

Center If you don't trust your hand to paint a straight line down the edge of the pane you can buy a metal paint shield with a straight edge. There's also a wonderful little gadget available — a scraper whose blade is automatically distanced about $\frac{1}{4}$in (6mm) from the frame so that you can get as much paint on the glass as you like and still scrape it away to a clean, straight line.

Upper left On woodwork, always paint moldings first, so that any runs can be brushed out as you come to paint the plain surfaces.

Lower left Lay gloss paint on generously and evenly over small sections at a time, then tip the brush off on the edge of the can and, with a near-dry brush, remove any excess paint from the surface, correct any remaining unevenesses with cross-strokes and make the final laying off strokes in the direction of the grain.

section of the surface and distributed evenly with cross-strokes before the brush is, for once, 'tipped off' on the edge of the kettle so that any excess can then be removed from the surface. With gloss you can tell whether the application is even by the feel of the brush: it will drag on poorly covered patches and slip on over-saturated areas. Correct the unevenness with cross-strokes before laying off with firm, even-pressured brush strokes. When you're applying several coats of gloss, you may like to try one decorator's trick of laying off each coat in the opposite **direction to minimize a build-up of tracks**, but the finishing coat should still be laid off with the grain on woodwork. Whatever paint you're using, each coat must be completely dry before you apply the next. Take note of paint manufacturers' recoating times, but remember that a cold and/or damp atmosphere will slow drying down. Perfectionists will also rub down between coats with fine abrasive paper — dry for water-based paints, wet-and-dry with a soap solution for oil-based. Dusting off is normally **sufficient before repainting latex, but flat oil paint, low-luster and gloss paints will benefit from a quick going-over with a tack rag to pick up any remaining bits.**

Below and **left** There is a sensible painting order for both doors and window frames. Remove handles and latches before you begin. For casement windows, paint the inside of the frame first so it dries first; the sill last since it is most likely to be brushed accidentally during the course of the work.

Broken color

Broken color is, very simply, using one or more colors in relief over a background. The various techniques, some of them centuries old, of giving a broken color effect to plaster and woodwork were, until fairly recently, used predominantly by professional decorators, some of whom guarded their secrets jealously. This is not without reason, since once home decorators discover how easy most of these techniques are, they will choose to do the work themselves rather than pay someone else. It really is true that to gain any of the effects on the following pages, your artistic sensibility, your sense of color and texture, is more important than technical expertise. Nearly everybody has this magic at their fingertips, and magic it is.

Paint has always been the cheapest and most immediate way to revive a tired room, but sometimes plain-painted walls can look a bit bleak and not everyone wants, or can afford, to bring them to life with pictures or even wallpaper, which is a more expensive way of giving a room patterns as well as color. However, these broken color effects offer an excellent option, which is much more than a mediocre alternative to plain color or pattern. Each technique has a different character, as well as an individual attraction, adding not only color but visual texture and depth. They also have some utterly practical properties: with the exception of dragging, which does demand a smooth, even surface, these color-textured finishes can help to disguise the superficial imperfections found particularly on older walls and woodwork, and are relatively tolerant of the finger marks and scuffs of wear. Also, because the choice of colors, materials, tools and touch are up to the individual, each person can virtually guarantee he will have the only finish of its kind.

Above and right Broken color can unite or distinguish different surfaces and, if the same colors and tones are retained for different techniques — as here, where ragging meets marbling — the result can be a delightful change of pace and contrast without clash.
Far right It can prove a practical choice, too. In a hand-made kitchen where units have been added over the years in a variety of different woods, simple dragging retains the 'woody' feel of grain but with a uniformity of coloring which stain could not achieve.

Materials and grounds

Two basic methods cover all the decorative effects in this section and it is these methods which, to a large extent, govern the materials used for both ground and top coats. To achieve the desired effect, paint is either added or subtracted. If it is added, as in sponging or spattering, the choice of materials is wider because they do not require specific drying times. You can therefore use an ordinary, matt water-based paint like latex, if you wish, as well as flat oil paint, undercoat, eggshell, glaze or a mixture of paint and glaze. If you are using a technique where the effect is gained by partially removing the top coat, either by stippling, ragging or dragging and combing, you need the material to stay 'open' long enough for the work to be carried out. For this reason, the quick-drying water-based paints are generally less satisfactory and more difficult to work for these techniques. They are not impossible to use, however, and you may prefer their cloudier patterning and chalkier texture. They are easier to manage if the ground is painted with one of the 'silk finish' varieties, whose less-absorbent surface will help the top coat stay open and workable longer. There is no doubt that it is more straight-forward to work in any of the oil-based materials mentioned above and the detail of the finished surface will be much finer, so that overall you have a more sophisticated result. Even when using these slower-drying preparations it's safest to paint on a band of color at a time — say 18-24 in (45-60 cm) wide, rather than painting the whole flank of a wall — and then work on it, so that you can keep a wet edge going. Otherwise you will find that the paint has dried before you have managed to apply any detail or are satisfied with what you have produced.

Where grounds are concerned the principle is usually to use a water-based glaze or wash over latex and an oil-based glaze over flat oil paint, undercoat or eggshell. An latex ground needs no undercoat, although two coats may be necessary to get a good surface on new plaster, but the ground coat must be clean and free from grease — best of all newly painted — if the decorative top coat is to take evenly. For the oil-based surfaces, professional decorators prefer the low-luster surface of eggshell for the ground (over a suitable undercoat, plus primer/sealer on new plaster), because it provides a smooth, non-porous surface, which discourages the top coat from drying out too quickly. When preparing the ground, remember the decorators' tip that two — or even three or four — thinned coats will look better than one thick one; it does mean more work but, in the end, you will have achieved a much, much smoother result. Also remember that whatever the preparation of the ground, it must be completely dry before glazing can begin. Otherwise you will destroy the work that you have already done — and there is nothing more soul-destroying!

Mixing and thinning

One of the economic advantages of these finishes is that the top coats are always thinned so that you generally only need between one-third and one-half the quantity of paint normally required for the room. Thinning is important, first for reasons of workability, and second for effect — the desired texture comes from the broken nature of the color, not from three-dimensional splotches of paint or glaze. The thinner the paint or glaze, the lighter and/or more translucent the effect, but obviously beyond a certain level of thinning the preparation becomes too runny and so unworkable.

Latex paint should be thinned with water — about one part paint to three parts water. Make it four parts water for greater translucency but, depending on the paint, you may find it runs too much and that more paint is needed to make it more workable.

Flat oil paint, undercoat or eggshell should be thinned with mineral spirits (the solvent sometimes called turpentine substitute). Start with a half and half mixture of paint and solvent, adding more solvent, a little at a time, until the desired consistency is reached. If, on testing, the mix is too liquid to hold the effect you're using, add either some more paint or a little proprietary drier: usually up to a tablespoonful per quart/liter of thinned paint will do the trick, but don't add too much or the finish may dry to a brittle surface.

Oil-based paint and glaze, thinned at least half and half with mineral spirits, is a mixture used by some decorators. This makes a very workable formula which holds out well (adding more glaze will make it less opaque and it will stay workable even longer), but the paint in the mixture can start to separate after a while, so don't mix up more than you can use in a day.

Glaze gives the most glowingly translucent of broken finishes. As the proprietary glazes vary in consistency, start by thinning half and half with mineral spirits. You will still get a workable consistency if you double the amount of solvent, but just bear in mind that the more solvent you add, the quicker the glaze will dry; so take care before overdoing the solvent.

Tinting

The cheapest way to buy paint is to acquire a large can of whichever medium you are using in either white or the palest of a pair of toning colors, and tint the paint to exactly the right shade yourself. Tint latex with the powerful universal stainers, or with artists' gouache, acrylic or poster colors. Make a solution of the color in a little water and add this to the paint before you thin it. Tint oil-based paint and glaze with universal stainers or artists' oil colors by dissolving a small amount of color in a little mineral spirit and, again, add this solution to paint or glaze

Left In this marbled hall it is the translucency of one thin coat of color over another and another, which builds up the surface and gives it depth and a kind of stylized realism. **Below** This richly-textured finish, spanning and integrating walls and woodwork, is merely the result of brushing a red-brown glaze over a beige background and dabbing at it with a bit of screwed-up rag?

before thinning. The important aspects of home tinting are to use small amounts of color concentrate at a time — they're surprisingly potent — and to make sure the color is fully dissolved before adding it to paint or glaze, and then to mix very, very thoroughly: unless, that is, you actually want streaks and splotches of intense color to appear in the finish. In the case of glaze, it will help color dispersion if you stir the dissolved color well into a small cupful of glaze before adding the rest of the glaze to it. This leaves a more even finish.

Varnishing

These finishes will benefit both practically and aesthetically from varnishing. Varnish brings out the colors in the finishes rather as salt adds flavour to food, but it also protects the surface, essential in the case of any thinned water-based finish, which can otherwise easily rub off. Use matt, semi-gloss or gloss polyurethane varnish. Matt has the least sheen — although it is not completely flat — and is therefore the kindest to uneven walls. However, it is the least hard-wearing, so take the trouble to apply at least a couple of coats. Semi-gloss and gloss are harder-wearing, but their sheen will show up an imperfect surface as well as every speck of dust left on it before varnishing. You would be well advised to wash down the surface first, then vacuum the room thoroughly and keep doors and windows shut, both while you apply the varnish and until it is completely dry. You are less likely to get streaks or ridges with semi-gloss or gloss varnish if you thin it with one-third its quantity of mineral spirits — this also makes it easier to brush on. Always keep one brush for use with varnish only, so that there is no risk of old paint coming off on the new finish. It is worth taking the trouble in the first place, as you will only regret even the tiniest of faults in the varnish later.

SHADING

The blending of one color into another across a wall or ceiling not only looks attractive, it can also visually affect the proportions of a room in a much more subtle way than flat color. In a high-ceilinged room, cream shading up the walls into buff, and the same buff covering the ceiling would be a much more sophisticated way of visually 'lowering' the ceiling than simply painting the walls cream and the ceiling buff. The same trick used in reverse would imperceptibly 'lift' a low ceiling. Shading walls in panels from a light center to dark perimeter can also be very effective and shading need not only be in the various tones of the same color; harmonizing tones of different colors can work well together, but the choice and sequence of color is crucial, otherwise, for example, by placing opposing colors next to each other you may end up with 'dirty' neutrals or dark bands between the two. Try shading blush pink into a delicate blue-green, for instance, and the area of overlap will turn a murky gray, whereas moving from pink through lilac to mauve would be a smooth and pleasing transition. Although shading in tones of one color can happily accommodate fairly dramatic shifts from light to dark, shading with more than one color generally works best in the lighter, pastel shades. This advice may be erring on the side of safety, but if you really want to try shading a wall from, say, yellow ocher through flaming orange to bright scarlet or crimson, just remember that you will also have to live with it!

Oil based paint

MATERIALS Flat oil paint is undoubtedly the easiest material to use for shading, but nowadays it is generally only obtainable through specialist suppliers and in a very limited range of colors. Undercoat makes a reasonably satisfactory alternative, is easy to apply and can be bought anywhere. Whichever you choose, it is more economic to buy it in a large can, either white or something near the palest of a set of toning colors, and tint it yourself to the exact shades required. As usual with oil-based paints, mix the pigment — universal stainer or artists' oil-colors — to solution form with a little mineral spirits before adding to the paint; add them gradually — they can color up the paint quicker than you'd expect — and stir well to avoid streaking. You will find the paint easier to both apply and blend if you thin it with mineral spirits first, but in this case don't thin more than one part mineral spirits to three parts paint because you need to retain the covering power of the paint to achieve the most even and effective finish.

TOOLS Ordinary paintbrushes are required for applying the ground coat and for applying and rough-blending the top coat, but the final blending needs to be done with a stippling brush. These are expensive to buy, but there are stippling-tool alternatives, which you may use such as bunched-up rags and sponges.

GROUND Always undercoat for flat oil paint and apply enough top coats of paint, in the lightest of your shading colors, to give a solid finish. Thinning the last of these coats a little with 1:2 mixture of linseed oil and mineral spirits will give it just enough gloss when dry to help you manipulate the shading coat. If there is to be much difference in the tone of the shading colors — for example, shading from *eau-de-Nil* through to deep turquoise — roughly blend the last ground coat, too, to stop the lightest color grinning through the darkest.

TONES FOR THE TOP COAT On normal- sized walls, three shades of color should be adequate, so tint up the lightest and darkest colors first and then mix some of each color together to form a middle tone. For very large or, especially, very high walls you may need to make up five, carefully graduated tones by mixing some of the middle one first with the lightest and then the darkest. Apart from careful coloring, the other important requirement is that the paint stays 'open' long enough for you to work on it. As thinning the paint with mineral spirits will only encourage it to dry more quickly, the process can be slowed down by adding some clear oil glaze to the paint (about one part glaze to eight parts paint) if you are dealing with relatively small patches, and, for very large areas, adding about the same amount of raw linseed oil.

METHOD Whether working in bands or panels, accuracy will be helped if the wall is divided up by snapping a chalk-line across and/or down the point at which the move from one color into the next occurs. (You can buy self-chalking lines, which are very convenient, but for a one-shot job you might just as well make your own with twine and pale blue chalk, using a spirit level and plumb to get lines horizontal and vertical.) Whatever direction the shading is to take, apply the lightest color first, then the second color, working it into the first and blending the two together with the paintbrush; if this is all left to the stippler, the colors will merge too suddenly instead of the ideal, almost imperceptibly graduated blend. Apply subsequent bands of color in the same way, brush-blending each into the previous one and use all colors liberally — they must stay wet for as long as possible so that the final blending can be done easily with the stippling brush. Once all the bands of color are brushed on, start stippling from light to dark, working gradually and evenly from band to band of color. If possible, change stippling brushes half way to avoid taking too much of the lighter color into the dark, or at least quickly rinse out the stippling brush in mineral spirits and dry it off before moving on. It will help speed up the process if you can enlist another pair of hands, so that one person can paint while the other starts stippling. But only one person should do the stippling work, as touch varies from one individual to another and will inevitably show up in the finished surface.

Water-based paint

This is a much dicier business than shading with oil paints, mainly because a water base encourages quicker drying, by evaporation rather than reaction, and so it is much harder to keep the wet edge that you need for successful blending. If you are going to attempt it, use a 'silk finish' paint to give a less absorbent ground coat. Before starting work on the shading, create as damp an atmosphere as possible, by shutting all doors and windows and sprinkling or spraying the floor with water, if you can do so without damaging it, or laying down dampened dustsheets over plastic sheeting. If you are painting on lining paper, wet it thoroughly with a brush and clean water before starting to paint. Work in narrow bands of color, starting with the lightest and adding a little more of the dark tone to it as you move from band to band. Brush and stipple between each band as you go. In this way you should be able to keep a wet edge 'alive' between bands. Although the lining paper will blister because it is so wet, it should shrink back satisfactorily as it dries, as long as it is well stuck to the wall. Chances of success with water-paint shading will be increased if you stick to smaller areas and it will greatly help if you satisfy some of the porosity of the wall by coating with an oil primer first.

COLOR-WASHING

For return on time, effort and money invested, color-washing comes high on the list of decorative wall finishes. When properly applied on a sound, dry, well-prepared wall, a tinted wash can give the surface a perfect matt finish, rather like the texture of blotting paper yet with a very unprosaic, almost luminous quality. The translucent nature of this medium is particularly useful where the walls require a glow — perhaps to warm up a north-facing room with yellow ocher or deep rose, without the dominance those colors would have is used solid in neat paint form. Although a color-wash effect is often con-sidered most suited to country-style rooms of pine and wicker furniture, coir matting and cotton prints, it can eas-ily take much more adventurous applications. For exam-ple, in Paris, one of the top interior designers 'dirtied' and aged his white wall with a buff wash as an absolutely stunning foil to his collection of classic modern furniture. In this case, the wash was the merest film of water color, but the texture of a wash can vary, depending on consistency and application, from translucent to near-opaque and from even to rough, the latter being a partic-ularly sympathetic ally to uneven walls — a useful tip for those who are despairing at the state of their walls.

Below On mid-gray, rough-textured walls an ultra-thin wash of charcoal breaks up the ground color and emphasizes the texture as it nestles in dips and hollows, and intensifies the natural effect of light and shade.

Distemper

Color-washes also have the advantage of being cheap. The traditional and perfect material for this technique was distemper, and although you can no longer buy distemper in Britain (it is still available in certain parts of Europe), it is easy enough to make. You need whiting (basically crushed chalk — powdered, washed and dried); glue size (the kind containing alum will help bind the distemper and prevent mold, but it is insoluble and therefore harder to remove when you want to redecorate); a tinting agent such as artists' acrylic, gouache or powder colors, or decorators' universal stainers; water and two buckets. Make the distemper by breaking up the whiting into smallish lumps in a clean bucket and covering it with cold water. Leave the whiting to soak for about 30 minutes before pouring off any excess water and beating it into a smooth, thick batter. Mix the size according to the manufacturer's instructions with hot water and blend it with the whiting knife while it is still in its warm, liquid state. Whichever kind of stainer you use, mix it thoroughly into a solution with cold water first; if it is added dry it is unlikely to disperse evenly and will produce unwanted streaks of pure pigment on the wall.

Since distemper lightens considerably as it dries, you may want to test the color first. In this case, mix the stainer thoroughly into the whiting — a little at a time, more can always be added, but not taken away — and brush a sample onto a piece of lining paper, drying it on a sunny window-sill or in front of the fire (otherwise you will not get a true impression of the color, as size tends to darken when it is artificially dried). Once you have reached the color you want, add the size. If for any reason the size was mixed in advance and has set to a jelly, heat it up in its bowl over a container of water on the stove. How much size to add is a delicate business and just about impossible to specify on paper. Size is the binder for the distemper — without it the distemper would dry as a loose powder that would simply rub off as soon as it was touched, but if too much size is added, the distemper could come off in flakes. The trick is to add a little of the runny size at a time, mixing thoroughly and allowing it to cool and thicken the distemper until it reaches the consistency of standard emulsion paint. Use it in this consistency for the full covering power of a ground coat, but for a superficial wash coat, thin it to a milky consistency with water. Either way, mix only as much distemper as you can use in a couple of days before it starts to go off.

PREPARATION Distemper can be applied on any sound, dry, flat finish except on top of old distemper, where it will produce a patchy result due to the old ground color 'pilling' as the new is brushed on. Wash off any old distemper thoroughly and prepare the walls for the new coat with

either a coat of pure size or claircolle — a straight mixture of size and whiting, which will give a uniformly porous white base coat and make a good ground for the first coat of tinted distemper.

APPLICATION The only problem with distemper, as with any water-based paint, is the speed with which it dries. This makes it harder to keep a wet edge going and avoid hard lines. Adding a small amount of glycerine — about one table spoonful per quart/liter (theatrical scene painters sometimes use molasses) — will help slow down the drying process, as will keeping doors and windows closed while work is in progress. Apply the distemper liberally and quickly, starting on the window side of the room and working away from it. Make your last 'laying off' brush strokes towards the light to minimize the chance of the strokes being visible and try not to miss out sections, as it's hard to touch up distemper without it showing. If you do miss a patch, it is probably better to sponge the color onto the bare area, rather than risk an odd, obvious brush stroke. Once the work is finished, it should be dried as quickly as possible, so throw doors and windows open

Above A thin, 'brushy' wash of salmon pink over cream softens the salmon and gives the whole surface a peachy bloom. On the left, a similar consistency of wash in corn over a cream ground produces a patchy effect which suits the random collection of earth-toned and metal *objets*. In both cases, the naturally rough nature of this finish is crisped out of tattiness by the fresh, sharp angles (**top**) and plans of white-painted woodwork.

Far left It can take courage to use a color wash — to adjust to and accept its naturally unfinished appearance. In this cottage bedroom, the condition of the surfaces has been not merely accepted but visually intensified — thick, white distemper washed with almost translucent buff to 'age' it authentically, deliberate 'damp spots' and the floor patchily stained to match.

and, if it's a ground coat, leave it to dry for a good 24 hours before adding the final, wash coat of thinned distemper

Other types of wash

There are one or two modern alternatives to distemper and choice depends on the effect you want to achieve. For an all-over, near-matt finish of translucent color, try well-thinned, flat oil paint (about one part paint to seven or eight parts mineral spirits) over an eggshell ground. If the work is done reasonably quickly, the wash will stay 'open' long enough for you to avoid hard edges and work out brush marks. If you actually want to get the 'distressed' and textured effect of criss-crossing brush marks, you could simply use latex paint, thinned with water. The most translucent of washes is made from pure pigment and water, with a very small amount of latex added just to give the mixture some body and make it more brushable. The quantities of color/water/latex will vary according to the desired richness of the finish, but in general, use about two tablespoonfuls of paint per quart/ liter of water. For the color, start with one small tube of gouache (it is expensive, but a little goes a long way), adding more if necessary. Whatever you're mixing, follow the same sequence of dissolving colors in water or solvent and mixing this solution with the undiluted paint before thinning. The importance of mixing thoroughly cannot be stressed too strongly; the tiniest speck of pure pigment can become a huge dark streak across a wall.

PREPARATION With the exception of the flat oil version, the washes mentioned above should be applied onto a flat, latex-painted surface: the flatter and more absorbent the ground, the easier it is to apply these very liquid washes over the top. But the surface must be absolutely clean and free of grease, or the wash will simply run off any of these patches. To check that all grease has been removed after washing, wipe the wall over with a solution of warm water and vinegar, rinse thoroughly and leave it to dry completely before applying the color-wash. Cover the floor with plenty of absorbent, protective layers and keep newspaper and/or rags handy for mopping up.

METHOD Slap the colour-wash on liberally and loosely, brushing in all directions and trying to keep a wet edge going as well as avoiding any heavy brush marks. If you want an open, more 'distressed' texture, deliberately leave some areas of ground color showing through on this first coat, or just skim some parts very lightly with the brush. Be prepared for this first coat to look awful, and wait until it is quite dry — about 24 hours — before applying a second. Distribute this second coat more evenly, so that it covers any previously unpainted parts as well as enriching the color in the already painted areas. Work as quickly and

loosely as possible, especially if you are adding one or more darker tones of wash for a richer effect. If the wash starts running down the walls, don't panic, work it in vigorously with a soft, dry brush and/or add a little more latex paint to the wash and use a sponge to fill any bare patches.

FINISHING The intermediate stages of color-washing can be rather a heart-stopping process, but it is unbelievable how well a couple of coats meld together when dry — and how different and much more 'deliberate' it will look once you have sharpened up the room's edges by repainting doors, windows and baseboards. Color-washed walls tend to look best if they are left in their matt, rough, rather unfinished-looking state, but if you feel the finish must be protected — for example, you may want to wash the walls, although this kind of 'open color' effect seems to survive dust and dirt with more resilience — use clear, matt polyurethane varnish. Just be prepared for the slight sheen effect that even the mattest of varnishes will give.

Above Even though brush-stippling, from a distance, probably comes closest to a plain surface, there is still a misty quality to the color and closer inspection reveals a very definite texture.

Below When brushing on the top coat, which is to be manipulated, over the ground, remember that the density and evennesss with which the paint or glaze is applied will influence the appearance of the finish.
Left Ragging is basically stippling with a rag. A clean, bunched-up rag is held against the wet top coat and 'rocked' very slightly to leave the impression of its folds in the glaze.
Far left In this dining-room a variety of techniques are combined with remarkable sensitivity. The wall on the left is brush-stippled, the far wall is ragged and the columns marbled. The secret of this room's success is not only the color-coordination between the techniques but, just as important, knowing when to stop.

STIPPLING

The traditional tool for stippling is a large, flat-faced, soft-bristled stippling brush which, dabbed onto a wet glaze, lifts just enough of it for the background color to show through, producing the fine, mottled, orange-peel texture typical of this finish. These brushes are extremely expensive, so you may well want to find an alternative. Experiment with a painter's dusting brush, a shoe brush, a soft-bristled hair brush, a worn down (or sawn off) broomhead; you could even try using a rubber-tipped stippling brush, usually used for textured paint, which is less expensive to buy but gives a much coarser finish. Each of these tools will produce a different texture, so it is worth testing them all to discover your personal preference but, whatever kind of brush you choose must have a flat bristle surface.

ALTERNATIVE TOOLS TO BRUSHES Brush-stippling can be quite a slow and exhausting business — although the bigger the brush, the quicker the ground can be covered, which makes the broomhead a popular choice, but there are several alternatives to brushes. You can stipple with clean, undyed, bunched-up rags, experimenting with different textures of fabric, or with sponges: the marine variety will produce a softer mottle, and for a crisp, granular stipple, cut a cellulose sponge in half to get a flat surface and keep twisting it from side to side as you stipple, to avoid too regular and hard-edged a pattern. Stippling can also be done with a roller — much the fastest way, although it's less easy to control the texture. Use lambswool, mohair (real or synthetic) or *coarse* polystyrene rollers (the smooth kind will just move the glaze about over the surface in nasty swirls) — each of these will give you a different finish, but they all leave a more blotchy, open texture than brush-stippling.

COLORS The classic color formular for stippling is to use a transparent or semi-transparent glaze over a white or at least light-colored ground. The clean, solid color of the glaze is lightened, softened and mottled by the tiny specks of ground showing through so that, for example, salmon pink over white or off-white becomes a velvety, pinky peach with a bloom that resembles the fruit itself; coffee on cream can look like natural suede. Only use this dark-on-light recipe as a guide rather than a limitation and experiment with your own color combinations. Also, try matt over shiny finishes as well as mid-sheen over matt. Multi color finishes are also possible since stippling enables you to blend, say, two or three pastel shades into each other so that there's no clear demarcation line between the colors and the results is a cloud of shifting color. You can stipple both walls and woodwork, but often it is better to keep one or other — that is, either walls or woodwork — plain, rather than treating both, to make a satisfying crispness of contrast.

EQUIPMENT Apart from your chosen stippling tool (brush, rag, sponge or roller), ground color, glaze and the material for thinning and tinting, you will need a couple of paintbrushes — use a wide, flat brush for applying the glaze — and plenty of clean rags or paper for wiping tools' and mopping up.

METHOD It really couldn't be simpler. Once the ground color is on and dry and the glaze mixed, you just brush on a band of glaze — about 2 ft (60 cm) wide is the most workable width — and then stipple over it. There are just one or two points to watch for, depending on which stippling tool is being used. If you choose a brush, rag or sponge it is much more helpful to have two people on the job, one to paint and the other to follow on stippling, so that there is no panic about keeping a wet edge going. The glaze should be brushed out thoroughly to a fine, even film and the stippling done by pressing the tool flat to the surface with a smooth but decisive dabbing motion, above all avoiding skids. Do not change roles half-way, as one stippler's touch is always different from another's and this difference will show.

Whatever the stippling tool, you will reach a point where it is so loaded with glaze that you risk putting more on than you're taking off. Clean brushes regularly by wiping them on clean paper or rags; change stippling rags frequently or clean the rags and sponge by rinsing them out in mineral spirits. Some people actually prefer to work with sponge or rags moistened with solvent as it tends to 'open out' the texture on the glaze. Keep a watch on your work, too: any missed patches can be filled by brushing a thin film of glaze across the bristle-tips of the stippling brush or the face of the rag or sponge and dabbing it on the bare patch. This is a safer rescue method than brushing on more glaze, as long as you clean any excess glaze off the brush/rag/sponge before moving on. A clean stippling tool should also reduce any over-glazed or twice-glazed

areas of darker color, although it may need to be moistened with mineral spirits for obstinate areas where the glaze has started to harden.

Roller stippling is so quick that it can easily be managed by just one person — it is actually quicker to stipple the glaze off than it is to paint it on. The only points to watch for are keeping the pressure even so that the texture remains regular and to avoid skidding — otherwise you will take too much color off and will have to re-cover the patch with glaze, then stipple over it again. As with the other tools, keep the roller clean by rolling it out regularly on clean paper to remove surplus glaze.

CLEANING UP Clean rollers on paper, as above, before squeezing them out in mineral spirits. Clean sponges and brushes with mineral spirits, too. If you throw the rags away, make sure you spread them out to dry first; when soaked with a mixture of paint/glaze and solvent, they are highly inflammable and could combust spontaneously if they are left bunched up in a waste basket.

SPONGING

Sponging is probably the quickest and easiest of all the broken color techniques mentioned here, largely because — unlike most of the others — it is being used to put paint on the ground rather than take it off. This makes the technique easier to control and there is no pressure from the drying time of the glaze. Try experimenting with a patch first and if it is not a success, you can quickly wipe it off an oil-based ground with a rag and mineral spirits although, as with the other techniques, it is better to use pre-painted lining paper pinned to a board for testing.

There are an inspiring number of possible effects that can be achieved with sponging, since you have three variables — the glaze, which can be opaque, translucent, shiny or matt; the texture of the sponge (and the way you use it); plus the colors you choose. Sponging can be done with one or more colors. The freshest combinations come from pastels or clear, bright colors like emerald or tangerine used over white, but using a variety of tones in the same color family, such as coffee over beige with perhaps a paler caramel sponged on top, produces a rich, mottled surface, often with the texture of rough stone. If the right colors are chosen, sponging can also look almost uncharacteristically smart and sophisticated. Imagine black sponged over a flannel grey, over electric blue or over scarlet. At the other extreme, you might want to create a soft cloud or color with a combination like mauve and forest green sponged over sage. Whatever mixture you choose, sponging in two colors works best with the lighter color on top.

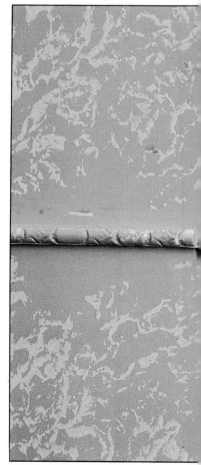

Right Sponge on one color or a whole sequence, letting each one dry before applying the next, depending on the complexity of color-texture you want.
1 The first, soft, semi-translucent green is sponged on airily.
2 Next, a slightly thicker gingery-beige, and rather more densely applied.
3 The third coat is a light, random sponging of butter yellow.
Below right The final touch proved to be a scattering of watery terracotta and sponging the radiator to match.
Below A complete face-lift for a pair of ordinary flush doors. First moldings were stuck on to create panels and then a ground of very dusty pink applied as a foil for a sparse sponging of jade green.

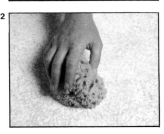

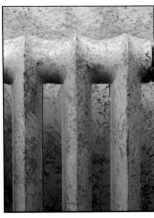

MATERIALS AND TOOLS This is one technique where it is both possible and easy to use latex but the effect with be cloudier and the print less defined than with an oil-based paint, which gives a crisper, cleaner texture. For a translucent, marbled finish, use a tinted oil glaze. The best sponge to use is the genuine marine variety. But you can use a cellular sponge (massage sponges have an unusual texture); with the ordinary cellular type, cut it in half to get a flat surface and keep twisting it, with a flick of the wrist between dabs to disguise the regularity and hard edges of the print. It is also possible to 'sponge' with bunched-up rag; try out different weaves from muslin to burlap to find a texture you like, but whatever is used must be undyed and lint-free.

As well as paint/glaze and sponge/rags you will need a flat container to hold the sponging medium. An ordinary paint-tray (the kind used for roller-painting) is ideal as it will hold a reservoir of paint or glaze at the 'deep end', which can be tipped every now and then to leave a fresh film over the surface of the shallow end, where it can be picked up on the sponge. Clean paper and rags are essential.

METHOD If you are using a marine sponge, soften it with mineral spirits first, or water if you are using emulsion, and let it expand to its full size, then wring it out thoroughly before using. Dab the sponge lightly onto the film of paint in the tray and test the print on clean paper before applying it to the wall. It will produce a wet, muddy print if there's too much paint on the sponge, so either squeeze it out or keep dabbing it on the paper until you get a soft but well-defined impression. Then start working your way over the wall with the sponge, refilling it as necessary and testing on spare paper each time, too, until you are confident of getting a consistent density of print without testing. If you are sponging with one color only, overlap the prints slightly for an even, all-over texture; if you are planning to use more than one color, keep the first sponge-prints fairly well spaced out, wait for these to dry and then fill in and partly overlap with prints in the second color. It is preferable to try and avoid the kind of regularity of pattern repeat found in bought wallpaper or fabric, so make sure you keep changing the position of the sponge in your hand or, if you are using rag, keep refolding and rebunching it. Clean both every now and then, to save getting messy prints, by rinsing out in mineral spirits (water for latex), but wringing both out thoroughly, otherwise you'll dilute both glaze and print.

You can also sponge new color onto a *wet* ground, which will produce an even softer print. In this case, follow the procedure for stippling, ideally working with two people, one applying the wet ground color in bands while the other follows after, sponging on the second color. If

RAG-ROLLING

Rag-rolling is one of the most dramatic of the broken color effects. It's related to stippling, dragging and, of course, ragging in that the relief patterning — which can look unnervingly like crushed silk or velvet — comes from partially lifting the wet glaze off the ground, but in this instance it's done by rolling a sausage of bunched-up rag over the wet glaze. The resulting pattern depends very much on the type of rag used. Cheesecloth, old sheeting or net curtain, lace, linen, jute and burlap are all possibilities as long as they are clean, undyed and lint-free. The pattern they produce varies with the softness of the fabric from a distinct but subtle marl to a crisp, definite marking, but all have a certain formality.

There is no technical reason why you shouldn't rag woodwork, but because its application involves a considerable amount of movement it is certainly easier — and generally more appropriate — to confine it to wide open spaces of wall and ceiling. It is particularly good at 'domesticating' these surfaces, softening angles, visually amalgamating oddly proportioned alcoves and extrusions and giving depth, interest and sophistication to otherwise boring expanses of plasterwork.

Rag-rolling has such definite markings that quite striking effects can be achieved with the gentlest of colors, so decorators tend to stick to the lighter neutrals and more off-beat pastels over a white or toning ground. A slightly

Far left It's easy to tell rag-rolling from ragging because the rolling technique produces a much more definite marl and a distinct feeling of movement.
Center Even at quite close range the visual effect simulates the way light bounces off the multi-directional pile of crushed velvet.
Left At the experimental stage, on lining paper, try rolling in different directions — horizontally, vertically or diagonally — and with different degrees of pressure (1). It's possible to roll rags over fairly straight-forward three-dimensional surfaces, like this radiator (2), but more complex items can be rag-stippled to match. Sponging is another alternative for co-ordinating adjacent surfaces, as on this molded board where bands of plain white emphasize architectural detail (3).

dirty white, tinted with a touch of raw umber and raw sienna, which browns and 'ages' it, makes a very sympathetic background for deep, faded pastels like caramelled pinks, dusty blues, grayish greens and that unusual half-gray, half-buff color that some people call 'greige'. Even rolling one shade of white over another can produce interesting results: a speck or two of black in a white glaze can produce something like the light-and-shade surface of an old damask tablecloth. So, experiment by all means with bolder combinations, but softer shades are a safer bet.

EQUIPMENT Apart from paint for the ground coat and mixed and tinted glaze for the top, ragged coat, the usual paintbrushes are required, including a wide, soft one for applying the glaze, and above all a plentiful supply of your chosen rag. But only use one *type* of rag for each job, otherwise you will get differing textures.

METHOD With this technique you can afford to apply the glaze over a fairly large expanse of wall before beginning work on it with the rags, as rag-rolling is quite a quick process. (The exception, of course, is when latex paint is used. This dries so quickly that it is better to both paint and work on a sequence of narrow bands as well as having two people on the job, one painting and one rolling.) Make sure the glaze is well brushed out to a fine film, preferably with

no brush marks. To lose all the brush marks, apply smaller areas of glaze at a time and rough-stipple them before you begin ragging. Roll the bunched-up sausage of rag across the glaze as if you were rolling pastry and, because, in this instance, you want an irregular effect, keep not only changing direction, but rebunching the rag so that you don't produce too uniform a pattern. Each rag will have to be abandoned as the glaze begins to harden it, but chamois leather can be washed out in either mineral spirits or water, depending on the glaze, wringing it out thoroughly before you start ragging again. Some people prefer working with rag or chamois moistened in solvent (or water) as it produces a softer marl. Keep watching your work as it progresses and dab the rag directly onto the surface to fill in any missed or unsatisfactory areas, and near adjoining walls, ceiling or woodwork to save smudging them — the difference really will not show. You can also, of course, roll on a second color once the first is dry, although sponging it on can look very pretty as it softens the ragged texture. As a general principle, a second glaze color nearly always looks best if it is lighter than the first.

CLEANING UP The danger of the solvent-and-glaze-saturated rags catching fire spontaneously if you leave them bunched up in a confined space cannot be stressed too strongly. Make sure used rags are left out to dry before disposing of them.

In spattering, experiment is really worthwhile, since every variation in technique will produce a different effect, including the exact point at which you knock the stock of the brush against the batten and the distance between brush and surface. Spattering can be done in one or more colors but it generally looks best if the whole effect remains fairly open.

1 The first, sparse spattering of red is showered onto a white ground.

2 Yellow and mid-green have been used equally sparingly and now a faint freckling of a watery dark green is being applied.

3 This darker green gives a bit of 'bite' to the final coloring, balancing the red and saving the whole from being too wishy-washy.

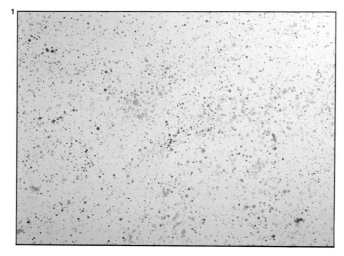

SPATTERING

Spattering has a very different feeling from the other effects, partly because it is generally a more casual and informal finish (although this also depends, of course, on the colors chosen) and partly because the 'spattering' of specks and flecks of paint onto walls or woodwork actually creates more of a texture, and a surface that is almost three-dimensional. It tends to be a messy process, so cover up anything that you don't want freckled with paint — including yourself — so that you can work freely.

COLORS If you use close tones of the same color or different colors of the same tonal value, a mist effect is created, which is much more suited to — and better achieved with — one of the other techniques such as sponging or stippling. Try spattering for nursery-like gaiety and freshness, using primary colors or the gayer and brighter of the pastels flicked onto white; for startling

Far right Spattering blends happily with other techiques and can, of course, be used for furniture as well.

combinations like yellow, pink and black flicked onto grey. Use spattering for sophistication, too, and for its ability to intensify or subdue an existing color: a brilliant cornflower over a calm saxe blue creates more surface 'tension' and excitement than either color could provide on its own, whereas spattering glossy black over a rich, mid-sheen bottle green changes the latter's rather claustrophobic somberness to the iridescent sheen of a bluebottle. The contrast of paint finishes is another important and useful element in spattering, because, luckily, any paint that can be diluted to a liquid, flickable state can be used. Run through color combinations in your mind and imagine how they would look if either ground or spatter were shiny, low-luster or matt.

EQUIPMENT A stencil brush is the ideal tool because of its stiff, squared off bristles, but an ordinary, rather coarse-bristled paintbrush will do if the bristles are sliced off squarely to about half their length. You will also need the relevant solvents and tinting agents for thinning and mixing paint, clean cans to mix it in, plus paper to experiment, pre-painted the color of your ground.

METHOD With spattering it really is a good idea to spend time experimenting first. You will want to test not only your own spattering touch, but paint consistency, too. For a good spray the paint should not be thicker than a milk-like consistency, but if it is made too thin it will run down instead of holding to the wall. Practice diluting a small amount of paint at a time, noting what proportion of solvent you need to add to get the right mix. To 'spatter', dip the bristle-tips of the brush into the paint then slide your finger, a knife or a comb steadily across the bristles to release a fine spray. With practice, you will be able to vary the size of the droplets in the spray and aim them with surprising accuracy. When spattering in more than one color, leave the first coat to dry before starting the next and protect the final result with varnish, which is especially important where water-based paints are used.

DRAGGING AND COMBING

These effects are decorative extensions of graining, with the main difference that the aim here is not to simulate 'the real thing' or even a stylized version of it. Nevertheless, both these techniques — and the distinction between them is made mainly by the equipment used — can definitely produce effects that resemble materials other than paint. One-way dragging of a wet glaze with a dry brush, normally used vertically, produces fine, slightly irregularly spaced lines as the brush reveals some of the ground color and leaves a surface texture like woven cotton with a heavily slubbed weft. But a second glaze color can be applied and dragged either vertically or horizontally, in

the latter case producing a texture like raw silk. And both the vertical and horizontal dragging can be in bands, so that something like a plaid effect is achieved.

Combing — either with proper steel or rubber graining combs or home-made versions cut from rubber or plastic flooring — obviously results in coarser lines than the dragging brush and a mixture of the two can produce some very exciting effects. The choice of both colors and paint finishes enormously changes the character of a dragged or combed finish. One-way dragging of tone on tone with flat oil paint or undercoat in, say, brick over terracotta can be subtle, formal and smart — a suitable setting for the elegant polished wood tables and chairs of a town house dining-room. But it can also look pale and bedroom-pretty in pastels on white and works equally well in more adventurous combinations such as charcoal over scarlet: At the other extreme, combing a shiny glaze in different directions all over a low-luster finish, so that the light is

Above and **top** By dragging with the flat-faced brush made for the job it is rather easier to obtain fine, clean, straight lines. But my own feeling is that, unless you are really doing a lot of dragged work, the difference in the result is not enough to compensate for the difference in brush prices. Here, you can see the effects produced by a dusting brush (a paper-hanging brush would do just as well) and by dragging first once and then a second time with the dry brush.
Left Even in close-up, dragging retains its resemblance to open-weave textile, although variations from the true vertical give it away. But these really don't matter, you're not trying actually to fake fabric and these imperfections, if not too frequent or at too marked an angle, can serve to make the surface more interesting.

bounced off the surface at all angles, produces a surface ripple like shot silk.

Both dragging and combing can be used on plaster and wood surfaces, even on floors. However, for one-way dragging in particular, it is important that the wall surface is sound, smooth and even as, unlike some of the other finishes, the lines created by dragging serve only to emphasize irregularities.

TOOLS AND MATERIALS Like many of the specialist brushes, those made for dragging are considerably more expensive than ordinary paintbrushes so it is only worth buying one if it will really earn its cost. Alternatives are a wide paper-hanging brush or a jamb duster. Graining combs are less expensive, but you can still make or buy alternatives. Make them by cutting V-shaped notches in plastic or rubber flooring, either at regular or irregular intervals. Buy large, wide-toothed plastic hair combs or metal combs, which can be adapted to produce an irregular pattern by bending back or breaking off some of the teeth.

Although it is possible to drag an oil glaze over an emulsion ground — a quick and unusual way of reviving a tired color scheme — dragging is most successful over a ground of either flat oil paint, undercoat or eggshell. This is not only because their non-absorbent surfaces make it easier to manipulate the glaze, but because, particularly with combing, their harder skins are more resilient to the pressure of rubber or steel. For the most clearly defined, dragged coat, with a shiny, washable finish, use a translucent oil glaze. The next best thing to this is a mixture of glaze and oil-based paint, which has more opacity. Some decorators do simply thin eggshell to near-transparency with mineral spirits, but the quicker drying of this mixture makes it harder to keep a wet edge going. For a flatter finish, use flat oil paint or undercoat; the stripes tend to merge together more, but you may like this effect. Dragging with thinned emulsion gives the flattest finish of all, of course, and very muzzy stripes, but again, it has its own charm and may appeal. Whenever you thin or tint paint or glaze experiment on paper or board with both tools and materials to be sure of color, paint/glaze consistency and the effect of brush and comb before starting. Keep clean paper, rags and mineral spirits handy for wiping tools and mopping up.

Walls

Dragging or combing a wall becomes a smoother operation with two people, one to apply the vertical bands of color, about 2 ft (60 cm) wide, the other to drag it straight and steady from top to bottom. With this technique, it is especially important to keep the wet edge 'alive' and the directional nature of the effect will only emphasize the patchiness of any overlap of wet color on dry. Keep the

glaze well brushed out to a fine, even film to prevent it running and always make the last, laying-off stroke downwards to avoid a criss-cross effect when the glaze is dragged. The hardest part in dragging is to keep the dragged lines straight and true. At the same time, being tense and apprehensive will only lessen your chances of success. Try to stay relaxed, relatively loose-wristed simply rest the bristle-tips on the surface and keep the pressure even as you drag the brush down the wall. If you doubt your ability to maintain a reasonably straight, vertical line, suspend a plumb from ceiling to floor an inch or so away from the wall, moving it along as you move yourself; or use the decorators' trick of a straight-edged board with nails knocked through to keep it off the wall (tie a spirit level to the board for level, horizontal dragging). If there is simply no way of doing top-to-bottom in one swoop, stop the down-stroke somewhere between waist-

Above Here, the glaze has been sparingly and brushily, but evenly laid over the ground and the dragged result is light and open.

Left This extraordinary, variegated plaid effect is produced by combing the glaze horizontally first, overlaid with wavy lines, and then vertically in straight lines.

Right In this bedroom the walls have been dragged vertically to resemble loosely woven cloth. The picture rail and cornice have been dragged but the edge-beading left plain.

Above Although dragging on woodwork does not really aim to simulate grain, it does simply look better if it follows its natural direction, as here where it sympathizes with the traditional structure of a panelled door.

requiring small brushes, the method is basically the same. The important point to watch with woodwork is to follow the direction of the grain — or the direction in which it would normally run, even if it cannot be seen. This is especially important on panelled doors and on windows, for even though you are not trying to simulate wood grain, it will simply look odd if the dragging is in one direction across all the broken surfaces. Follow the painting sequence and glaze/drag in one grain-direction at a time, masking off the other section and waiting until the first set of dragging is dry before working on the next. Emphasize the joins or joints between sections either with a fine, painted line (in a slightly deeper tone of the dragged color or in a watery neutral like gray or buff to suggest shadow), or you can make a light knife-score, which is then lined with the sharpened point of a lead pencil.

Floors
My own feeling is that dragging is rather too fine and subtle an effect for a floor, whereas combing can add pattern, color sophistication and gaiety to both floor-boards and chipboard or hardboard floors. Although, if they are laid close enough together, the directional nature of floor-boards can be disguised with painted panels. Boards look good simply combed in one color over the ground, in the direction of the grain. This still leaves you plenty of decorative scope, as color possibilities can range from light and pretty, like mid-gray dragged over white, to something dark and dramatic like black over red. Hardboard and chipboard panels can take some very jazzy treatments and it's astounding the range of designs, from simple, straight-line geometrics to complex curves, that a simple tool like a comb can produce. One way to think of such a project is as if you were creating your own, large- or small-scaled, 'tiled' floor, and, with this in mind, carry out the combing accordingly.

MATERIALS Stick to flat oil paint, undercoat or eggshell for floors. Prime new wood, then undercoat the floor and apply at least two coats of undiluted, or only very slightly thinned, paint to provide a good, solid ground. The combing coat should be thinned less for floors than for other surfaces (about a 1:3 mixture of mineral spirits to paint), again to give adequate 'body' to the finish .

METHOD Whatever type of floor you're painting, don't forget to paint yourself out of, not into, the room! With floor-boards, start in the opposite corner from the doorway and follow the principles for one-way dragging, painting and combing a couple of boards at a time. The advantage of laying a new hardboard/chipboard floor, is being able to paint and comb the panels before you lay them. If the panels are already down, the easiest way to

level and baseboard — that is below eye-level, standing or sitting — and brush upwards to meet it, feathering the join lightly and staggering the level of these joins so that you don't get a stripe of feathering across the wall.

When dragging, wipe the glaze off the dry brush between strokes or you will be putting color on rather than taking it off and the definition of the stripes will vary. Watch, too, for a build-up of glaze at top and bottom of the wall — lighten pressure here and around switches and moldings and keep a mineral-spirits-soaked rag handy for smudges. If you are planning to add a second, dragged coat, let the first dry thoroughly before reglazing and give the final surface a coat of clear matt or semi-gloss varnish — optional for oil-based glazes, essential for water-based.

Woodwork
Although the scale of the job will differ from walls,

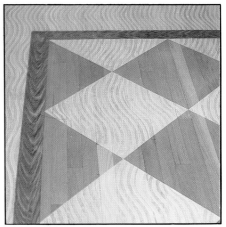

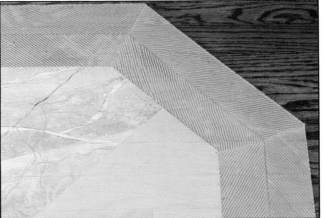

keep the edges neat is to do them a checkerboard sequence (as if you were working first on all the white squares on a chessboard, then on the black), masking the edges each time and waiting until the first set is dry before masking, painting and combing the second. Either way, plan the floor out on paper first, so you know exactly what you're doing, and use chalk lines to snap the position of panel edges onto the floor if they won't correspond exactly with the panels as laid: it may be, for example, that the chipboard is laid in rectangles where square panels are wanted. Once the combing coat is dry, protect the finish with polyurethane varnish — two coats will give you a certain degree of protection, but three coats will give real durability against the inevitable wear and tear that a floor that any floor will receive. It is always worth taking the trouble to apply these extra coats.

Top and **above left** A daring and imaginative treatment of a woodstrip floor, almost entirely combed in biscuit over cream, but leaving the original floor showing through in a diamond relief pattern, contained by a straight-dragged and wavily combed green border to resemble a rug.
Above Combing can disguise both the condition and direction of old floorboards.
Left A superb combination of combing and marbling over a previously-bleached section of a wood floor.

Fakes and fantasies

Such are the miraculous properties of paint that it can be used, and has been by generations of decorators and craftsmen, to simulate natural materials, from everyday substances such as wood and bamboo to exquisites like fine marble and tortoise-shell. Paint can also be used to simulate age — the patina of decades, even centuries of wear, newly created. It is these types of finishes that are covered by this section, together with two basic suggestions to anyone attempting them. The first is that, as a general principle, you confine your use of these finishes to surfaces that might just conceivably be made of their originals. This is not a hard-and-fast rule and the second point can explain why. Although some of the decision-making about how and where to use what is down to aesthetic instinct, the innate behavior and traditional use of the original material — such as whether it normally has a flat or curved face, whether or not it can be carved — act as a useful guide. The second suggestion, then, is don't aim for perfection. It takes not only talent but years of practice to reproduce the appearance of these natural materials so exactly that they might be mistaken for the real thing. The amateur decorator is unlikely to be able to achieve this degree of verisimilitude and anyway, it is unnecessary and probably not what is wanted.

The essence, or fantasy, of these finishes is their impressionistic quality: in using the appropriate patterning and color, they offer a general impression of the original material, but the purpose is decorative effect, not a mirror up to nature. This allows for a certain amount of license, within reason, to use these 'fakes' on some surfaces where the original would have been either impossible or ridiculously extravagant — for example, in tortoise-shelling a wall. Practically, these techniques are within the reach of anyone who has the confidence and will take the care to try them.

Far right If you work in naturalistic colors, you don't necessarily need to employ the full panoply of graining techniques to achieve a stylized replica of wood. On this door, simple dragging does the job and tatty hinges are first dragged and then sponged to blend in (**right**). In fact, this simpler treatment is a wise choice in a hall which is dominated, despite the pale colors, by large areas of marbling.

GRAINING

The practice of faking wood surfaces with paint is literally as ancient as the Egyptians and has taken many different directions over the intervening centuries. The most skilful and faithful copies, sometimes indistinguishable from the real thing, were often inspired by the shortage or high cost of the material itself, as well as by the irresistible challenge the job represented to the craftsmen. But a great number of liberties have been, and still are, taken with this technique — from stylized versions that retain the natural colorings of the wood, but discipline its random figuring into un-natural order, to fantasy versions that present the grain and other markings in a loosely realistic fashion, but depart entirely from its natural coloring.

Painted wood grain that seeks truly to deceive the eye is one of the fine arts of the decorators' craft, if that isn't a contradiction, and employs a large repertoire of techniques that can take a lifetime to learn and practise to perfection. But by acquiring just a few of these — and keeping your tongue in your cheek — you can have enormous fun creating wood-inspired finishes which, if nothing like the real thing, have definite decorative value. For those who want to try their hand at the real, representational finish, there's a chart suggesting ground and graining colors for a variety of woods. For the rest, choose colors to match your decoration scheme — safe color bets are tone on tone, but some very pretty effects can be made with pale-to-mid-tone pastels or neutrals over a different colored, lighter ground such as a silvery gray or beige on off-white, a cream or any of the sugar-almond colors on white, tinted with just a speck of the color to tone. I've also seen striking contrasts work well — black on terracotta and on emerald. Whatever combination you use, keep the ground color several tones lighter than the graining color so that the latter does not become overpowering. For the graining itself, it obviously helps to study the figuring of any wood you particularly like. Taking a rubbing of the grain with charcoal and paper is a useful way of isolating and becoming familiar with some of the more prominent markings. So is playing with a dry graining brush over the grain to see and feel exactly what angle and movement is needed to follow it, as well as practicing the various techniques on prepainted board or paper. But don't get too perfectionist or over-intense about it; you're not training to be a master grainer and this type of decorating should, above all, be enjoyable.

MATERIALS AND PREPARATION Graining can be done with either oil or water color, or both. For graining in oil, use a transparent oil glaze over an eggshell ground: it's important that the ground is hard, smooth and non-absorbent, so although flat oil paint can also be used, it's worth giving it a protective coat of clear shellac or satin-finish

varnish before graining. This is an essential step if you are graining on bare wood such as white-wood, and over stain on any other water-based finish, including water graining color. This water graining color is made in two ways, either as a 1:2 mixture of stale beer and water, or similar proportions of vinegar and water with a little sugar added to help it stick to the surface. Use powder pigments to tint it, mixing them to a smooth paste with a little of the combined liquids before adding the rest gradually, stirring them in well. This is the traditional 'cheap and cheerful' country cousin to glaze graining, although this does not dismiss its possibilities. Used sensitively, it can produce some very sophisticated results and some craftsmen prefer the special translucency of watercolor. Apart from being inexpensive, other plusses are that you can actually wash

Simple graining (above)
1 A coat of glaze is laid over the ground and dragged first with a dry brush to give the surface a basic texture.
2 Combing inserts more definitive straight grain.
3 A fitch is used to fidget in the outline of the heart wood.
4 A simple but effective method of adding knots — rag-covered forefinger placed straight down on the glaze and then slightly turned and rocked, as if trying to press a drawing pin home.

it off if you're not satisfied with the effect, providing you've sealed the ground beneath, and that it's quick drying — usually in about 15-20 minutes. This, of course, is also a disadvantage, giving you less time to work on it. It's therefore best kept for smaller or isolated areas like door panels. If it's drying too fast, you can usually brush on more of the solution without causing patchy color and adding a few drops of glycerine will also help slow the process down. The ground for water graining needs to have a flat finish for good adhesion. Flat oil paint or undercoat is best, sanded smooth with fine, wet-and-dry abrasive paper and soapy water. If you use eggshell paint, sand extra thoroughly to flatten the sheen and give the surface some tooth. To prevent this water-based color cissing (forming globules) on an oil ground, rub the ground over with whiting on a damp sponge and, when dry, dust off the loose whiting powder. Adding a drop of detergent to the color (some people actually mix the color with hot soapy water) will also help prevent this problem. Rubbing the ground over with a soap solution just before applying the color will help kill any remaining grease and prevent the color moving where you don't want it to. It's really worth experimenting with both these types of graining color, separately and in combination, as they each have different qualities which can complement each other to produce wonderfully subtle results.

TOOLS The right tools — or near approximations of them — are essential for graining. Professional grainers use a whole army of specialist brushes with extraordinary names, some of them aptly descriptive like a 'mottler', which does just that to put in highlights, or a 'flogger' to beat the surface, usually to simulate pore marks. But some of them are mystifyingly obscure: why, for example, would a brush that blends and softens be called a 'badger'? It also took me some time to realize that a 'pencil' wasn't that at all, but a brush sometimes also known as a sable writer — both names which, once you're in the know, exactly explain their fine-pointed performance. For most of the expensive, specialist brushes, the amateur can find or make adequate alternatives. If I had to choose one proper brush it would be a 'badger' softener because it can be used not only to soften and blend hard markings but to stipple, flog and even drag, too. A poor man's version is the ordinary painter's dusting brush, or 'jamb duster' whose bristles can be squared off, if necessary, with a hammer and the blade of a craft knife.

For the rest, you will need: a medium size decorator's brush for applying the graining color; a graining brush — make your own from a stiff, preferably thinly bristled paintbrush by chopping the bristles off square about 1 in/2.5 cm from the stock with hammer and knife blade, as above, and cutting out clumps of bristle from each side of

the brush, alternating the clumps and leaving a slight space between them; a graining comb — cut irregularly spaced notches out of a piece of strong cardboard or plastic (for regularly spaced grain, buy a cheap metal comb, which will also be useful for separating the bristles of the graining brush); make a knot tool by notching a cork or coring the center bristles from a stencil brush and removing clumps around the edges; a wide, soft-bristled paintbrush will serve for mottling and, at a pinch, for softening and blending too; a fine-pointed artists' sable brush is useful for teasing out, or in, individual lines of grain; back-up equipment could include a marine sponge, chamois leather and clean rags.

METHOD The character of every species of wood is basically defined by its color, grain, pore marking and mottling. In painted versions there's no need to even attempt to interpret these accurately, as long as they are combined in a form which roughly represents the natural texture of wood and the rhythm of its figuring. If you look at a piece

Far left Knowing when to stop is so important. The lining and shelves in this corner cupboard, sponged in a watery blue on cream to set off the blue and old-white china, makes a refreshing change.

Left One of the advantages of graining over real wood is that you can choose where knots appear and use them for decorative interest.

Below Fine, darker lines emphasize joins and, brushed and blotted in molding recesses, prevent panels looking too brash and new by suggesting the natural build-up of a little dust in the appropriate crevices.

Above A room full of character, but all of it superimposed and at a fraction of the cost of real wood panelling and custom-made cupboards. What makes this room work is scrupulous attention to detail and a degree of restraint. The walls and cupboards are trimmed and panelled with molding, the likely direction of real grain faithfully adhered to on each different section, markings have balance and symmetry where they occur and joins are shown clearly (**left**) as they would be on the real thing. But the graining itself is kept simple and the areas of definite patterning well-spaced.

of wood, you'll see that there is a definite pacing of the markings, but that they are never exactly evenly spaced nor exactly repetitive. Notice how the grain changes from light to dark, thick to thin, wide-spread to closely spaced, straight to curved; smooth-edged to jagged or blurred in outline; how it is stronger and darker as it curves around the knot and becomes straighter and fainter as it veers away from it; how it gets broader and spacier as it curves again into the long, ragged oval shape of the heartwood. In painted versions, you can place all these separate elements in a form to suit you and the surface you're working on — just try to keep a balance between the absolutely regular, which would look unnatural, and the absolutely random, which would look equally unrealistic and aesthetically unpleasing. The following sequence of methods will give you one kind of woody impression, but by experimenting with each one and with different combinations and in different sequences, you find that a considerable variety of effects can be obtained with the same basic collection of tools and techniques.

Texture Brush on the glaze and then rake it through from edge to edge with a dry graining brush; for a heavier texture, rake it through again with a comb. In both cases, undulate the graining tool slightly from side to side as you draw it down the surface to give the grain a gently waving quality.

Pore marks Hold the dry dusting brush — or the flogger if you have one — almost horizontal to the surface and beat it lightly all over, as if you were using a carpet beater. Beating with the grain will produce one effect, against the grain another. An alternative method for introducing pore marks is to hold the dusting brush perpendicular to the surface and stipple it all over or push it backwards and forwards over the grain to break it up, beating it afterwards against the grain with a dry brush to soften the markings. For a different type of pore marking, protect the otherwise completed finish with a coat of clear shellac, then spatter a fine spray of color lightly over the surface and soften it by whisking it immediately with the bristle-tips of a soft, dry brush in the direction of the grain. Experiment with these methods and take your pick.

Mottling Mottles are the silvery highlights that run across the grain to give many woods a satiny sheen. Again, here are two methods which each produce a different effect. Either fold a chamois leather, dampened with either mineral spirits or water (depending on whether you're using an oil or water graining color) and roll it down the surface, or dampen the bristles of a clean brush with the wet chamois, rest them lightly across the grain and rock the brush from side to side. In this way you can take the color off in irregular, horizontal patches down the surface; overlap each patch to avoid getting regular, vertical divisions, which do not do anything for the finish.

Knots These are put in with the cored stencil brush or notched cork by placing the end squared against the surface and twisting it. The surface may then be grained again to show stronger markings curving round the knots and straightening out between them. The stronger, darker markings can also be painted in with a fine-pointed artists' brush. The graining brush can also, of course, be used to put color on as well as taking it off. Separate the bristles with a comb after loading it with color and, whether you're using the brush wet or dry, play with its versatility. Changing pressure will alter the marks it makes from narrow to broad, close- to wide-spaced. This is particularly useful for putting in rings where, by varying the position, pressure and direction of the brush, you can move from dense, dark grain at one side to broad, widely spaced grain at the top of the curve before it narrows and tightens again on the other side. This can be done in one movement, with the process repeated to fill in the bottom half of the ring. Feather joins with a dry brush, so that they are unobtrusive and well finished off.

Heartwood These are the sets of distinctive, concentric ovals that sometimes contain a knot and sometimes do not. For these you can take the color off either with a fine-pointed artists' brush, the edge of a cork or with your thumb-nail wrapped in clean rag. On different woods, the grain is jagged or smooth; for a jagged effect, just wobble the tool gently as you draw it through the color. When the patterning is in, soften and blend hard lines by lightly whisking across the surface along the grain with the bristle-tips of a soft, dry brush. This will give a much more authentic end result.

FINISHING OFF Graining done in the water medium will need two or three coats of clear varnish for protection. Oil glaze, while less vulnerable, is also more durable under varnish and you may, anyway, want to use a tinted varnish to mellow the surface.

BAMBOO

Bamboo is another example of a technique where,

although it's as helpful, informative and inspirational as ever to study the original, nature is only the beginning of the painted art. As long as the two basic styles are loosely adhered to — that is, the typical patterning of male and female bamboo — fantasy can take over at any stage of this technique and, used with imagination and taste, prove stunningly effective.

To the Chinese, the bamboo has always been both a decorative inspiration and a practical material for the construction of buildings and furniture, but it wasn't until the seventeenth century that the burgeoning China trade brought its possibilities home to Europeans. Since it was initially too expensive for those other than well-heeled high society, craftsmen literally 'turned' to copying it in wood and these turned and decorated pieces became an art in themselves, reaching the peak of popularity in the eighteenth century when they were painted not only in **subtle colors to simulate the natural maerial, but in bril**liant hued fantasy versions, too. The fashion for real bamboo was revived in Victorian and Edwardian times — often decoratively scorched rather than painted — and it is furniture from these periods that most often turns up in junk shops, ripe for renovation. But the decorative features of bamboo can be used just as effectively on other surfaces around the home as it can on furniture, making a very pretty treatment for any suitably rounded picture or mirror **frames, or woodwork moldings such as those on archi**traves or the balusters along staircases and landings. To prevent it looking silly, the distinctive markings of the female bamboo, which has dark spines and 'eyes' as well as the knotty joints, should only be painted either on real bamboo or on turned wood that echoes its shape, even if not exactly simulating it. The simpler, tone-on-tone ring markings of the male bamboo can be used on any type of round mouldings — and these can also be added to the **'female" type for effect. Colors are really up to you: dark on light, woody colors to simulate the real thing, pastels on white or off-white for a pale and pretty effect, different** tones of the same colour for subtlety or brilliant colours and dramatic contrasts for drama and sophistication. The 'female' bamboo figuring generally looks best if the knots, **spines and eye centers are painted in the same color and** one which is darker than the ground but, again, these conventions can be broken with impunity: you might, for **example, use a mid-gray for knots, spines and eyes on a black ground, dotting in the eye-centers alternately with** black and scarlet It is really entirely up to individual taste and preference.

Far left This staircase from Brighton Pavilion, cast in iron in bamboo shapes, is further decorated with paint to emphasize the bamboo look.
Left and **above** Real bamboo can be embellished with paint to bring out the distinctive details — thin, parallel rings for male bamboo; dark spines and eyes for female bamboo.
Right Decorative treatment for bamboo can vary from picking out realistic features to more fantastic treatments. A length of real bamboo can be a useful source of ideas, but nature need not be copied slavishly.

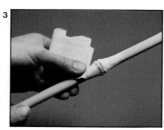

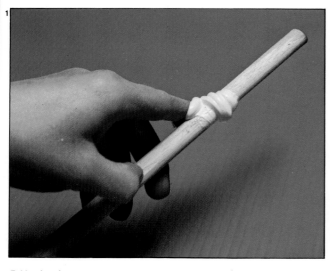

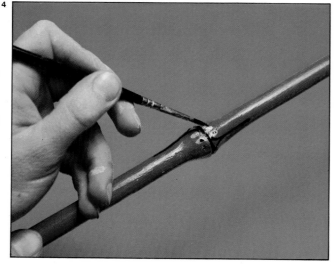

Faking bamboo
1 Build up the fake bamboo joints using plaster of Paris on ordinary wooden doweling. Plaster of Paris sets quickly, so can be readily built up in layers.
2 Use a sharp craft knife to carve the precise shape you want.
3 Sand smooth with a very fine abrasive paper.
4 Paint in the decorative details using a fine brush.

PREPARATION If you are merely adding decoration to natural bamboo, give it a preliminary wash with methylated spirits to remove any grease or oil, and any old French polish. If you are both painting and decorating bamboo, wash as above before applying at least three coats of thinned flat oil paint or undercoat, sanding carefully between coats with fine wet-and-dry abrasive paper and soapy water. If you're working on turned wood, you can leave out the wash (although a quick rub over with either methylated or mineral spirits is always a worthwhile safety precaution against grease on previously painted surfaces) and paint as above. Whatever ground you're working on, protect it with a coat of thinned, clear matt varnish or shellac; this will not only seal surface porosity but enable you to quickly wipe off any decorative mistakes with the appropriate solvent before they dry. It is certainly worth taking the trouble to achieve a smooth ground coat, as delicate decoration will not only be difficult to achieve and wasted on a rough ground, it will also serve to emphasize surface imperfections; so do take the trouble with the ground coat.

MATERIALS Although you can use flat oil paint, thinned to the consistency of cream and tinted with universal stainers, for decoration, these take so long to dry that an otherwise delicate and delightful job can become a bore. The quick-drying signwriters' colors are ideal, as are artists' acrylic colors: thin these to a creamy consistency with mineral spirits or water respectively, so that you get color that is smooth-flowing yet still opaque. For the subtle, more naturalistic and near-transparent ring markings of male bamboo, use 'sharp' color — that is, artists' oil color dissolved in a little mineral spirits, mixed with varnish and then further thinned with solvent. You'll need three tones — the darkest one for the knot, plus two paler ones. Mix the lightest, most transparent tone, first, thinning the varnish about 1:1 with solvent and get the two darker tones by adding more color and more varnish, using about half the amount of solvent to varnish for the mid-tone and a 4:1 mixture of varnish and solvent for the darker of the tones.

TOOLS You will need two ordinary paintbrushes for striping the male bamboo, one ³/₄in (1.9 cm) and one 1in (2.5 cm), and two fine-pointed artists' sable brushes — a No 3 and No 6 are the most versatile combination — for the decorative detailing.

METHOD **Female bamboo** With the No 3 sable brush, paint in the knots between the bamboo sections, pressing the brush so that the paint extends up and over about ¹/₁₆in (1.5 mm) of the rings at each side of the knot (the rings look like lips in profile, so it's easy to see where the 'lipstick' should stop). Paint in the spines in the same color. These start from each knot as two lines about ¹/₄-³/₈in (6-9 mm) apart and curve towards each other to meet and form one straight line, which tapers to a point as you gently lighten the pressure on the brush. The spines can vary in length, but traditionally never extend more than one-third of the length of the section and, where there are two spines pointing away from a knot, it looks better if their bases overlap or just touch rather than being absolutely symmetrical. The open area between the two branches of the spine can also be filled in with color if you wish. Next to be added are the eyes, using light but firm pressure with the No 6 brush to create slightly oval dots of color, usually in a mid-tone which contrasts with both knots/spines and ground. When these are dry, use the No 3 brush and the knot/spine color to place a tiny dot off-center in each eye and two or three dots around it. The placing of both eyes and dots is important: the eyes should be near enough to the spines to relate to them, but randomly spaced to create a more lively effect, and the dots should relate to the eyes in the same way, placed usually in singles or pairs, but with their formation changing from eye to eye.

Male bamboo Apply sufficient pressure on the ordinary $^3/_4$in (1.9 cm) brush, using the thinnest, palest of the colours (see above), to paint in an even, translucent band which is centered on the knot and extends about $^1/_2$in (1.2cm) each side of it. When this is dry, add enough color and varnish to this mixture to thicken and darken it to a mid tone and, with the 1in (2.5cm) brush, paint a second, narrower ring over the first, again centered over the knot. Add more varnish and more color to make your darkest tone to paint in the knot with the No 3 artists' brush, as for the female bamboo above.

ADDITIONS AND VARIATIONS The knots on female bamboo can be further emphasized with a single, broad band of translucent color, as in the lightest of the stripes for male bamboo. The sections between the knots can be lightly dragged with toning or contrasting color before the detailing is painted on or, after decoration, the entire piece can be brushed and/or dragged with tinted varnish or antiqued by any method, including freckling the area either side of each knot with a fine spattering of paint in the same tone. A fantasy version of male bamboo can be achieved by striping the whole length of the shaft with rings in a contrasting color to the ground: use the No 3 and No 6 brush to vary both the width and spacing of the rings for a random effect, or paint on the second color all over and comb the rings on, either straight or in jagged zig-zags. Real fantasy female bamboo can be achieved by retaining the positioning of spines and eyes but replacing the traditional figuring with a suitable pattern of your own choice, such as leaves and flowers of some description.

FINISHING TOUCHES Whatever treatment you use, wait until the decoration is completely dry before adding two or more coats of clear varnish. Whether you use matt, satin or gloss may be needed to bring out brilliant colors and give painted pieces will look better under matt varnish, satin will most resemble the natural sheen of real bamboo while gloss may be needed to bring out brilliant colours and give a lacquer-like finish to fantasy pieces. These are useful hints on the best finishing treatments if you are unsure of yourself.

This gilding method uses silver leaf, which is much cheaper than gold leaf. The surface is painted gold afterwards to adjust the color.
1 First paint a base coat on the surface.
2 Take out a sheet of silver leaf from the book.
3 Brush the sheet down onto the base.
4 Burnish it with cotton batting.
5 The method for laying gold leaf is exactly the same.
Left A restrained use of gilding, picking out the details at the top of this column, creates a rich, warm look, reflecting light from the wall lamps.

MARBLING

There are as many paint techniques for marbling as there are types of marble. No decorative technique relies so heavily on the natural behavior of paint and its reaction to the materials used with it; no technique is so full of surprises and delights and, in some ways, there is no technique in which it is easier to produce such extraordinary results since, to a large extent and with the aid of a few simple tools and accessories, the materials do the work for you. However, it is fairly essential to know what these materials are and how to use them.

It is also helpful to understand something of the basic structure of marble in order to attempt even a merely decorative facsimile. The most important thing to understand is that marble was originally created by movement: by the action of heat and pressure on limestone, which caused crystallization in black, white and other, sometimes brilliant, colors; by mineral substances running through the original molten strata and cooling in vein-like form; by the fragmenting of layers like leaves in a book, whose cracks became filled with other, variegated matter before the whole welded itself together as solid stone. But marble isn't, in fact, 'solid' — at least to the eye. Its translucent quality results in some veins and colorings showing clearly and strongly on the surface while others are seen more vaguely beneath it. Real marble has movement, a directional flow and a mixture of opacity and translucency; and so, of course, does paint.

Marbling has long been an inspiration and a challenge to painters, proven by examples dating back as early as 2000 BC, and some exceptionally fine examples exist where only obvious misapplication or touch call their bluff. In today's interiors, marbling works well on walls, baseboards, mantelpieces and floors — and best, with the possible exception of matching mantelpieces and baseboard, if its use is restricted to one of these areas per room. As with the other techniques in this section, the aim is not necessarily to reproduce the original exactly or even attempt the accuracy of the grand marbling masters. Merely approximating some of the colors and forms can produce delightful and different effects, which have a decorative value in their own right, and marbling can, actually, be anything you make it.

Sicilian marble

This is one of the simplest marbles to imitate; it is white with tinges of light greeny gray, yellow and soft, but with distinctive veins in black and a dark, warm gray.

MATERIALS The ground should be in a dead white flat oil paint, eggshell or undercoat and well rubbed down with fine abrasive paper when dry to eliminate brush marks and leave a smooth, flat surface. For marbling you will need

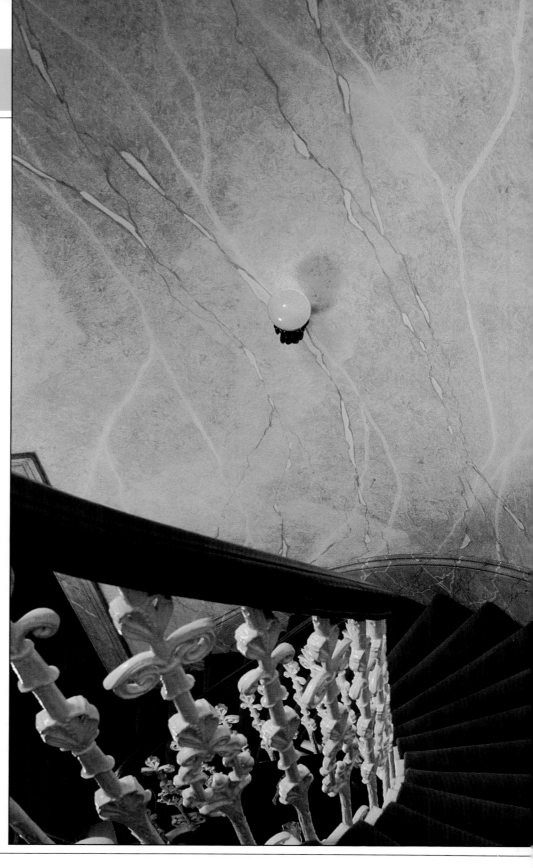

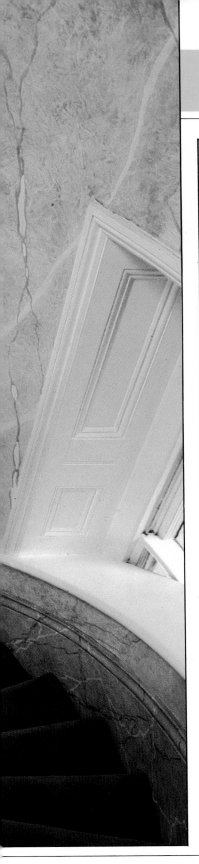

Far left This marbled stair-well attempts a fake finish. Because it's done in a stylized way (see close-up, **below left**), it comes off.
Top This marbled fireplace has been sponge-mottled and feathered.
Above Marbling does a good job at integrating ugly objects.

transparent oil glaze; boiled linseed oil; artists' oil color in Chinese white, black, raw umber and pale yellow ocher; two oil crayons, one in a warm gray and the other black; a small marine sponge; a softening brush (the specialist version, again quite expensive, is a hog-hair softener but a soft 2 or 3 in (5 or 7.5 cm) paintbrush will do); saucers, screw-top jars, clean rags and mineral spirits.

METHOD I Prepare all the materials in advance. Blend a little of the white oil color with the oil to make a milky, near-transparent mixture. Prepare small amounts each of two pale shades of glaze — a gray-green (white plus raw umber plus a little black) and a yellowish gray (white plus raw umber plus a little yellow plus a little black) — by dissolving the oil color in mineral spirits and adding an equal amount of glaze. Now, use a rag to rub the surface all over with the white oil mixture. Then use first the gray crayon to draw in the inner veins, followed by the black crayon to add the more prominent outer ones. The veins should meander across the surface diagonally, branching to left and right from a central point and then linking up again to make quite large-scale, rough and irregular diamond shapes. Veining lines are never straight but vary, rather like an erratic old sewing-machine, from patches of quite frantic zig-zagging to calm ripples across the surface. The end result should look very much like the wanderings of rivers, streams and tributaries across a map, with one exception: the veins always have a beginning and an end, they do not just appear from nowhere, nor do they disappear into nothing. Keep the veins well spaced out, with just occasional busy patches where one set crosses another, but err on the side of too few veins rather than too many. Fill in the patches between them by sponging in areas of the gray-green and yellowish gray glaze but, again, be sparing and don't entirely cover the white ground. The last step is, with the dry paintbrush, to stroke the whole surface diagonally, first in one direction, then the other. This is where the transformation occurs and as the crayon lines soften and the glazes blend, the whole thing suddenly does begin to look like a piece of marble.

Top right Marbling made simple: on a white ground another, almost indiscernably different white is added and crumpled newspaper dabbed on and rocked against the surface to 'break up' the color.
Top Watery black veins are painted on and softened by teasing them diagonally with a feather.
Right and **above** The starting point for this marbled pillar was a plain, creamy-white ground. The steps for achieving a similar effect are shown opposite.

METHOD II Another method, which produces a very similar effect, involves covering the ground with a thin, pale, greeny gray paint glaze. A 1:2 mixture of paint and mineral spirits, plus a little raw umber and black, it should have just enough colour to show against the white ground when it is sponged on. Veins can then be added — in two different mixtures of raw umber and black to give a lighter and darker shade — with a fine, pointed artists' brush. The brush is teased against the direction of the vein to produce the more excited, zig-zag lines; for the smoother, rippling lines, hold the brush straight out, like an extension of your hand and, with palm upwards, rotate the brush as you draw it towards you across the surface, varying the pressure to vary the line width. These lines can be sponged lightly and a little of the dark color transferred from the sponge to the areas between them before softening the surface with diagonal brush strokes.

Veins can also be drawn in with a feather, either by using the tip as the finest of paintbrushes or by irregularly serrating the broad edge. Dip this edge first in water, then in mineral spirits, comb it to separate the fronds, brush some oil color onto it and draw it across the surface. It will leave a set of fine lines which, when the feather is turned sharply, will branch off in all directions; and by simply changing your hand to the other diagonal, the movement will be along rather than across the feather, the lines will all join sharply at different points to become a single vein.

Serpentine marble
This is one of the most dramatic marbles which, for painting purposes at least, has a black ground, mottled with slightly dusty emerald and streaked with a random criss-crossing of straightish, thread-like white veins. This is almost simpler to simulate than Sicilian, except that this technique needs to be executed on a horizontal surface or the paint and solvent will run. Lay the ground as before with black oil-based paint. Mix a top coat of green paint glaze — emerald with just a touch each of raw umber and black to 'dirty' it, thinning no more than one part mineral spirits to two parts paint, so the glaze has a reasonable amount of body. Apply the glaze and then flick random splashes of mineral spirits over it with a stiff stencil brush. Wherever these splashes fall they will magically open up the glaze to reveal the ground. This penomenon is technically known as 'cissing' and the shapes produced can be varied by flicking on methylated spirits or plain water (keep cotton buds handy to neatly soak up any over-enthusiastic splashes). Now, squeezing a marine sponge out in thin white paint glaze, dab it here and there on the revealed areas of ground so that there is the occasional, light mottling of white. Lastly, coat lengths of cotton twine with white oil color laying them on the surface to produce a loose, random lattice-work of fine, diagonal veins.

1 An ochre glaze is laid brushily over the creamy-white ground, so that a lot of the background still shows through, and then supplemented by diagonal loops and swirls of dark brown.

2 Colors are blended and brush-marks partly obliterated by dabbing the surface, while still wet, with crumpled newspaper.

3 The whole effect is softened with a dry brush, drawn diagonally across the surface first one way and then the other.

4 Veins are fidgeted in with a slim artists brush in sepia and blue glaze, so near transparent that some color is taken off the surface as these are added.

5 The new veins are teased with a feather to soften their lines.

6 As a final touch, the whole surface is softened and blended again with light, diagonal sweeps of a soft-bristled, dry brush.

Below and **center** Marbling before and after it's been varnished. Varnish not only provides a vital, protective coating but seems visually to unify the finish so that several different layers fuse into one. Several coats of well-thinned varnish, rather than one, will not only offer additional protection but give more depth.

Multicolored marbles

Real marbles may contain some or all the colors of the rainbow and will provide inspiration and example enough for anyone to follow. However, there is no reason why you shouldn't create marbled finishes with a blend of colors and forms entirely of your own choosing. You can, for example, marble on a dry ground, using the standard paint glaze (white, oil-based paint, thinned with half its volume of mineral spirits). Make up two or three different colors by tinting with artists' oils and dab them in a rough patch-work over the ground, then blend and 'distress' them in a variety of different ways. Dab the whole surface with a marine sponge or crumples airmail paper; this will blot up some of the glaze and roughly blend the colors, as well as adding surface texture. Then stipple across the colors to blend them more subtly and thoroughly.

Another method is to cover the whole surface with newspaper and stroke it firmly with a stiff stencil brush. This will remove color in some areas and create a movement of color in others. If the newspaper is creased and/or pleated first, it will take up the glaze under the creases, leaving fine, vein-like lines. (This is also a useful trick for creating the dramatic relief contrast of some of the black, gray and white marbles.) When you want pure, definite contrast, protect the ground from marbling with an intermediate coat of clear varnish or thinned, white shel-lac, which also enables 'mistakes' to be wiped off with a rag and mineral spirits.

By adding you will create a translucent oil-glaze of a lighter or deeper hue than your ground, the impression of looking through one color into another. or you can sponge on a faint mottling of paler colors over darker, dark over pale by loading (but not over-loading) a marine sponge with color and lightly dabbing it or rolling it over the surface. You can also spatter random showers of color in fine flecks or spatter mineral spirits, methylated spirits or water to open up the surface in different ways. Add fossil shapes by carving notches into the face of a cork or a cut apple, potato or carrot. These can be used to lift color off (clean the face of the 'stamp' each time) or put it on: dry the face of vegetable stamps with french chalk or blotting paper first. Other vegetables can create different effects — for example, the cut-flat head of a cauliflower floret.

Finish with a sparse fretwork of light and/or dark veins, traced in with a fine, pointed brush, a toothpick or orange stick, cotton thread or a feather. Just remember that, while veins can approach and recede from the surface, appearing stronger and weaker, thicker and thinner, sometimes even disappearing temporarily under a patch of color, they always reconnect and begin and end only at the edges of the surface itself.

Marbling on a wet ground allows colors to 'float' and flow into each other with greater mobility, forming other colors as they meet and merge. To make a suitably slip-pery surface, brush the existing, prepared, dry ground first with flatting oil (a 1:6 mixture of boiled linseed oil and mineral spirits) and then with a really watery dilution of the ground color. Use two or three colors, also thinned

Far left Fake marble need not aim to ape nature exactly to be effective.
Left Marble comes in a surprising range of colors — and this fireplace marbling draws inspiration from the striking moss green variety.
Above The classic proportions of this wood fireplace lend themselves marvelously to marbling and the bonus of making, rather than inheriting.

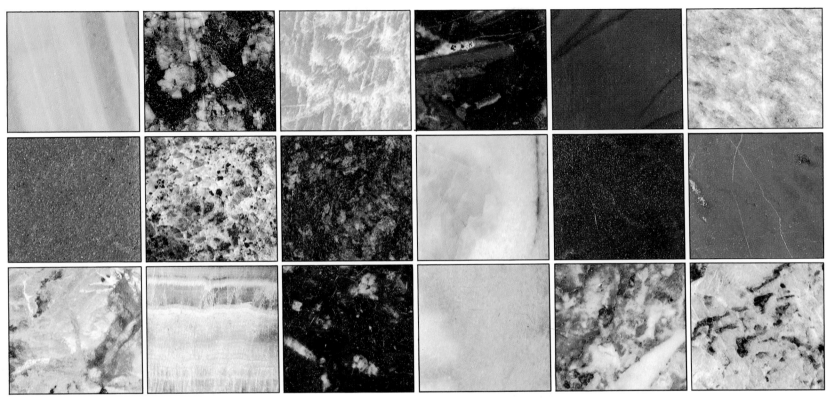

practically to water, and ¼ and ½in (6 and 12 mm) paint-brushes to drip or dab them onto the wet ground. Watch how the colors move and merge — you may want to check the flow of some with a cotton bud of cottonballs squeezed out in mineral spirits, or encourage the flow of others by dripping more color or mineral spirits onto them. Hard edges of color can be blended either with cotton balls as above or by stippling with a brush, and the colors can then be further blended or textured by any of the methods already mentioned.

FINISHING OFF On walls or woodwork, leave the finished marbling to dry for at least 24 hours before adding a coat of clear matt or satin finish polyurethane varnish. On wood-work especially, the soft sheen so typical of a marbled surface can be achieved by applying two coats of thinned varnish and, when these are dry, polishing first with a paste made of baby oil and rotten-stone, then with dry flour using a soft cloth or the palm of your hand. If you are marbling a floor, up to five coats of varnish will be needed for protection. Whatever the surface, one trick to obtain the feeling of looking through rather than at it is to use a final, more matt-like coat over a shinier one — in this case satin finish over gloss.

Above Truth is indeed stranger than fiction and if imagination runs out, there is more than enough variety in real marble to supply fresh inspiration.**Left** Two different marbles meet at skirting level; color makes the contrast but style and tone are the co-ordinators.

Above The entire surface of this panelled door has been tortoise-shelled — a treatment which may be a little extreme for some tastes, but is obviously not intended to look realistic.

TORTOISE-SHELL

The practice of using tortoise-shell for decoration stems from the Far East, reaching Europe in the seventeenth and eighteenth centuries along with the craze for all things oriental, and inspiring both cabinet-makers and decorators to reproduce its distinctive colouring and marking on everything from ceilings and cornices to finely lacquered furniture, accessories and objects. Anyone wanting to create even an impressionistic version of tortoise-shell would be well advised either to obtain even the smallest piece or object covered in it (protect these from the drying effects of central heating by rubbing regularly with a mixture of olive oil and senna powder, applied with a soft, warm cloth) or to visit a museum or stately home where both real and fake examples have been preserved.

The colouring of tortoise-shell ranges from golden browns and tawny tones to an almost fiery red through to deep browns with near-black markings. There is no need to feel restricted to these naturalistic colorings, however, as many people in the past have experimented by retaining the characteristic diagonal markings of tortoise-shell, but imposing them in, for example, dark brown on an emerald ground and in black on cerise, with stunning results.

The scale of patterning that you use will be influenced by the size of the area to be worked. This in turn is influenced by the medium: the distinctive element in the technique is the method of working the markings into wet tinted varnish and any piece being worked on, even a large wall, will need to be finished in one shot. Unless there are at least two people on the job — and bear in mind that everyone makes different marks — it's sensible, and can be very effective, to divide the wall up into a series of panels (3 ft (90 cm) is about the maximum workable width). Give each panel definition by separating them with a fine painted line in, say, black or dark brown, and perhaps changing the direction of the diagonal markings from panel to panel. If you're doing this, mask off and paint alternate panels and wait until these are dry before doing the ones in between; wait until all are dry before painting the dividing lines. Smaller areas such as doors will cause less of a problem, but it is much easier to control the behavior of the wet varnish and paint if they can be taken off their hinges and worked on a horizontal surface. Doors are, in fact, a perfect example of where and when not to use tortoise-shell: flush doors can look superb, panelled doors would look awful unless the tortoise-shell were contained within the panels. Painted tortoise-shell looks best on either flat or rounded surfaces. It simply doesn't look right on broken or carved surfaces, which were obviously never made of tortoise-shell in the first place. For tortoise-shell panels you can simulate settings to look like metal, ivory or ebony, as indeed they might have been. However you use tortoise-shell, bear in mind that it is an opulent finish and overpowering on a large scale, and therefore it is probably best kept — and certainly more easily applied — to small rooms like bathrooms, dressing-rooms or tiny halls, or smaller areas of a larger room, such as doors.

MATERIALS For a rich, golden-tinged, mid-brown tortoiseshell, use a ground — which should be of the low-luster/eggshell type of oil-based paint — in a juicy yellow like yellow ocher. For the tortoiseshell coat the crucial material is tinted varnish in a dark oak color (undiluted for plaster-work but for a smooth finish on woodwork, thinned with about half the varnish quantity of mineral spirits), plus artists' oil colours in a deep, reddish-brown, like raw umber, and black. Two ordinary paintbrushes are also required, one for the wet work of applying the varnish and a dry one for brushing it out (size from 2-5 in/ 5-10 cm depending on the area to be covered) and two small artists' brushes, about $\frac{1}{2}$ in (1.2 cm) wide, clean rags and spirits.

METHOD Apply the base coat and let it dry. Working diagonally, use one of the big brushes to apply a liberal coat of varnish as quickly as possible so that there is time to work on it before it starts drying. When this coat is on, use the same brush to tease the varnish into broken diagonal bands, zig-zagging the brush lightly as you draw each band through the varnish, but trying to avoid too regular a pattern. (To achieve a more natural look the bands should radiate slightly, as if they were all coming from some central point way off, up and to one side of the work area). At this stage the varnish will be very much 'alive', moving as the brush is laid on and removed, and possibly bubbling slightly too, although don't let this bother you.

The next step is to quickly and gently blot off any excess varnish with a clean, bunched-up rag, which will also help to slightly blur the marking on the varnish, more so if the rag is moistened with mineral spirits first; slightly fraying the end of each dark varnish stroke with the rag will also make them loos even more natural. then, with the small brushes and oil colors, insert diagonal squiggly lines of smaller scale and sharper definition, the dark brown being punctuated by a lesser amount of the black. Use the small brushes either by rolling the tips over the surface of the varnish or with a flat, zig-zag movement, as if you were shading paper with a wax crayon.

Once all the markings are down, soften them — blending paint and varnish together — by very gently stroking the whole surface across and back in the same diagonal direction with the remaining large, dry brush. Then repeat this gentle brush stroke down and back diagonally across the 'grain'. Repeat this two-way sequence as often as necessary to soften and blend varnish and paint to your satisfaction, but always make the last stroke in the direction in which you first applied the varnish.

Left This detail of a tortoise-shell panel shows how effective it is to pick out frames or trim in different colors. The warm, pinkish red tones well with the more traditional honey color of the main panel.

Alternative colors and markings

For a 'blonde', golden-brown tortoise-shell, use a lighter, sharper yellow for the ground and either thin the dark oak varnish with mineral spirits or use light oak instead; use two different shades of dark brown oil color for the markings. For dark brown tortoise-shell, use a red-brown ground, dark oak varnish and brown and black markings as above. For a distinctive red-and-black tortoise-shell, use a deep, brick-red ground and black markings, but mix some of the varnish with a little of the black oil color to insert the first, broader diagonal strokes.

Depending on how 'busy' and 'fantastic' you want the finish, there are other ways of adding marks. You can apply 'accents' to the first broad, diagonal bands, either in the lighter or darker of the oil colors or in the two mixed together. Make accents by dipping the artists' brush in the oil color and pressing it down onto the varnish to form small, irregular ovals, circles and dots. Place these so that they are still in the same general direction of the diagonal, but at a slight angle to the broad, zig-zag bands, either slightly overlapping or between them and either singly or

in clusters. Circles of color can also be created by using an eye-dropper to drip a spot of mineral spirits into a circle or oval of paint. This will 'open up' the oil color and when the mineral spirits dries, another, tiny dot of paint can be dripped in the middle. Adding a drop of water will produce a slightly different effect and methylated spirit or undiluted alcohol will slightly fray the edges of the spot of oil color. Keep cotton buds handy in case you need to quickly and neatly mop up an over-spill of drops — although this in itself can turn out to be something of a happy accident and cleaning up unnecessary.

FINISHING OFF Since you are actually working in varnish, an additional coat of clear varnish is not strictly necessary. But for further protection and durability, you could apply a coat of semi-gloss or gloss polyurethane varnish (matt will kill the quality of the finish). For a really perfect finish on woodwork, after the varnishing sand down with very fine (600), wet-and-dry paper and a solution of mild soapflakes and water and polish up with a paste made of rotten-stone and warm linseed oil.

PORPHYRY

Porphyry is an igneous rock whose granitic texture comes from the many minerals embedded in its fine-grained mass. Although its name comes from the Greek word for 'purple' and was originally used to describe a particular reddish-purple and white variety, often used for sculpture because its hard surface can be given an almost glass-like polish, porphyry is now used much more loosely to cover a whole family of this rock-type, members of which are found in many different colorings. Other typical combinations are: brown, veined with near-transparent white and flecked with pink, red and green; dark green flecked with gold and black; violet, flecked with gold, black and iron-gray; reddish brown flecked with light brown and black or with reddish purple, black and pale pink. It is always worth studying the originals for information and inspiration for decorative purposes, as with the other techniques, but considerable artistic license may also be taken with color combinations as long as the characteristic granite-like texture is observed. This is easily represented by spattering a sequence of watery colors over a plain or sponged ground. The recipe given is for a gray-green porphyry with distinctive flecks of off-white and black, but with the technique at your fingertips, the colors can be varied to suit your taste.

MATERIALS The ground color requires a white flat oil paint or undercoat, tinted to a beige-gray with artists' oil colors in raw umber and pale yellow ocher (proportions are roughly one part of each oil color to six parts of paint). Make enough of this mix so that, together with some of the plain white oil paint, it may also be used for the spattering coats. For the spattering colors, make up six different shades from the paint, artists' oil colors and mineral spirits.

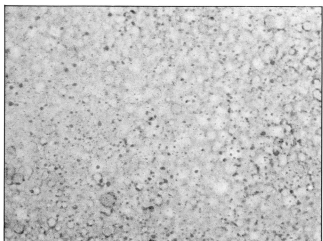

Above After laying the glaze on over the ground, crossing brush-strokes start to give the surface a more definite texture.
Above right The surface is then softened by criss-crossing diagonally with a dry, soft-bristled brush.
Far right After spattering terracotta flecks across the surface by knocking a paint-loaded brush against a wooden batten, the same technique is used to spatter small amounts of white spirit, which 'ciss' on the surface and open it up.
Below right The final result uncannily resembles a granite-like stone, saturated with fossils and minerals.

The first three evolve from the ground color, one being the same, one lightened with a little white and the third darkened a roughly equal degree with a little black. Then make up a slightly off-white shade by adding a speck of raw umber to the white paint. For the fifth color, add to some of this off-white enough pale yellow ocher and green chromium oxide to make a pale, milky, yellowy green. The last color is simply the black artists' oil color, dissolved in mineral spirits. All colors are thinned to the consistency of skimmed milk with mineral spirits (above 1:3 mixture of paint and solvent).

METHOD Apply two coats of ground color and, when they are dry, sand down with fine abrasive paper to provide a tooth. Then spatter all over with each of the colors in turn in the same sequence as they are given above, but waiting for each spattering to dry before adding the next. Bear in mind that porphyry often shows drifts of different crystals, so there is no need to try to achieve a uniform dispersal of each color. Similarly, although most of the spattering should be finely sprayed, passing knife or finger across the loaded bristle-tips of the brush, it looks more natural if there are occasionally larger and more irregular dots of paint. For these, knock the stock of the loaded brush against a block of wood, which will release larger, different-sized particles of paint. You can vary size and texture still further by adding a little more solvent to the paint. The finest spray of all will be achieved by using a diffuser, bought from artists' suppliers. This extremely basic piece of equipment — simply two short, slim tubes connected at a right angle — relies on one of the fundamental laws of physics to produce a remarkably sophisticated result: by resting the end of one tube in a jar of watery color and blowing through the other end, a vacuum is created which draws the color up to the top of the first tube; one further puff will spray it onto the surface.

For this particular, very granite-like porphyry effect, keep the spattering of grays fairly regular, with just a few lighter and darker areas, using the knife- (or finger-) across-brush technique. Use brush-against-block to spatter the off-white, making freckles of a more random size and in a sparser arrangement; spatter the green in fine, hazy drifts — ideally with a diffuser — and use a mixture of the first two techniques for the final, light spattering of black.

FINISHING OFF Protect porphyry finishes with two coats of clear varnish. Whether to use matt, satin finish or gloss depends on preference and surface — you may, for example, want a matt, more stone-like finish for walls. For a more reflective finish, apply enough coats of gloss to level the surface. This should give a high enough shine to obviate polishing, which could unsettle the fragile surface.

ANTIQUING

Familiarity with some of the basic antiquing processes is an advantage to those interested in decoration, because they have a far broader range of usefulness than mere nostalgia or for the creation of a strictly period environment. This may be a very personal view, but I prefer rooms that look as though they just happened or grew into what they are, however newly, deliberately or smartly done. The judicious use of a few of the antiquing techniques can be a tremendous ally in achieving this effect and can often work as well with an ultra-modern furnishing style as it does with any of the more traditional types, from country-cottagey to austere and elegant antique.

What you should be trying to do — in fact, *all* you're

Above The effect of making new paint-work appear old and blend into a period setting is shown here in this painted wooden fire surround. The paint has been carefully shaded and the edges dragged back to reveal a yellowish gray undercoat; mid-sheen paint works particularly well in this case.

trying to do — with any of the antiquing techniques is to give the treated surfaces the feeling of having been around a while. You are basically adding to subtract, to give colors the appearance of being age-darkened or sun-faded, to give protruding curves and angles the attractively worn look they naturally acquire after much handling and rubbing — the subdued sheen that is the result of years of polishing, while recesses and crevices show the same evidence of a lazy duster by being darker and even a little dustier by contrast, without actually looking dirty.

Most of the antiquing processes rely on other techniques already explained, so turn to the relevant sections for specific instructions if they're not given below. The secret of successful and natural-looking antiquing is to use each technique sparingly and to use several different ones with restraint, rather than going overboard on any single method. The thing they all share, and which makes them peculiar to the antiquing process, is that they are generally carried out in neutral, natural or earthy colors, sometimes mixed with darker tones of the ground color on which you're working. In fact, if there's any general principle for antiquing colors, it is that they should be both duller and darker than the ground. One of the few exceptions is black, which is best aged and warmed with a dark brown like burnt umber or sienna.

Walls
Just because of the relative size and prominence of the wall area in most rooms, any aging or antiquing of the surface must be done with subtlety if they're not to look ugly or just plain silly. The two most useful finishes are either color-washing or glazing, although you can also add any of the standard antiquing colors to varnish coats, too. Which you use will depend on the condition of the wall as well as personal preference. Walls that cannot be brought forward to a smooth, flat surface will find the matt, chalky texture of a color-wash more forgiving, and my own feeling is that they work better in the paler neutral and pastel colors rather than darker ones. Try a water-thin wash based on burnt umber to warm and age white, off-white, dusty pink or beige; a raw umber wash to give a faded, graying look to pale blues; mix burnt umber, raw under and a speck of black to warm and age a grey wall; wash a green ground with a slightly darker self-tone to which you've added a little burnt umber for warmth or raw umber for coolness.

Oil glazes lend themselves well to antiquing because of the way their pure, transparent color can change the quality of the surface to suggest age with depth as well as tone. They'll look good on any wall smooth enough to bear highlighting with their slight sheen, and have the advantage that they work well through both light and dark tones. You can also try using the more opaque, paint-based glazes. As with color-washing, you'll find the standard earth colors of raw and burnt umber most useful, plus raw sienna, burnt sienna, some of the warmer grays and occasionally a very small amount of black. But tint sparingly, a little at a time for antique glazes and always test first, remembering that what you are trying to do is soften and subdue the color, not kill it outright. Adding a darker tone of the ground color to the glaze is very often the best way to hold the color in the finish as it enriches it at the same time as aging it.

Woodwork
Any of the following techniques can be used to antique woodwork and they are presented in approximately the sequence in which you would apply them. It is worth re-emphasizing that using several different techniques with restraint is the recipe for success, rather than stretching one beyond visual credibility. Apart from stain antiquing, where you are working directly either onto raw wood or wood that has been prestained to a color you want to age, it is a useful safety measure to apply a thin protective coat of clear shellac or matt varnish over the ground first, so that any antiquing errors can be wiped off before they dry, without affecting the surface beneath. This does make very good sense since the whole antiquing process involves as much wiping off as it does putting on. Even with staining, once the groundwork is right, you can protect it with an isolating coat of sealer before adding any further stage such as glazing or speckling. The standard antiquing colors have already been mentioned, but you might try adding rotten-stone to the collection; this polishing powder is the beigey gray color of dust, so its useful-

Water stain It is rather ironic that, whereas normally you're doing your best to get the stain even, in this instance you're trying to achieve exactly the opposite effect, and it can be just as tricky. However, your aim is not for the stain to look patchy, but rather as if the color has been faded by the light or worn away in the center parts of panels and on the high points of moldings, while remaining more intense towards panel edges and in corners, cracks and crevices. There are two methods for achieving this effect. The first is to apply an even amount of stain all over the surface, then immediately wipe over panel centers and high points on moldings, leaving the stain to penetrate a bit longer in the other areas before wiping all over lightly to remove excess stain and blend any hard edges. The second method is to apply the stain evenly, leave it to dry and then very gently flour-paper the color back in the appropriate areas. Again, you're trying to avoid the hard edges which would look unnatural; one way of minimizing these with either of the above methods is to subsequently give the whole surface another very weak coat of either water or oil stain.

Left Here, the deteriorated condition of old surfaces has been emphasized, rather than any attempt made at disguise. But, although it seems hard to believe, a very similar effect could be achieved on new surfaces. Think about it ... Rough-plastered walls given a couple of patchy coats of white distemper and a brushy buff wash; unfinished, unprimed beams and boards given a scant coat or two of thinned, flat white paint, brushed well into the raw grain in some places, sanded off when dry or half-dry in others with some patches buff washed like the walls; the varnish on floorboards similarly sanded away in some areas to simulate wear. Perhaps not everyone would choose to deliberately sabotage the surfaces around them in this way, but the point is that it is possible, if that's what you want.

Above The walls and woodwork in this vaulted gallery look so right for the room that it's hard to imagine them any other way. But that's just the point about antiquing — it should make surfaces seem absolutely settled in their setting. This room would have missed so much of its atmosphere had the walls simply been plain-painted beige or biscuit, instead of brushily washed in one color over the other; or if the woodwork had simply been sanded, sealed and varnished instead of being painstakingly layered with stain, tinted glaze and varnish, dragged, sanded and wiped until the dark-on-light patina of age seems to seep out of its pores.

Glaze Use either a transparent oil glaze or the more opaque paint glazes. You can also try tinted varnish or a 3:1 mixture of paint and matt varnish, tinting the paint first (as for paint glaze) before mixing it with the varnish. All of these mixtures can be thinned to a greater or lesser degree with mineral spirits, depending on the effect you want to achieve. The important thing to remember with any glaze containing varnish is that it can only be worked on once it is touch dry, unlike oil or paint glazes which can be wiped when wet or rubbed when set. For wiped and blended effects with wet glaze, use either clear and tinted glaze, or tinted glaze only. For the first method, paint the centers of panels with clear glaze, then brush on the tinted glaze in a wide stripe round panel edges and over any adjacent moldings. On panels, work the tinted glaze into the clear with the paintbrush first, then blend colored glaze evenly into the clear glaze by stippling the surface from edges to center. On moldings use a soft, lint-free rag to wipe the glaze lightly from high points, leaving it nestling in recesses and crevices and stippling again to kill any hard edges. If you use tinted glaze only, simply wipe it gently from panel centers and tops of moldings and blend by patting it with a soft cloth and / or stippling as before.

When you're working on dry glaze, the degree of dryness will dictate whether the antiquing effect is slight or pronounced. For a light effect, work on the glaze when it is touch dry and no longer tacky; for a more pronounced effect, leave the glaze to dry for about a day, or at least overnight. Use fine steel wool to rub the glaze away from panel centers and high points on curves and moldings, blending gradually from covered to uncovered areas. As with staining, a second coat of well-thinned glaze may help to achieve a softer and more subtle shading. You can also try a combination of wet and dry techniques, by working a texture such as dragging or sponging into the wet glaze and rubbing it down when dry.

Spatter Spattering is not only another subtle method of shading, it's the way to achieve those neutral-colored, light and dark specks that often freckle old woodwork. Use a much thinner version of any of the media already mentioned, or black or brown ink (shellac or varnish the surface first if it's the 'permanent' type) and any of the spattering methods. With practice, you will find that you can direct the spatter with remarkable accuracy, first lightly dusting the surface, wholly or partially, with a fine spray, then spattering again when the first coat is dry to make denser areas around panel edges, deepening this effect in the corners and in the recesses of moldings. Don't make the spattering too regular and vary the techniques as described to achieve a different size and density of freckle, bearing in mind that the amount of liquid on the brush, the distance you hold it from the wall, the number of bristles you release at a time, the speed with which you release them, and with which you move the brush across the surface, will all affect the result. For example, releasing just a few bristles from a brush well-loaded with ink, while moving it quickly across the surface, will produce the familiar, sparse, random scattering of heavy spots sometimes known as 'fly-specks'. For more subtle freckling, use well-diluted color, blot or stipple the surface, or whisk the tip of a soft, dry brush over it any time from immediately after spattering to just before it sets. If you wait until the spatter is nearly dry, then spatter again with solvent, this will both 'open' and soften the freckling. Alternatively, wait until it is completely dry and rub it gently with fine steel wool; this can be used to 'knock back' overdone areas or simply to soften others. Experiment with these tricks separately and together, as each permutation will produce a different effect.

FINISHING OFF Antiqued surfaces should whisper at you, not shout. Look at an ordinary surface through half-closed eyes and you'll get a fair idea of the effect you're trying to achieve. Nothing is hard-edged or strident — even decorative detailing needs its bright newness dulled or delicately defaced. The same applies to varnish: antiqued woodwork looks completely wrong with a bright and shiny surface, so use several, thinned coats of clear, matt or satin-finish, polyurethane varnish, tinting it if you want an even mellower tone.

Left On the door and frame, moldings are crisply picked out in white to create a visual break between the two areas of broken color, but (**below**) some planes are sponged to soften them.

Decorative detail

These are 'finishing touch' techniques — a variety of ways in which, on both plaster and woodwork, you can add detail that is lacking, emphasize existing detail, display or disguise proportions and tidy or tighten visually 'loose' areas. It is often these tiny touches, at the end of the decorating job, that pull a whole room together and tell you it's done.

LINING

This is one of the simplest ways to add interest to plain surfaces and emphasize or visually alter their proportions. A series of lines can be painted onto an expanse of wall, to break the area up into panels. The placing and scale of the lines can be used to make the wall seem taller or shorter, wider or narrower, or to contain areas of, say, broken color, marbling or tortoiseshell. On woodwork, lining can be used to transform a set of nondescript flush doors into prettily panelled pieces, or simply as decoration — a fine line along each side of a balustrade or around the top edge of a mantelpiece. It can also be used to emphasize the straight and curved relief on moldings in either wood or plaster.

The choice of color for lining is an individual matter, but as a general principle, it should either tone with the ground — on plain walls, for example, the same color but a shade or two deeper — or at least be sympathetic to some other element in the decoration: on tortoise-shell panels where the deepest and most dominant color is dark brown, this would also be the most suitable choice for a fine, containing line.

MATERIALS The lining color needs to be fairly thin to flow, although obviously where lining a light color over dark, it must be substantial enough to cover the ground. Dissolve artists' oil color or universal stainer in a small amount of mineral spirits and mix this solution with a little varnish, or quicker-drying goldsize, to give it 'body' and hold the bristles of the brush together for a clean edge. Thin with mineral spirits, and if the mixture doesn't flow quite smoothly enough, add just a drop or two of raw linseed oil. Perfectionists will also strain the color before use to be sure there are no particles of undissolved pigment, or anything else.

The professional's tools for lining are especially made, hog-hair fitches, round or flat for different purposes; the short-haired fitches are easier to use for the beginner, but the long-haired ones hold more paint so you don't have to pick up color as often. Artists' sable brushes are a perfectly satisfactory alternative for the amateur and two sizes should provide sufficient versatility, a No 6 for broader lines, $\frac{1}{8}$-$\frac{1}{2}$in (3-12mm), and a No 3 for lines of $\frac{1}{16}$in (1.5mm) or less.

METHOD Lining can often frighten people because it seems to demand artistic ability and, above all, a steady hand. The first thing to remember is that you are not being asked to do a technical drawing — decoration is a handicraft, not a mechanical skill, and the evidence of the hand of the craftsman is part of the charm. Second, it is easy enough to practice on painted board or lining paper. Thirdly, there are both preventative and curative measures for imperfect lines. A coat of clear varnish before lining will enable you to wipe off mistakes before they dry with a rag moistened in mineral spirits. On other surfaces, keep paper tissues handy to wipe off the worst of any slips; when the paint is dry, rub out the mistakes with fine abrasive paper, steel wool or a pencil eraser. Try to avoid rubbing through into the base coat, because although you can retouch lines — lightly to avoid color variation — retouching the ground will almost certainly show, as paint starts to fade in a matter of days. If it is necessary to retouch the base coat, gently feather the patch into the surrounding area, either with a very fine abrasive or with your finger.

There are a variety of tricks to ensure a true line, straight or curved. For short, straight lines, turning the bevelled side of a ruler to the wall will keep its edge clear; some decorators glue corks to the underside of longer straight-edges to hold them off the wall, and maintain a steady

Far left The unusual ceiling detail in this room has been picked out in electric blue, echoing the neon lighting.
Left Skilfully done, outlining panels in darker colors can emphasize (or create) a sense of three-dimensionality as demonstrated here in these kitchen units.
Below The cool elegance of classical detailing is brought out in this treatment of the panels, doorcase and architrave of this entrance. Choosing the right toning shades is just as important as skill in execution.

hand by resting the middle finger on the straight-edge as the brush is drawn down or across the wall. Snapped, ruled or freehand chalk lines are an ideal way not only to guide hand and eye when it comes to painting in the lines, but to judge initially whether they are in the right position and quantity. Be sure not to leave too much chalk on the surface; lightly dust off any loose surplus before you paint, or it could clog the brush. Whatever method you use, wipe the painting edge regularly to minimize the risk of blobs. When lining an edge freehand, especially curves on woodwork, use a notched card as a guide for placing little dots of paint every few inches to mark the position of the line. When it comes to painting the line, rest your little finger against the edge of the piece you are working on to steady your hand. To keep both hands free for this sort of work, some painters carry the color in a mug, strapped through the handle and around the waist!

All precautions and remedies apart, sooner or later the time comes when you've actually got to paint that first line. Pick up enough color on the brush so that it's well but not overloaded, or it may produce a blob (press the brush gently against the inside of your paint pot to release excess color). For a long, single stroke, hold the brush as far up the handle as possible while still feeling comfortable with it. Stand far enough away from the painting surface for extended arm and brush to reach it easily and, keeping your arm relaxed — let your shoulder muscles do the work as you literally draw the line. A little practice doing it this way and then using wrist, elbow and so on will demonstrate how much easier it is with this method to get a free, steady and continuous line. Once the brush is on the surface, keep going — even if the start is wobbly — because any hesitation or stopping and starting will show. Another trick is not to look at the brush, but to keep looking ahead to where you want it to go; trust the hand to follow the eye and it will. The amount of pressure, rather than the brush itself, will determine the width of the stripe, so keep pressure even for an even stripe and, for fine lines, use only the tip.

Once you become confident with the technique, a variety of effects can be tried. Using water-thin paint can produce lines that look faded with age. This effect can also be achieved by using thicker paint and, when it's dry, sanding it

Above An original use of molding — with recesses picked out in gold but the top, curved edges left to stand out in white — changes not only the dimensions but the entire status of this ordinary flush door.
Right Grilled cupboard doors concealing radiators are given the same treatment.
Far right This small corner shows a collection of interesting techniques. As a general principle, the high relief work on moldings is best left in a lighter color, which follows the natural effects of light and shade. But the heaviest strip of molding here would have stood out in too great a contrast had it been painted white, so the normal distribution of light and dark is reversed to integrate it with the other detail-work around it.

Fake panelling

This is an extension of lining, but, in this case, you really are trying to deceive the eye rather than just create an honest decorative effect. As with lining, this *trompe l'oeil* technique can be used on walls, to add interest to a set of plain flush doors or to any woodwork surface — for example, the panel that typically fills in the triangular area between stairs and floor in a hall. For this job, use paint to match the ground, tinted with either artists' oil colors/ universal stainers for oil-based paint or, for water-based paint, with universal stainers or artists' gouache, acrylic or powder colors. You will also need a ½in (1.2 cm) brush with a square end (either a proper decorators' fitch or an artists' brush), a straight-edge, chalk or a sharp pencil, and masking tape if there is any doubt about your freehand painting abilities. When you have decided what kind of panels you want and where, mark their position with the straight-edge and pencil or chalk. Each panel requires a rectangle of parallel lines, ½in (1.2 cm) apart and with

'mitered' corners. Tint the paint to give two shades, one just a little darker than the ground color and one about the same amount darker again. The aim is to create an effect of light and shadow, so on each panel, use the light shade to fill in the tracks on the bottom and the side away from the main light source, and use the darker shade to fill in the others, making sure the shades meet neatly — use masking tape if necessary — at the 'mitered' corners.

This technique for creating light and shade is enormously versatile and can obviously be extended. You might, for example, want to create a very elaborate effect on 'panelled' doors and give them a dragged or grained finish. On walls, the panels could contain areas of a paint finish that differ from the ground. They could suggest a window where none exists, either by filling in the panels with mirror or by painting panes of blue sky, sponged with scudding, stylized gray and white clouds. Alternatively, the scale of the painting could be enlarged to suggest a deeper recess, framing either an object or a view.

Far left Picking-out colors do not need to contrast greatly with those surrounding them to be effective. Tones close to those of the main surfaces can often throw them more elegantly and naturally into relief.
Left Glazing and wiping is the most subtle method of emphasizing the details of cornices and other similar molding work. The glaze is applied over the whole of the molding and then wiped from the highlights, leaving it nestling in hollows and recesses. This not only exaggerates the natural effect of light and shadow but gives the cornice an elegantly 'weathered' look by suggesting the dust of ages collected in its crevices.

Above Painting in the details results in a much crisper effect with cleaner definition, although in this instance painted mouldings are flanked by glazed and wiped strips for an interesting contrast in texture.

PICKING OUT

The sole purpose of picking out moldings and enrichments is to show them off. However, the detailed coloring work used in public buildings, churches and so on, would not generally be at all suitable for domestic interiors — but a certain amount of emphasis can be made of pretty features without becoming overpowering. Basic picking out can be done in two ways — a 'positive' method with paint and a 'negative' method with glaze.

The choice of paint colors depends on the shades used in the rest of the room. In general, avoid making too strong a contrast — moldings are an accessory to the room, not a separate element. Tones of the wall color are always a safe bet, or a subtle echoing of the color chosen for woodwork. The choice of coloring becomes obvious once you think about it. If the raised section is painted a darker color, it would be flattened to create a silhouette, whereas painting it a lighter color, with the dark color used for recessed areas, makes it stand out because it intensifies the effect of natural light and shade. On the practical side, picking out is usually done by professional decorators with a selection of round or flat, hog-hair fitches but, as with lining, artists' brushes can be used instead. Remember that rather than painstakingly painting in both light and dark colors separately, it is often simpler to paint over everything in the lighter color and then fill in the background with the darker one.

The 'negative' method, using glaze, works on the same principle of emphasizing light and shade, but is a good deal more subtle in its effect. If cornices, or other moldings, are first painted with an oil-based paint, they can be coated, when dry, with a paint or oil glaze of a slightly deeper tone. The glaze is brushed on, then stippled down to even it out and eliminate brush marks, before wiping with a rag moistened with mineral spirits. This removes the glaze from the raised areas, leaving it nestling in crevices and, again by emphasizing the naturally shadowy areas, throwing the decorative details into relief.

STENCILLING

Like several of these decorative finishes, stencilling is a legacy from very early civilization. In more recent history, it is probably the American settlers whom we have to thank most for keeping the tradition alive, bringing it with them from Europe and using it on walls, floors and furniture where, in the absence of other decorative traditions and before the advent of instant decoration such as wallpaper, it acquired status and value. It's seldom that one can attribute the revival of a craft to a single individual, but if anyone has been responsible for renewed interest in stencilling in our own time, it is Lyn Le Grice, who gave up a career teaching art to pursue her passion and now makes and sells ready-cut stencils as well as advising on and supervising their use in interiors in Britain and Europe.

In these days of mass-produced pattern, stencilling is a uniquely satisfying way to introduce small or large areas of individual design to just about any interior surface. If stencilling whole walls seems to demand too much time and patience, panels and borders are a relatively quick and easy way (the preparation actually takes longer than the execution) to add a restrained amount of enlivening decoration to a plain plaster or wood surface. These can often play a valuable architectural role, too — emphasizing good proportions and distracting the eye from the less-than-perfect by, for example, running a frieze at picture-rail height around the walls of a room whose ceiling is too high for its size, or breaking up large, bare expanses of wall into stencil-defined panels. Stencilling is also the perfect way to pattern a plain wood floor where you don't want carpet, and it still surprises me how just a stencilled border, a mock 'rug' or an all-over design of even the smallest, simplest pattern repeat can transform ordinary, rather boring boards into a surface that plays a real decorative role in a room.

Color and design

On natural wood surfaces like floors or stripped, panelled doors, patterning usually looks best if the colors are kept in sympathy with the surface — either mid-to-dark tone neutrals and earth colors or the more somber shades of other colors that contain warm, earthy undertones, like khaki and olive, mustard, brick red. On painted surfaces, almost every degree of contrast can work if you choose shades and motifs carefully: I've seen two pale grays on white looking like a damask border and brilliant primaries on a black grid looking very like Mondrian. My eyes tell me that bolder colors and stronger contrasts work better on plain simple shades and that more complex designs need more delicate coloring and subtler contrasts. My general advice is — keep it simple and err on the side of restraint: not too many colors, not too complicated a motif. This will not only look better, it'll also take less work. You can

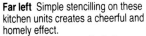

Far left Simple stencilling on these kitchen units creates a cheerful and homely effect.
Center A more complicated treatment is displayed in this floor stencilling.
Left A stencilled pattern on the floor, combined with a mural painted on the door, gives an all-over 'folk art' look.
Below This stencilled pattern painted on the wall around a wood architrave is subtle and decorative.

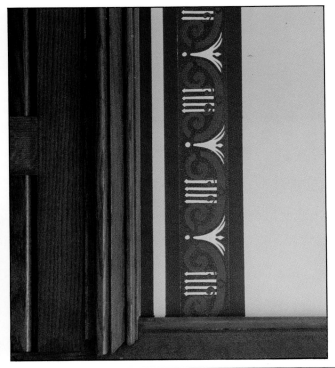

cut out one whole stage of the job by buying ready-cut stencils from the much improved ranges of both traditional and modern designs now available. If you want to make your own stencils but don't trust your artistic ability, copy a design from one of the books of patterns also available or 'borrow' a motif you like from a fabric or wallpaper. You may need to scale it up or down, easily done with squared paper and it's always worth testing the size, color and position of stencils first. Use colored paper cut-outs, stuck to the wall with masking tape to avoid harming the surface, or paint, stencil and pin up a length of lining paper.

Making stencils

MATERIALS You will need an oiled stencil board or some clear acetate, together with a fine-tipped felt pen or a rapidograph — a special drawing pen necessary if you use acetate. A scalpel and cutting board of hardboard, ply, chipboard or glass are also essential. Tracing paper is required if you're copying another design; carbon paper and a small-gauge knitting needle are needed where you're transferring the design to an oiled board. Use masking tape, to hold tracing paper steady over a design and over carbon/oiled board. A ruler, preferably metal is needed for any straight-edge work you do.

Right Both naturally finished and painted floorboards can be stencilled with repeating motifs for a lively 'folk art' effect.

Below Stencilling need not be limited to producing regular, repetitive borders or patterns. This unusual design accentuates the sloping ceiling.

METHOD The advantage of clear acetate for making stencils is that it cuts out the need for tracing paper, since you can place it over a design and trace directly onto it with the rapidograph. This is especially useful when you're stencilling in several different colors and need to make a separate stencil for each area of color. Acetate is also slightly easier to cut, although it can split on very sharp curves and corners, and larger sheets have an unnerving habit of trying to curl up as you work on them. On balance, I actually prefer the solidity of the board (it's cheaper, too) and the fact that you can cut it at an angle to produce a bevelled edge (like the up-market picture mounts), so paint is less likely to creep under it while you're stencilling. If you're using oiled board, copy the chosen design with a fine-tip felt pen onto tracing paper, then transfer the design, using the point of a small gauge knitting needle, through carbon paper onto the board. On either board or acetate, leave a good margin — 1-2½in (2.5-6.3cm) — around the design, or the stencil will be weak and floppy.

To cut the stencil, fix the oiled board or acetate to the cutting board with masking tape so that it won't slip about. (The advantage of glass as a cutting board is that the knife won't suddenly be sent off true by previous score marks, but protect glass edges with masking tape). Hold the knife firmly and cut slowly, smoothly and decisively. It will help to keep a steady line if you rest your little finger on the board while cutting towards yourself and, on curves, if you turn the board rather than your hand. Cut small, detailed areas first (use nail punches around holes, but not on glass!) to save putting too much strain on the board when larger areas are removed. When the cutting is complete, check for any rough edges and smooth them down with very fine sandpaper. On multi-color motifs, it's best to use a different stencil for each colour. Lining up presents no problem on acetate, where you can simply draw in a few other lines of the design to help you position subsequent stencils accurately over the first one. With stencil board, you'll need to take a few more precautions: trace and cut each stencil first, then align them exactly one on top of another and trim all the boards to the same size; cutting notches in the sides of the boards or punching a couple of holes through them will then enable you to make tiny pencil marks on the wall as a guide for the exact position of each stencil in the sequence. Where motifs are so close together that part of one will be covered as you stencil the next, it will also help lining up if you draw the position of the covered part of the motif on the face of the board. But always contain the cut for each motif within a single piece of board — joins will show — and, above all, remember to incorporate sufficient interconnecting 'roads' of board between the cut-outs, otherwise your design will simply fall apart along with the board. If you want to add more detail, even in the same color, make a separate stencil.

Applying stencils

PREPARATION For once you have a reasonably large range of paint possibilities for the base. You can stencil onto virtually any type of painted wall as long as it is in good condition, although obviously gloss paint has the least 'tooth'. Natural wood will need a couple of thinned coats of matt or satin varnish to seal it before stencilling. Painted wood is normally best in a flat or eggshell, oil-based finish, although there's no real reason why you shouldn't stencil onto latex, matt or silk finish, as you'll want to varnish the whole thing afterwards anyway to protect the pattern.

Paint There is a similarly wide choice of paints for the actual stencil work. If you want to get the job done quickly, use the fast-drying, signwriters' colors, thinning them with matt varnish and mineral spirits, or artists' acrylic colors, which can be thinned to various degrees of trans-lucency/opacity with their own acrylic medium or water. Latex paint, tinted with universal stainers or artists' acrylics and thinned with water, is the next quickest, suit-able drying medium; flat oil-based paint or undercoat, or even eggshell, tinted with stainers or artists' oils and thinned with mineral spirits, are other options and espec-ially suitable for woodwork, but they will take longer to dry — add a spot of drier to speed the process up. Whatever you use, thin it to the consistency of light cream — not too watery or it will creep under the stencil (you can add a little latex to acrylics to thicken them) and dense enough in color for a thin coat to show up clearly against the ground.

Some people use aerosol spray paint for stencilling and in some ways it does speed the job up. But, you have to hold the stencil down very firmly, follow the manu-facturer's instructions for spraying distance and spray directly onto the surface, not at an angle — and even then you may not be able to avoid seepage. Another problem, apart from the cost, is that it may take you two or three attempts to get an even coverage without runs, which almost cancels out the time advantage. All in all, I think these sprays can cause more trouble than they save.

Stains These can be stencilled in the variety of methods that you would apply straightforward stain. The basic principle for stencilling with stain is to create a resist, usually with a spirit-based varnish such as shellac, which will prevent the stain spreading beyond the stencilled area. In addition to the methods already described, this can be done by cutting an exact 'negative' of your stencil — or using the discarded pieces of board from the stencil itself — as a reverse stencil for applying the shellac. Once the stencil itself has been put in, the shellac — and any seepage — will come off with a rag soaked in methylated spirit. Obviously this works better and is easier with simple motifs. If you're applying the stain with a brush, be extra

Above left An alternative to using carbon paper to transfer the traced design onto the stencil board is to pencil in the design on the under side of the tracing, too. Then, when you place the tracing on the board and go over it again with a blunt pencil or knitting needle, the lead underneath will be transferred on to the board.
Above This will only produce very faint pencil lines, so it may be wise to strengthen them by going over them again with a sharp-pointed pencil.
Left The advantage of using clear acetate is that you can trace the design on to it directly with a rapidograph (drawing pen) and then proceed immediately to cutting the stencil. The disadvantage of acetate is that it's floppy and therefore needs to be held very firmly against the wall when you're applying the stencil to prevent paint creeping under the edges.

Right In applying the stencil, pounce directly down on to the cut-out shape with a dabbing motion. Do not get too much paint on the brush each time or you will risk it bleeding under the edges of the stencil.

Below right With more complex designs, cut a different stencil for each color. Complete all the stencils in one color first and let them dry before applying the next.

Below left Stencilling has been used to create this repeating border pattern on floorboards.

Far right If you want to soften the coloring of the finished stencil, to make it look as though it has faded a little with age, apply a translucent glaze containing a very small quantity of white pigment.

Center Alternatively, varnishing will enhance the colors and, if you choose one with a slightly yellowy tone, it will mellow them, too.

careful not to overload it; you may find you have more control over the stain if it is applied with a rag, folded into a swab and moistened rather than saturated with the medium.

EQUIPMENT Purpose-made stencil brushes look like shaving brushes except that the bristles are stiff and cut off short and square. These are generally the ideal tools for the straight-on dabbing motion — known as 'pouncing' — as they are less likely to push paint under the stencil edge. They come in various sizes — for very detailed work get the small, similarly shaped brushes called fitches — and leave the paint with a slightly stippled, 'orange-peel' finish. If you don't want this texture, you can use an ordinary decorating brush, a paint pad, a sponge or a folded rag. Each of these will give you a different texture — the important thing is not to overload any of them.

Extras You will also need a hardboard palette for paint, solvent (appropriate to the paint), clean rags, masking tape, a spirit-level, a straight-edge, chalk, T-square and a plumb-line.

METHOD First mark the position of the stencils. For friezes, use a spirit-level, straight-edge and chalk to mark horizontal lines; take vertical lines from this horizontal with a T-square, checking them with a plumb-line. Don't take any of your guide-lines off floor, walls, corners or ceilings as these are so often out of true. Mark the exact position of each stencil with a pencil, using notches on the board to line it up. You may need to band the stencil to take the design round corners. If so, score it lightly with a knife and straight-edge first, to make a smooth fold. To save having to work with a stencil that has been bent, it's worth making a paper pattern just to mark corner positions (or make more than one stencil to begin with) and save actually stencilling the corners until last.

For all-over or 'rug' type stencils on floors, make a plan on squared paper first, then square off the floor with chalk to match, using snapped lines and/or a straight-edge and chalk in the position of each stencil. Borders will normally need to be equi-distant from baseboards all round (draw chalk 'tracks', the depth of the stencil board apart, as a guide), but if the room is really off square, you should be able to compensate at corners, 'fudging' the border towards a more acceptable right angle, without it showing too much. However, you can't take motifs around flat corners in the same way as you can with friezes, so space them out evenly (divide the length of the border by the number of motifs) and mark the central point of each on both stencil-board edges and 'tracks'.

Now comes the moment you've been waiting for and may have thought would never come. Fix the stencil in its first position with masking tape. Pour a small amount of paint onto the palette, just dip the face of the brush in the

paint and stamp it out on a clean part of the palette to distribute the paint evenly and lose any excess. Dab the thinly coated brush straight onto the cut-out areas, working from the edge to the center of each. Rock the brush slightly to transfer color evenly, but don't smear it across the surface. When all the color is on, leave it to set for about half a minute before carefully lifting the stencil off the surface and moving to the next position. If the board overlaps adjacent stencils, apply them alternately to prevent smudging the wet paint. When stencilling in several colors, complete one color at a time and let it dry before applying the next. If you're applying the paint correctly, you shouldn't get a build-up on the stencil itself, but it's worth cleaning both faces off from time to time with a rag, moistened with the appropriate solvent if the stencil is badly clogged. When the job's done, clean and dry stencils and store them flat, separated with tissue paper or baking parchment. You've taken time and trouble to prepare them and you may want to use them again, so it's worth looking after them.

FINISHING OFF When the stencil work is dry, brush any remaining chalk from the surface and remove pencil marks gently with a clean eraser. Varnishing walls isn't essential, especially if you've used oil-based paint, but it's advisable for water-based media and will protect and prolong the life of other finishes. It's definitely worth varnishing any woodwork that gets wear and on floors it's an absolute must: give the paint or stain at least a day to dry (two days for oil stains) and then apply at least three coats.

Translucent and transparent

STAINING

Staining is an alternative to paint in the decorative treatment of woodwork. The prime reason for using a stain is because, being tinted with dyes rather than pigments, the various media used remain translucent, so that the wood can be colored without obscuring its texture or grain. Staining is also quicker, and often cheaper than painting, but among the reasons why it's not more popular is, of course, that it doesn't cover a mixture of surfaces or a multitude of imperfections with the same *sang-froid*; although staining can do much to perk up a piece of rather plain wood, the smooth, sound, uniform, clean surface must already be there. Another reason more people don't use stain is because they don't realize the wide range of both colors and types available. Most shops only stock a very limited range and usually only in the 'natural' wood shades (often in the very ill-formulated varnish stains, usually made from oil stain mixed with gloss varnish, which leave a nasty sludge on the surface), plus a few bright colors, if you're lucky. Yet just a little investigation will discover water stains, spirit stains, oil stains, even wax stains. Some are ready mixed in solution form, some come as crystals to be mixed with water or spirit (usually methylated spirit). There is a considerable range of colors, which can in themselves be blended (although not, obviously, between different stain types), some manufacturers will make up colors to order, or match color samples, and you can make up your own wood-dyes from the standard range of textile dyes sold in the shops.

Water stains This type of stain has several advantages: it usually fades less noticeably than other types, it is inexpensive and it forms an even color with relative ease. Ready mixed color ranges can be slightly dull, but it is simple enough to make your own from the powder textile dyes, giving you access to a considerable range of clear, bright colors. Follow the manufacturer's instructions for dissolving the dye but, for staining, use about half as much water as they suggest. Test colors out on spare pieces of a similar wood before applying and be prepared to apply two or more coats before the color really begins to show. The main disadvantage with water stains is that they tend to raise the grain of the wood. A variety of measures can help minimize this effect. Working conditions can be a great help: wood that has been acclimatized to an atmosphere of reasonable warmth and humidity is less thirsty than dry, cold wood. Wood that has been sanded really smooth with fine sandpaper has a tighter, less porous surface texture than rough, or roughly sanded wood. The tendency for the stain to dry streakily because of uneven absorption (although this can sometimes be a pretty effect in itself) can be helped either by giving the surface a coat of thin size or very thin shellac first. This tendency to patchiness does mean that water stains are best used on light, close-grained woods rather than on the porous, open-grained softwoods, where the paler, spring-grown areas will drink up the stain and the hard, autumn-grown grain remains almost impervious.

Spirit stains These hardly raise grain at all, but they are penetrative stains that dry very quickly, making it difficult to keep a wet edge going and avoid patchiness. It is especially important not to cover the same area twice in a single application, or there will be some patches that are darker than others.

Oil stains These stains are by far the easiest to apply, and, because they dry more slowly, they are the most likely to give an even color, which makes them particularly suitable for floors. The drying time does, however, have its own disadvantages: it can take as much as two days and it must be completely dry before you apply varnish.

PREPARATION Stains are generally best applied to clean, untreated wood, with the exceptions mentioned above. Before staining, the surface should be scrubbed, sanded with fine sandpaper and rubbed over with a rag moistened in mineral spirits to cut any remaining grease. Take care always to sand with the grain; cross-scratches will show in the finish and they will have to be removed with a scraper and the surface sanded again. When using water or spirit stains, fill deep scratches, scores or nail-holes before staining with one of the suitable proprietary fillers and touch up the filled and sanded areas with thin knotting to prevent them taking up more stain than the wood. Also remember that end grain will take up more stain so either apply the stain sparingly or wet the surface just before staining with mineral spirits. When using an oil stain, it's better to fill after staining with tinted wood filler.

METHOD A brush or rag-swab can be used to apply all the stains, and a clean rag should be kept handy to wipe off any excess and even out the color. Apply water and spirit stains quickly and methodically and do not cut corners, such as trying to avoid second or third coats by putting too much on at once. This will slow down the drying time and only encourage patchiness. Oil stains should be thinned and applied more liberally, especially on hard woods where you can risk leaving them to soak in for a few minutes before wiping off the surplus with a rag. Wiping-off is something many people neglect, but it is this that actually makes the difference, on all staining, between a densely colored surface where the grain is partially obscured and one where both grain and texture show attractively through the color.

Left Stain is the perfect way to marry up mis-matched wood surfaces, although sometimes you may need to bleach dark woods back to make the match. In this kitchen, custom-made units have been stained and varnished to a similar 'old pine' finish to the beams, table and chairs. Both units and furniture, although the latter is obviously by no means new, have been sympathetically treated with a variety of antiquing processes to high-light handled or rubbed areas, deepen shadows and suggest dust lying in hollows and crevices and generally simulate the effect of years of well-worn use, which somehow subdue a setting into somewhere where we feel much more at home.

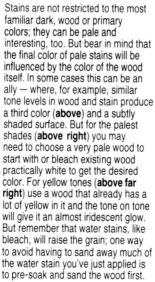

Stains are not restricted to the most familiar dark, wood or primary colors; they can be pale and interesting, too. But bear in mind that the final color of pale stains will be influenced by the color of the wood itself. In some cases this can be an ally — where, for example, similar tone levels in wood and stain produce a third color (**above**) and a subtly shaded surface. But for the palest shades (**above right**) you may need to choose a very pale wood to start with or bleach existing wood practically white to get the desired color. For yellow tones (**above far right**) use a wood that already has a lot of yellow in it and the tone on tone will give it an almost iridescent glow. But remember that water stains, like bleach, will raise the grain; one way to avoid having to sand away much of the water stain you've just applied is to pre-soak and sand the wood first.

Decorative staining

Although it is harder to contain stain than paint in specific, chosen areas, there are several methods that will allow different colors, depths and patterns to be achieved on a single surface. You can make clear or colored patterns on a stained ground by stencilling them in knotting or spirit varnish, tinting these if you want color, and then using water stains, which will not affect the patterned areas. If a coat of clear size is put onto bare wood, patterns can be painted on top, and the size may then be washed off and then the surrounding surface stained. Outlining areas with fine dark lines of oil-based paint will keep different stain colors apart and is another way of making patterns. If you want the lines to show as natural wood through the stain, you will need to size the wood first and use a 'resist' of Brunswick black to paint the lines; let them dry, wash off the size, water-stain and then use a rag and plenty of mineral spirits to remove the lines.

Various areas of a wood surface can also be stained to different depths of color using water stains and clear spirit varnish as the 'resist'; stain the whole area with the lightest color (or leave it bare if you want natural wood showing through), then varnish the areas you want to preserve in that color. Stain with the next, deeper shade, then varnish again the parts you want to keep in that shade and continue with this sequence until your deepest stain color has been applied. Then, either leave the varnish areas if you want a mildly embossed appearance, spirit-varnishing the whole surface, or remove the varnished areas with methylated spirits before applying one or more coats of polyurethane varnish.

Bleaching

You may want to bleach wood, either to leave it in its natural, lighter state to apply a lighter colored stain than would show up on the original, or to give a faded look to a newly stained surface. The traditional bleach materials for wood are oxalic acid and sodium hyposulfate (a concentrated version of domestic bleach and particularly good at removing red tones), bought from drug stores and used separately or together. To use separately, dissolve 2 oz (57 g) of either crystal in $1\frac{1}{4}$ quarts (1.2 liters) of hot water

the proprietary, two-pack alkaline-plus-peroxide bleaching system, available from builders' suppliers, although of course it is more costly. Any and all of these processes can be repeated until the desired shade is reached, but the washing off stages are vital. In the case of bleaching, there is no preventative measure against the inevitable raising of the grain, so be prepared for a considerable amount of sanding.

Special wood effects

Limed oak is oak which has been treated — or rather mistreated — in a way that turns it a distinctive gray-brown with white grain and pores. For a very pale version, bleach it first by one of the methods above before whitening the grain and pores. Otherwise, brush on a paste made of garden lime and water and leave it to dry before washing and sanding off the dry coating. (For a more pronounced effect, wire brush along the grain first to open it out.) Fill the grain and pores with plaster or proprietary filler, leave this to dry, then sand the surface smooth and clean so that it remains in the cavities only. To avoid getting the slightest yellowy tinge back, finish with well-thinned white shellac rather than polyurethane varnish. Apply two or three coats, sanding between each coat and after the last one, as this finish is traditionally matt. If you want a slight sheen on it, polish with a little white wax.

Weathered oak For this silver-gray look, do not fill the grain but simply treat the wood with lime, in this case allowing the sediment to settle before pouring off and using the solution. To preserve this delicate coloring, finish with white shellac as above.

Pickled pine looks like ordinary pine from which the paint has been stripped, leaving it both a more 'distressed' and paler version of its normal self. It is a shame to use this effect on a piece of well-grained pine with a good color, but it can make nondescript pieces more interesting by intensifying the natural contrasts in the grain. The 'pickling' solution is made by adding one part nitric acid to eight parts water (don't mix the other way round); brush this evenly over the surface and let it dry. Sand down with very fine abrasive paper and, to kill any remaining yellowish tinges, brush over again with a mild solution of bichromate of potash. Rinse thoroughly when dry. Sand lightly again, if necessary, and protect with thinned white shellac as above or, for a more durable finish, with acid-catalyzed lacquer. If you want a slight sheen on it, polish the dry, lacquered surface with fine steel wool and wax; this should bring out a good color.

It is extremely important to note that the materials used in bleaching and for the special wood effects can damage skin and other materials. Wear gloves, protective clothing, cover the surrounding area with suitable material and also organize as much ventilation as possible.

Above This section of a pickled pine dresser shows the particular color obtained when using this technique.

and brush the solution on, when cool, with a fiber brush — you will ruin good bristle. For really good penetration, try sanding in the solution with fine wet-and-dry abrasive paper. When the surface is dry, brush off the crystals and neutralize it with a borax solution (one cup to one quart of water) or with methylated spirits, then wash off thoroughly with lots of vinegared water. (If anything, neutralize and wash off early rather than late to prevent the bleach drying in the grain, where it could affect both color and quality of subsequent finishes. If the color is not as pale as desired, you can always repeat the process.) If you use both solutions for a more thorough bleaching, use the oxalic acid first and let it half dry before applying the sodium hyposulfate, and try to do this in a well-ventilated area as the combination gives off powerful fumes.

To achieve a grayish tone on the wood, a weak to medium solution of permanganate helps kill yellow tones. Apply this before the neutralizing wash with borax solution, then follow the final washing stages as above. When really drastic bleaching is wanted, it is probably best to use

GLAZE

In general terms, a glaze is any transparent or semi-transparent color applied over another to enrich or intensify it, to subdue it, to 'age' it or to modify it in any other way. To narrow this field down slightly I — and many other professionals — tend to use the word 'glaze' to indicate transparent color of the oil-based type, which differentiates it from, for example, the water-based materials used for color-washing. However, glaze is also sometimes called 'scumble' or 'scumble glaze' — especially in Britain — and the two should not be confused. Scumble can be oil- or water-based, but is always and only made from semi-transparent pigments, so that it has a degree of opacity. The ground coat therefore shows through to a much lesser and often random degree so that whether or not it is to be 'distressed' to produce a broken colour effect, it usually needs working on in some way, if only with a fine hair-stippler, to get even coverage. Don't try using scumble, therefore, when what you want is clear, translucent color and don't confuse glaze with varnish, either; glaze is purely decorative, varnish is basically protective and although it's also used for various levels of shine and can itself be tinted, it cannot generally be worked on in the same way.

Oil-based glazes — which can be glossy, satin-finish or flat — are slicker, more sumptuous and more transparent than water-based washes. It is most likely that decorators first learned about their properties from artists who have traditionally used transparent color to deepen shadows, enrich dark color, highlight the lustre of silks, satins and the brilliance of jewels and give a pale translucency to skin tone, for glaze can do all this and more. In the decorator's craft, translucent color on color is used for atmosphere — for softness, richness and depth on surfaces, and to give a 'spacy' feeling to walls and the patina of age to woodwork — as much as for the practical purpose of modifying an unsuccessful color or the pure aesthetic pleasure of seeing color through tone on translucent tone.

The effect of opaque color is much easier to imagine and understand than that of transparent color, not least because opaque color, in the form of paint, is what most of us are more accustomed to working with. It is not so much that glaze is more unpredictable, as paint can be full enough of surprises, but rather that it has an entirely different quality. If you're unfamiliar with glaze and the performance of transparent color, it's especially useful to experiment on sealed or painted lining paper or board first, as you may find you want to change the tone of the ground color as well as the glaze. As a general guide, you'll find that translucent glazes that are darker than the ground will add warmth, that a slightly lighter tone of a bright color will add brilliance, that a glaze in a dark, cool color over a warm ground will contribute richness and depth and that a

glaze which is very much lighter than a dark ground will give it a cooler tone.

PREPARATION The low-luster, hard, nonporous surface of eggshell paint makes the ideal ground for all types of glaze as it provides some 'grip', but won't be softened or in any other way affected by it. Flat oil paint is the next best ground and although you can apply these glazes over emulsion, its porous finish makes the glaze harder to manipulate and achieve good, even results.

MATERIALS **Oil glaze** You can buy ready-made glaze in a range of colors, but I prefer to buy the clear variety and tint it myself. Off-the-shelf, it comes in a variety of fairly thick consistencies; these can all be applied undiluted, as long as they're brushed out well. If you apply too thick a coat, it can form a surface skin which prevents the glaze beneath drying out properly and leaves it permanently soft. The level of sheen also varies according to the amount the glaze is thinned and I find the softer sheen of a well-thinned glaze much more attractive. You can thin glaze up to 1:2 with mineral spirits, but start with 1:1 mix and test

before adding more solvent. The more you add, the quicker the glaze will dry, which is obviously a disadvantage if you're planning to work on it with brushes, rags, combs and so on. If you want to slow the drying process, try thinning with one part raw linseed oil to two or three parts mineral spirits — this will only slightly increase the level of shine. If you want the glaze to dry more quickly, particularly when the weather is exceptionally damp or cold or you've tinted with one of the slower drying pigments, add just a little liquid drier; but watch the amount carefully or you could end up with the surface-skin problem mentioned above. The other problem with oil glazes is their limited availability. They tend to be stocked only by specialist or trade decorators' suppliers. You can make your own by mixing one part boiled linseed oil with between one and three parts pure turpentine. The glaze dries more quickly with a higher ratio of turpentine, so if you're using only the same amount of turpentine as oil, add an equal amount of drier and be prepared for it still to take a week or more to dry out completely. Commercial glazes normally dry out overnight, although they'll take two or three days to harden off.

Far left A translucent glaze, tinted to tone with the ground, intensifies plain color — even pastels — and gives them a depth of luster which is more than either sheen or shine. In this room, the boarded ceiling is glazed to complement the walls, but with the tinted glaze applied brushily over a paler ground, then lightly and roughly dragged in the direction of the grain for surface texture.

Left A daring treatment where two coats of blue-tinted glaze have been used to give depth to the surface of walls already color-washed in dark-on-mid blue. Although, for walls, glaze can be a finishing coat in itself, these walls were varnished for additional sheen. But for any floor on which a glaze is used, like this marble 'tiled' version, varnish is a must — at least three coats for protection and durability.

Above Glaze is here used more for texture than for sheen, or even color, to add a light, dragged surface to these kitchen units. Part of the charm of this treatment is in the balance of plain and textured surfaces and although a definite method has been followed, the impression is actually of a random, refreshingly arbitrary choice of which bit to treat in what way.

Paint glaze Neither of the two glazes mentioned here are completely transparent because they contain opaque pigment, but for this reason they have a softer effect and are both suitable for a variety of 'distressing' effects. The first type is a 1:1 mixture of flat oil paint or undercoat and oil glaze. Thinning the paint/glaze blend with an equal amount of mineral spirits makes a very easily manipulated mixture that stays wet long enough to be worked on; adding more glaze will make it less opaque and help it hold out even longer. This glaze dries to a slight sheen, but gives a flatter finish than transparent oil glaze on its own.

For the flattest of paint glazes, simply use flat oil paint or undercoat well-thinned with mineral spirits. The disadvantage of this glaze is the speed with which it dries, but practice and, if you're distressing the glaze, having two people on the job, makes it an absolutely practical proposition and many people prefer the flat, almost sheenless finish. Thin the paint from 1:1 to 1:2 with solvent, starting with equal parts and testing before adding more solvent. If the glaze gets too runny to hold the effect you're working into it, simply add a little more paint or, if you don't want to increase the opacity, a little drier.

Varnish glaze This is simply tinted varnish — a useful way of giving woodwork, in particular, a clear coating that is both decorative and protective with an easily available material. Follow the instructions given for tinting, thinning and applying varnish, bearing in mind that adding color will thicken the varnish so that it may need a little more solvent to thin it sufficiently to achieve a fine film of transparent color. If you're tinting with any of the slower-drying pigments, you may need to add a spot or two of drier to speed the drying up.

Tinting glazes All of these glazes can be tinted with either universal stainers or the larger, better range of artists' oil colors. Dissolve the colors in a small amount of mineral spirits, stirring them well until you have pure, thick liquid color, containing no bits. (Some professionals insist on straining glazes to double-check for undissolved pigment which could streak the work surface). To get proper color dispersion, stir the unthinned glaze or paint into the color a little at a time (not the other way around). In a paint/glaze mix, tint the paint rather than the glaze and for any of the paint glazes, buy white paint to make pale glazes but, for darker color, buy the nearest you can get to your chosen tone and make the final tinting adjustment yourself.

METHOD Glaze can be applied with either a brush or a rag. Over large areas a brush is faster and makes it easier to control the amount of glaze you're applying and achieve an even distribution. Brushing technique is much the same as for normal painting. Use a 3 or 4 in (7.5 or 10 cm) brush so that you can apply the glaze as quickly as possible. Pick up a small amount of glaze at a time, brush it on and smooth it out quickly to a thin film with the brush tip to avoid runs. If you're using a rag, bunch it up in your hand, dip it into the glaze and simply wipe it on thinly over the surface. If you're planning to use more than one layer of transparent/semi-transparent color, let each coat dry out overnight before applying the next. Whether or not you intend to distress the glaze for a broken color finish, you can even out patchy color with a hair-stripper, which is an attractive finish in itself. Remember, too, that glaze is a decorative, but not a protective finish. If you want proper protection for your hard-won decoration, it's only sensible to give it one or more coats of clear varnish.

VARNISHING

Varnish is almost as large and complex an area as paint. There are innumerable specialist products, most of which you don't need to know about, but there are two or three which between them give the adequate variety of finishes normally needed and wanted in interior work. The choice between them is not only a matter of practicality but aesthetics. Each finish has a different quality as well as a different performance and is used as much to visually enhance the surface beneath as to protect it.

Polyurethane varnish This is the modern, jack-of-all-trades among varnishes. It is the easiest one to use, the most economical and the most versatile, in that it is applicable to practically all interior surfaces, except plastics and those that may contain alkaline residue from insufficiently neutralized treatments such as stippling with caustic soda. As a finish, polyurethane doesn't perhaps have the

Left Different levels of sheen in a room play as much a part in textural variety as the more obvious rough and smooth, but varnish can get so stuck with its 'protective' image that its relative visual possibilities are forgotten. In this bedroom, the varnished surfaces are understated — nothing shines — and their relationship is unconventional: the furniture is satin-finished and the floor is actually matt, although over several coats of gloss varnish for durability.
Below A more conventional treatment uses gloss varnish for the wood-block floor but for aesthetic as well as practical reasons, for the high shine emphasizes the unusual design.

subtlety of some of the traditional varnishes, although if you are prepared to work patiently with it, laying on thin coats one after another, and playing around with the various degrees of sheen available, you can achieve a high quality finish, which is unbeatable for surface protection and durability. Polyurethane varnish comes in clear, wood and some coloured finishes; you can also tint it yourself by dissolving artists' oil color in mineral spirits and adding varnish to it, a little at a time and stirring well. Today's clear polyurethanes are virtually colorless. The palest — and you need to check that is what you are getting — have only a very slightly yellowish tone which make them suit-

able for covering all but the most precisely and delicately colored surfaces. To compensate for the yellowish tinge either modify the color beneath it or the varnish itself with a small amount of cobalt blue oil paint or artists' oil color, but you may prefer to use a 'water-white' protective finish, such as shellac, mentioned below.

Polyurethane varnish is normally obtainable in three finishes: matt, which has almost no sheen at all, satin, which has a sheen similar to that of eggshell paint, and gloss, which is just what it says — a hard, high shine. The level of shine goes hand-in-hand with durability, gloss being the most durable. However, you may not want a high-gloss finish, not least because it demands a near-perfect surface as it shows up every imperfection and speck of dust or grit. In this case, the way to achieve a high level of protection and durability and a low level of sheen is to build up the surface with two or more coats of gloss and finish with a satin coat — or even a matt coat, although it

will take a couple of coats of matt over gloss to achieve an even finish.

Varnish is like paint in that several thinned coats make a smoother, more even and glass-like surface than a couple of thick ones. The only exception is in varnishing floors when two undiluted coats should be applied after a well-diluted sealing coat (up to half and half with the appropriate solvent), to set up a really durable base. The 'proper' tool for applying varnish is an oval varnish brush, specially made to hold more varnish than an ordinary brush and so improve its flow; but, as with other finishes, there are alternatives. A 2 or 3 in (5 or 7 cm) paintbrush will do perfectly well, with the addition of a smaller artists' brush — 1 or ½ in (2.5 or 1.2 cm) — for detail work. Whatever you use, keep the brush exclusively for varnish work; clean brushes in mineral spirits and twirl them dry. Shaking varnish can cause it to froth and the same thing happens if you shake the brush — both could create bubbles on the

Above and **above left** Hiding under many a peeling, painted surface is good wood and this, of course, applies as much to furniture as to interior woodwork. The transformation that can be achieved with thorough stripping, meticulous sanding and several careful coats of varnish is little short of miraculous.

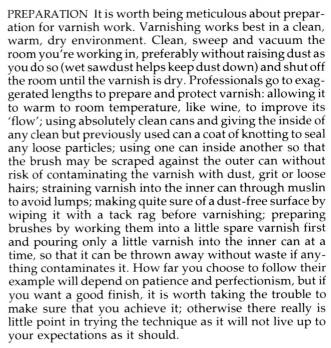

Below Be aware of how adjacent finishes relate to each other. Contrast in shine can be nearly as striking as contrast in color — the two together can really startle. In this collection of surfaces the new wooden floor was given a satin finish, over several protective coats of gloss, to blend with the matt and sheeny finishes surrounding it and leave the gloss-varnished, pillar-box red railings and spiral staircase to stand out as the only element with a hard, high shine.

varnish surface.

Polyurethane varnishes are normally touch-dry in a couple of hours and can be recoated in five to six hours. The next coat should be applied as soon as possible after this, as it is less likely to adhere properly once the varnish is completely dry. In traditional varnish work, 'flatting down' between coats is an integral part of the process, but polyurethanes are less elastic than some of the older types of varnish and therefore need to be rubbed down and polished with care. Matt varnish does not really need rubbing down between coats; the first coat of a satin and gloss varnish should definitely not be rubbed down and preferably not the second either, or there is a risk of breaking through the fine film to the surface beneath. Observe the recoating time strictly, as this will help adhesion, and on subsequent coats, use fine abrasive paper or steel wool.

PREPARATION It is worth being meticulous about preparation for varnish work. Varnishing works best in a clean, warm, dry environment. Clean, sweep and vacuum the room you're working in, preferably without raising dust as you do so (wet sawdust helps keep dust down) and shut off the room until the varnish is dry. Professionals go to exaggerated lengths to prepare and protect varnish: allowing it to warm to room temperature, like wine, to improve its 'flow'; using absolutely clean cans and giving the inside of any clean but previously used can a coat of knotting to seal any loose particles; using one can inside another so that the brush may be scraped against the outer can without risk of contaminating the varnish with dust, grit or loose hairs; straining varnish into the inner can through muslin to avoid lumps; making quite sure of a dust-free surface by wiping it with a tack rag before varnishing; preparing brushes by working them into a little spare varnish first and pouring only a little varnish into the inner can at a time, so that it can be thrown away without waste if anything contaminates it. How far you choose to follow their example will depend on patience and perfectionism, but if you want a good finish, it is worth taking the trouble to make sure that you achieve it; otherwise there really is little point in trying the technique as it will not live up to your expectations as it should.

METHOD When varnishing *walls*, thin satin or gloss varnish 3:1 with mineral spirits — it will run on more easily and leave a smoother finish. Dip the brush into the varnish to about half-bristle length and then transfer it straight to the surface. The feel of brush against wall — whether it drags, or slips too easily — will indicate whether the loading is right. If you have overloaded the brush, press the bristles against the inside of the can to release the surplus, but do not tip off the excess on the top edge of the can or you will risk getting bubbles. Applying the varnish generously will help to give an even coverage. Dip the brush in three or four times and cover the first section quickly with easy, decisive but light strokes, to avoid creating bubbles, and pick or flick out any foreign bodies with the tip of the brush. Leave this section to settle for as long as it takes you to brush on the next and then, with an empty brush (scraping it off on the outer can, if you're using one, otherwise on clean paper), return to the first section, crossing your brush strokes to lay the varnish in and finishing with a light, upward stroke. To avoid getting beads of varnish on areas such as picture rails, the top inch or so can be finished horizontally.

The same general principles apply to varnishing *woodwork*, but there are a few specific precautions and procedures worth knowing. Varnish does not adhere well to a greasy surface and may even start to 'ciss' in places. Bare surfaces can develop their own form of greasiness in a matter of days so, if there is any doubt, give the surface a wet rub with either vinegared-water and wet-and-dry abrasive paper, a chamois leather and water mixed with a little whiting or a rag moistened with mineral spirits. Try to avoid touching the surface subsequently — fingers contain a surprising amount of grease. If you are varnishing all the woodwork in a room, follow the normal painting sequence doing doors first, and ending on baseboards this is a fail-safe method for making sure the brush is worked in and clean by the time you reach the largest, and most obvious flat surface, baseboards being the area where you are most likely to pick up dust again. Doors should be taken off their hinges where possible, working on the flat allows the varnish to 'flow' over the surface rather than being simply brushed on. Work with a full brush on horizontal surfaces from the middle of each section, easing the varnish out to the edges, before actually brushing it out lightly and evenly over the whole area and laying it off in the direction of the grain. How many coats to apply is simply a matter of patience — or rather, lack of it — versus perfectionism, but the greater the number of well-laid, thinned coats of varnish, the better protected and more mirror-like the surface. Matt varnish should need no more than three coats, but satin can take up to five and gloss up to seven. However many coats you use, the proper, professional way is to lay off alternate coats against, and finishing coats with, the grain.

One of the big advantages of polyurethane varnish is that it does give a reasonable finish with a brush, unlike many of the traditional ones which need to be applied with a rubber. Nevertheless, however careful you are, brush strokes may still show on the finished work. For a soft, smooth sheen, sand the last coat when dry with very fine abrasive paper and then with very fine steel wool and liquid wax, both with the grain. For a brilliant polish, wet-rub along the grain with very fine, wet-and-dry abrasive paper and wash off any residue with clean water. When the surface is dry, make a 'rubber' out of lint-free cotton wrapped around a pad of cotton batting; moisten the pad with oil (warmed linseed oil is ideal, although lemon, olive or baby oil will do), pick up a little rotten-stone on the pad from a saucer and rub this in a circular movement over the surface. Don't rub too vigorously or too long in the same place or you may heat and soften the varnish with the friction. The final stage is to wipe the surface clean and then rub it with dry household flour, using either a soft cloth or the palm of your hand.

Polyurethane varnish can be applied over any well-seasoned, well established and sanded wood *floor*. Because the aim is to build up an exceptionally well-bonded, durable surface, varnishing is treated a little differently on floors. It is worth applying a sealing coat first; diluting the varnish half and half with mineral spirits. The first couple of coats are then applied undiluted, brushed on against the grain, and laid off with it. Subsequent coats can be thinned and applied with a rubber, if you wish, but leave each coat to dry overnight and sand down before applying the next, vacuuming thoroughly and preferably using a tack rag to make sure the surface is spotless. The number of coats is a matter of personal preference, although three is the absolute minimum, and five or six are advisable on a floor that receives much wear and tear. This applies whichever type of varnish you are using. The prime aim with floors is protection and gloss varnish, although the slowest drying is by far the most durable. The high shine will dull with wear, but if you prefer not to have it from the start, either finish with a satin coat or wait until the last coat is really dry and hard (this will take up to a week), then rub it along the grain first with medium, then fine steel wool.

SHELLAC

Shellac is probably best known as the material used for French polishing for which, to quell both hopes and fears immediately, I have decided not to give the instructions. These are as complicated and patience-stretching as the method itself which, although it does result in a sheen of a particularly beautiful character, is a highly-skilled operation, not adequately taught by book and also more suitable to fine, old pieces of furniture than structural or decorative interior surfaces. Shellac is also not particularly durable; imaginative use of modern varnishes will not only give a very close approximation of its finish but a much better level of protection. However, this does not entirely rule out shellac as a finishing coat and I have given a couple of methods below for those who want to use it as such. It can also play other very practical roles in the decorating process.

Liquid shellac is a spirit varnish made from an insect-derived resin dissolved in methylated spirits. Since it is soluble only in methylated spirits (and, therefore, alcohol) it makes an extremely useful barrier coat between different stages of decoration, preventing one layer 'disturbing' another with unwanted chemical reactions and allowing mistakes to be cleaned off without damage to the ground. Its fast drying time — about one hour for each coat, but increasingly faster the more it's thinned — which is precisely what makes French polishing so tricky, is one of its main advantages in other applications. Its sealing properties are also often used in the preparatory stages of decorating: the best knotting, which prevents resinous knots and streaks in wood from 'bleeding' into subsequent finishes, is pure shellac, and it will also seal off new plaster patches, plaster board before papering and filler before painting, the only proviso being that its glossy surface has insufficient key for oil-based primers and should therefore be sanded with medium abrasive paper or touched up with sharp flat paint first ('sharp' means very well thinned with mineral spirits). Shellac is also used as a kind of 'invisible mend' filler on unpainted wood: flowed in, liquid shellac can fill minor depressions caused by over-zealous sanding and, in its solid form of shellac sticks, which come in various colors, can be melted with a hot iron into cracks or areas of exceptionally open grain.

BUYING AND USING Shellac in varnish form comes in a variety of colors including the orange-yellow type known as 'button polish', a brown sometimes called 'garnet', a light amber known as 'pale', a milky white and a near-transparent water-white; solutions of Bismark brown are sometimes added to give it a reddish color, spirit black for black polish and you can tint shellac yourself with spirit-soluble dyes. The most useful of the commercial varieties is the water-white, as it has just about the least self-color of any clear finish available. It has a shelf life of about six months maximum and after that may not dry properly, or at all. It's therefore worth getting it from a well-patronized, specialist shop, looking for a date on the tin and even asking if you can test it on a piece of wood. For most purposes, thin shellac from 2:1 to 1:1 with methy-lated spirit, several thin coats being better than one thick one. Ignore manufacturers' instructions to shake the tin before opening it: shellac should always be stirred, not shaken, otherwise you'll cause bubbles which will show up on the surface of the work. It's also important to use shellac in warm, dry conditions — a damp atmosphere may cause a white bloom in the finish — and to observe the same dust-eliminating precautions as for varnish. And as with varnish, keep one brush especially for shellac: a soft-bristled $1\frac{1}{2}$ or 2 in (3.8 or 5 cm) brush is best, cleaned with methylated spirits after use. Soften hard brushes in a mild solution of ammonia, but never use soap.

METHOD **Brushing on** The most important aspect of brushing shellac on is that you work as quickly and methodically as possible. Shellac begins to dry almost before the brush has finished each stroke, leaving you no opportunity to fill in missed bits or overlap wet edges — at least until the next coat when you may, anyway, start to get a patchy build up of film. Practise applying shellac on a spare piece of wood until you can apply it quickly, evenly and confidently, without panic. It also helps if you can work on a flat surface so, for example, take doors off hinges first.

Take up a full brush-load each time, pressing any excess out against the inside of the can to avoid bubbles, rather than across the rim. Place the tip of the brush in the center of the surface and, working with the grain, draw it lightly across to one edge; then go back to the center and draw the brush out to the opposite edge in the same way. If you've loaded the brush correctly, there should be enough varnish left in the small, central pool to repeat this stage once, before, pressing slightly harder on the brush, you level this area out by brushing right across the surface from edge to edge. Take care not to stop short of the edge — imagine the brush is a plane landing and taking off, so that the movement of the brush begins and ends well clear of each edge. Try not to overlap brush strokes and re-load the brush quickly as and when necessary, repeating the whole process above each time. Rub down between coats with very fine abrasive paper or fine steel wool, dusting off residue with a dry cloth and tack rag. Use steel wool and soapy water to even out any patches on the dry sur-face, or use a rag moistened with methylated spirits, which softens the shellac and allows it to flow together again quite smoothly and evenly.

If the shellac is to be a final coat, you may want to kill some of its shine. Wait until the surface is completely dry and hard, then sprinkle on a little flour-fine pumice powder and, with a soft-bristled brush such as a shoe-brush, work backwards and forwards over the whole surface, from edge to edge with one stroke and staying absolutely true to the grain. This will give you a fine, matt finish with no criss-crossing effect. On dark woods, mixing charcoal dust with the pumice will stop any powder stuck in cracks from showing up. You can also use felt or a soft rag, moistened with a mixture of baby oil and mineral spirits and sprinkled with pumice for this process, which will leave you with a fine, dulled, satin-smooth, satin sheen.

Rubbing on In French polishing proper, the shellac is traditionally applied with a rubber — a piece of fine, soft, lint-free cloth, such as old sheeting, wrapped around a wad of cotton batting (which acts as a reservoir for the polish) to form a pad. There is an easier approximation to this process for clear-finishing wood that is sometimes called 'dip and rub' and which produces a finish with a rich, soft gloss. First brush on a 1:2 mix of shellac and pure turpentine, leave this to dry and then sand down with fine abrasive paper or steel wool. Make up the 'rubber' as described above and dip it first into a saucer or small bowl of turpentine, then one of shellac and rub it onto the wood with circular or figure-of-eight movements. In this process you will inevitably be overlapping strokes, but try to work your way across the surface methodically, don't go back over areas you've left and above all, keep the rubber moving continuously until the whole surface is evenly covered. Let the first coat dry for three to four hours, then repeat the process at least three times to make quite sure that you have a well covered and, also, an even, smooth finish for the most satisfactory result. It really is worth taking the trouble with this number of coats, to achieve the desired effect and one which will last.

LACQUER

Strictly speaking, none of the finishes below can be called 'lacquer', since the original, fine oriental lacquer-work depended on the sap of the lac tree and the patience of saint-like craftsmen, prepared to coat, rub down and polish a surface several dozen times. The result was a finish as smooth as satin and as hard as glass which, however brilliant or somber the color, created the illusion that you were looking into or through rather than at it. No techniques we have devised in the west, despite the efforts of skilled craftsmen to simulate the work of their eastern counterparts with paint and shellac, quite match the wonderful ambiguity of this oriental finish, which is simultaneously hard and soft, brilliant and subtle. However, I also question whether it is even sensible to attempt this level of finish on most interior surfaces, especially those subject to wear and tear like doors. Hard as it is, it is not invulnerable to chipping and the slightest damage shows up painfully on such a high sheen surface and can make it look shabby in a trice. Lacquer-type finishes make heavy demands on preparation for the same reason. Walls and woodwork must be absolutely smooth and even and it's better to confine a high-gloss finish on walls to rooms with good, plain proportions, as light bouncing in all directions off different angles, extrusions and alcoves will confuse and disturb rather than please and satisfy the eye. Yet all this is said to be cautionary rather than off-putting, as there are a variety of fairly simple ways to produce something like a lacquer finish, modern varnishes to protect them and the results are far from the thick texture and hard shine of a coat of gloss paint. The secret lies in the number of coats of clear or tinted glaze and varnish you have the patience to apply, for every extra coat will add to the depth and subtlety of the surface.

Walls

Since the instruction for surface preparation as well as mixing and applying the various materials are detailed elsewhere in the relevant sections of this book, all that needs to be said here is which blend of materials will give you what type of finish. If you are satisfied with the coloring of the walls and merely want to give them sheen or shine, a couple of coats of satin or gloss varnish will do the trick. But by tinting the varnish you can modify the base color: adding a small amount of color that tones with the ground to gloss varnish can give it a jewel-like intensity, while adding a small amount of one of the more earthy colors to satin-finish varnish can have a softening and aging effect. To build up a surface which has both depth of color and shine, apply a number of coats of tinted glaze, modifying each coat through different tones of the ground color, before you finish with clear or tinted varnish.

Far left Traditional lacquer-work has a quality of shine which no other finish can approach and the point is made very clearly here in the visible difference between the hard-soft depth of sheen on the surface of the lacquer cabinet and the more brittle, superficial shine on the varnished wall behind.

Left Probably the nearest we get to a lacquer finish today is by having a surface commercially sprayed with one of the modern artificial versions, such as nitro-cellulose lacquer, and this really does need to be done professionally. But the level of finish achievable by hand should still not be dismissed, if you're prepared to lay on several coats of glaze — up to a dozen.

Right Another inspirational piece of lacquer-work designed by Leon and Maurice Jallot in the late 1920s, as was the cabinet, left. For smaller pieces of areas of 'lacquer', like this little table, you may find the sheen of shellac more sympathetic than, say, satin-finish varnish.

Woodwork

Despite the *caveats*, 'lacquering' can completely transform the most nondescript piece of wood and is therefore particularly suitable for those plain, ordinary, very modern flush doors. But preparation is all. Unless wood has a sufficiently fine grain and smooth surface to need undercoat only, be prepared to fill, sand and prime until it is really hard and completely flat. Use wood filler or all-purpose proprietary filler to correct any major, obvious gouges, chips, scores or other defects, then mix the all-purpose filler to the consistency of cream and brush it on like paint, first across and then with the grain; a sponge can also be useful for filling door sides. On brand new flush doors — especially those made of foreign ply — you may have not only grain to contend with, but a kind of 'furry' texture which will persist through the first filling/sanding at least; but once you've primed it, then filled, sanded and primed again, it should disappear. Keep following the fill/sand/prime sequence until you have as near a glass-like, hard smoothness as possible, then give the surface a couple of well-thinned undercoats before painting.

More expensive — and therefore perhaps more suitable for smaller areas — but with a china-glaze quality of finish to match is synthetic gesso, available from artists' suppliers. This is the stuff artists use to prime canvases and in decorating it will provide a smooth, hard shell even over previously painted surfaces, as long as they're well sanded first to give them tooth. With synthetic gesso, you can leave out the priming stage of the raw-wood process above, brushing on thin coat after thin coat, leaving each to dry before sanding well with medium abrasive paper or steel wool and dusting off between coats. Seal the last coat with well-thinned shellac before painting. Whether you're using proprietary, all-purpose filler or gesso, use old brushes that you will never again need to use for paint. Don't skimp on the sanding — as with paint, it's the many fine layers which will build up to a good, hard, smooth surface — and sand especially well along the closing edges of doors or windows, even to the point where the old finish just shows through or they may not shut properly.

The method for achieving a 'lacquered' wood surface relies on paint and varnish and/or glaze in much the same way as it does for walls. The ground-work is important: apply two or three thinned coats of flat oil-based paint or undercoat, rubbing down between coats with fine, wet-and-dry abrasive paper and soapy water. Rinse off thoroughly each time, allow the surface to dry and go over it with a tack rag. Then apply two or three coats of gloss or satin polyurethane varnish, thinned 3:2 with mineral spirits, rubbing down between coats as above. As with 'lacquered' walls, tinted glaze and varnish coats will give greater depth of color. Polish the last varnish coat either with oil and rotten-stone or, for a higher shine, with wax.

WAX

Every wood surface benefits from protection, whether or not it's varnished, but wax is also used for the particular quality of finish it gives to the surface, which can vary from a subtle luster to a hard, glossy shine. But wax should never be applied to new or raw wood without sealing it first; by waxing directly onto wood, you may be rubbing dirt in, too, and anyway, wax is not completely impervious — there is a greater chance of getting a stain out of a wood surface that has been sealed before waxing. Use a proprietary sealer, working it well into the surface and, when it's dry, sanding it smooth along the grain with fine abrasive paper. Dust thoroughly before waxing.

Some people feel that proper beeswax polish is the only respectable wax with which to treat good wood. On the plus side, it has an incomparable smell and its golden tone is particularly sympathetic to woods of a similarly yellowish tendency, like pine and elm, which can be waxed and buffed several times, eventually to a rich amber glow. On the minus side, it requires much elbow-grease, is expensive and, personally, I am not convinced that the end result is good enough to justify either effort or cost. It also obscures the wood in a way that oil does not, which is illustrated when you touch a waxed, wood surface, as what you are touching is not the wood but the wax. In any case, there are any number of commercial wax polishes on the market — paste, liquid, clear and colored — which will very nearly do as good a job for a fraction of the time, trouble and effort.

However, for those who must be martyrs, the polish is made from real beeswax, bought from a drug store or hairdressers'/beauticians' wholesaler (there is a bleached beeswax if you don't want the yellowy colouring) and real turpentine, bought from artists' supply shops; the addition of a few lumps of resin will harden the wax and give it a better shine. If the beeswax is not already in smallish lumps or flakes, break it up or shred it into an old can and cover it with a roughly equal amount of turpentine. Heat and melt the two together (plus resin if you are using it) by placing the can in a saucepan of water on the stove — and keep all materials well away from a direct heat source as they are highly inflammable. Stir the melted mixture well and let it cool until it reaches the stage of soft, warm paste; then, using a brush with fairly stiff bristles, scrub the paste vigorously into the grain. Leave it overnight, to allow the turpentine to evaporate, before polishing, first with a clean, soft-bristled brush and then with a soft cloth, folded into a pad. If you want to repeat the process, wait for about a week to let the first coat settle.

If you are beeswaxing a floor, some back-ache can be avoided at polishing stage by using either a long-handled polisher or an electrically powered version (these can usually be rented). Long-handled applicators are also avail-

Left Wax can provide a subtle, mellow finish highly suitable for surfaces such as these stripped pine kitchen units. Be sure to seal new or raw wood before applying wax.

Stripping a pine table

1 Many proprietary brands of stripper are available to ease the chore of stripping. Apply with a clean soft rag. Always wear protective gloves when using stripper.

2 In stubborn cases, subsequent coats of stripper can be worked in using an old paintbrush.

3 Steel wool can also be useful for stripping intricate areas.

4 The top of the table near completion.

5 Restoration work is particularly satisfying when the natural beauty of the wood finally emerges from layers of poor quality finishes. A couple of coats of oil, well rubbed in, is all that is required to show this piece at its best.

able, some with hollow handles and a lever to dispense wax evenly, for putting on the commercial liquid, polishing or self-polishing waxes. Self-polishing waxes do not need buffing — they use water as a carrier for the tiny particles of wax and dry, leaving a film of wax on the surface. They are not particularly durable and more suited to floors that need frequent washing and easy rewaxing. Better for wood floors are the liquid polishing waxes; many types both clean and shine — although they do need buffing — and leave an attractive, smooth sheen and water-repellent finish. Some people don't believe in waxing wood floors at all, but rely on one of the enriched floor sealers and polishing to produce a natural, dull sheen on the surface. The great advantage of these is they can be renewed without any arduous preparatory work except thorough cleaning.

For varnished finishes, particularly on well-loved pieces of interior woodwork and furniture, use a thin wax with a high proportion of turpentine (you could adapt the proportions of the beeswax recipe for this). Rub the wax in with a damp cloth, allow it to dry for about 30 minutes, then add another coat. When dry, this second coat can be polished to any level of sheen you want; it should be left as it is for a matt finish; for an even, soft sheen, polish it once a day with a damp cloth for about a week; for a high gloss, buff with very fine steel wool, then with the damp cloth.

OIL

There is a tendency today, to move away from wax towards oil. It is easier to apply, it penetrates and protects the surface more thoroughly without in any way obscuring it and, although it can take repeated applications to build up to a high sheen, once there you will find that polishing will suffice for maintenance with just the occasional addition of a topping-up smear of oil. Which oil you use depends on your preference and the color of the wood. Linseed oil is the traditional material — easier to apply and more penetrating if you warm and mix it with half its volume of pure turpentine in a double-boiler — but it can take time to dry completely. Teak oil is a good substitute, with Danish oil or even olive oil for lighter woods.

You can apply the first coat of oil virtually any way you like, but the secret is to apply as much oil as the wood will absorb. Saturate the surface, leave it to soak for 20 minutes, then wipe off all excess oil with a rag while it is still wet. This last stage is simple but crucial, because as soon as the oil starts to dry, wiping it will only result in a sticky mess.

Leave this first coat to dry for a day or so before adding a second. Apply this more carefully, with a clean, lint-free rag around a pad of cotton batting, acting as a reservoir for the oil. With this coat you are just wetting the surface, not flooding it, and working it in as you go. When this coat is dry, buff it for a shiny finish, but otherwise leave it. You can always re-oil and if you get any marks on the surface, rub with fine steel wool until the mark has disappeared, oil the patch, buff and your perfect finish is back with relatively little time or effort.

SURFACES

There are literally, thousands of alternative surfaces to paint now available for applying to walls, floors and ceilings. The choice of surfaces is truly bewildering, but I hope that by outlining the options here, together with their characteristics, merits and disadvantages, aesthetically and practically, I can save both the heads and legs of a few home decorators!

WALLS

Walls represent by far the largest surface area in any room, to such an extent that they can easily dominate through sheer size. So if you want the strongest element in the room to be its decoration, or if this is the only way it's going to develop any degree of character, by all means envelop the walls with pattern. However, you may prefer them to play a more retiring role. Or the room may be so pleasing architecturally that the best way to show it off is also the simplest, with white, off-white or light, neutral-colored paint or a plain, minimally textured wallcovering. If, on the other hand, the walls leave something to be desired, but you personally dislike pattern, the best choice then may be a heavy-textured, stone-finish paint or relief wallcovering or rough textured fabric which will give walls surface interest and disguise irregularities.

Sometimes what you want can be obscured by what you've got. This can happen just as easily in a new environment, where someone else's taste holds your imagination in check, as it can in an old one which is so familiar that you can no longer see it objectively. Take your time over the decision and, if you're absolutely stuck, the way to move on a step towards a choice is temporarily to paint everything white or off-white (but not brilliant white, there's so much blue in this that it's no longer really a neutral). You'll then have a view of the room and its proportions that is uncluttered by idiosyncratic decorative style — yours or anyone else's. If you live with it like this for a while and consider all the options (bearing in mind color, textures and pattern), I think you'll find that the decisions will more or less make themselves without you having to force them.

Practical considerations

You may, of course, be limited in practical ways too — limited by the state of the walls and what's already on them. Most inherited surfaces can be dealt with one way or another and the Basic Preparation section of this book tells you how to remove, disguise or otherwise adapt the old surfaces to make way for the new. But there may be some inherent problems that are nothing to do with any previous decorative treatments. Damp needs to be dealt with at source and there's no sensible alternative to calling in a professional, although pitch-coated lining paper may keep minor damp patches at bay for a while. Some rooms suffer from excessive condensation; here again, take professional advice but if you can't solve it by increasing the ventilation and/or overall warmth in the room, you can at least counteract it by your choice of wall finish. For serious cases, special anti-condensation paints exist, containing cork flour, which reduce the amount of heat conducted but usually need to be sprayed on. Otherwise, try lining the walls with an insulating skin of expanded polystyrene (it comes in rolls as well as tiles and panels) before painting or papering, but observe the special fire precautions necessary when using polystyrene. In less serious cases of condensation, finishing the walls with a warm, naturally insulating material — heavy wallpaper, paper-backed natural fabric, cork or wood panelling — may be all that's needed.

What most of us get at some time in our decorating lives — especially those of us who insist on living in older properties — are walls in every state of unevenness from the odd minor undulation to something resembling the cratered surface of the moon. How you deal with these depends on the degree of unevenness, whether they're dry or damp, the money available and how long the walls are likely to be yours. If they're damp, badly pitted and you expect to live with them for a long time, the only sensible course is to trace and cure the cause of the damp and, if necessary, replaster completely.

If walls are dry but far from flat, you could consider covering them with any of the batten-mounted panels described below, but be prepared to pack the battens out from behind in places to get them flat, true and also stable. Walls which are rough but otherwise relatively flat and in good condition can often be adequately smartened up with one of the matt, textured materials such as wood-chip paper, embossed relief papers, burlap, linen or jute, or try one of the textured, 'stone-finish' paints. I can understand why these paints have acquired their reputation of being rather 'unaesthetic' finishes, because the manufacturers tended to concentrate on the high-relief effects — of stipples, swirls, whorls and patterns — that can be obtained with them. These are indeed generally horrid, but used plain and simple, and laid on generously with brush or roller, this type of paint can disguise imperfect walls perfectly.

Visual options
The introductory section of this book deals with the general principles of handling color, texture and pattern, the three main ingredients of decoration but here are the specific considerations that will shape your choice of wall-treatment on visual grounds.
● What is the aspect of the room: Can it take a cool treatment or is it north-facing and a bit bleak and cold-looking and crying out for some warm colors?
● How big is it? Will it feel cramped with too dark and dominating a color or pattern, or are there large expanses of wall which desperately need to be made more interesting? What is your preference as far as adding that interest is concerned? All-over pattern or a plainish texture punctuated by collections of pictures and objects?
● Will your chosen treatment suit the architectural character of the room?
● What role do you want the walls to play in the scheme as a whole? Do you want the room's decorations to stand out and be it's main feature, will this clash with its contents or should the decorations make a more neutral, less demanding background for furniture and accessories?
● How will the decoration of this room link with that in adjoining rooms, the rest of the house?

Left Walls whose natural condition leaves a lot to be desired are prime candidates for emphasizing rough plaster with the liberal use of filler and a couple of coats of textured paint. This type of wall treatment has a naturally Mediterranean ambience.
Above The condition of this wall becomes irrelevant because, thanks to the magical properties of mirror, it simply disappears. The sparkle within the mirror surface is transferred to the reflected images so that everything it touches becomes instantly more glamorous.
Right The modern miracle — a bathroom whose walls appear to have been lined with some kind of rare, mineral-saturated marble. It is, in fact, a decorative plastic laminate with a hand-finished abstract metallic design and a mirror-like shine.

WALLPAPERS

Wallpaper has been with us, in Europe, at least, for over 450 years. The earliest example of European wallpaper is said to date from 1509, the first year of Henry VIII's reign (1509-1547), although it took nearly another 200 years — until 1692, according to the records — for the first patent to be issued for manufacturing wallpaper in Britain. Today's wallpapers are mostly machine-printed by feeding paper through large, inked rollers, which transfer colors and designs onto them. The only significant limitation in this process — hardly likely to matter to most of us — is the circumference of the roller, which necessarily dictates the maximum size of any pattern repeat. It is this limitation which, to a certain extent, encourages the on-going practice of hand-printing. These hand-printed wallpapers are very much in the minority and are considerably more expensive; you're paying partly for the fact that very much smaller quantities can be produced in the same amount of time and need more labor to produce them, partly for better quality paper and more individual colors and designs.

However, if wallpapers today fall into these two basic categories, machine- or hand-printed, that's by no means the end of the story. There are wipeables, washables, pre-pasteds, textured or relief papers, flocks, foils, fake fabrics and genuine grasscloths. When is a wallpaper not a wallpaper, you might ask. The answer's not an easy one, since so many wallcoverings today contain a substantial or even predominant quantity of materials other than paper. This section, therefore, includes any type of wallcovering that is not strictly a decorative textile, outlines the main varieties, their general characteristics and any specific hanging requirements. You will find instructions for hanging wallpaper on page 102, but I'll emphasize here one point made to me by an expert. When things go wrong, it's most often because insufficient time has been allowed for the paper to expand after pasting. All papers expand to a greater or lesser degree and unless you leave them to complete this process (usually five to seven minutes) they will continue expanding on the wall, causing bubbles and uneven shrinkage as they dry.

Machine-printed

The cheapest types of machine-made wallpaper are called 'pulps' in the trade, because the design is printed straight onto the raw paper, the color of which forms part of the pattern. These papers are often very thin and more difficult to hang because, unless you handle them very gently, they may over-stretch in places while wet and therefore shrink unevenly and distort as they dry. Don't put them in any room where the walls get wear and tear or expect them to cover even minor surface defects satisfactorily. Most better quality papers are coated with a ground color first (which is why they are called 'grounds') before being over-

Wallpaper is seen here in just some of the many, many disguises in which it's capable of appearing today. Only one of these wallcoverings, the fresh, green fronds on a white ground in this light and airy kitchen (**far left**), remotely resembles coventional wallpaper. But this, too — along with the co-ordinating tile-effect paper — has the built-in benefits of today's technical knowledge because its deceptively fragile-looking surface is actually a tough, scrubbable vinyl. Today, foil wallcoverings are used with great subtlety, as in this bathroom (**above left**), where thin strips simulate burnished metal inlay between plain painted panels. Burlap papers (**below left**) are virtually indistinguishable from the real thing and make walls warmer and more welcoming. But wallpaper imitates and co-ordinates with more ornate fabrics, too — even reproducing texture as in this traditional dining-room (**right**).

printed with their patterning — although this is sometimes done in one operation. (This and the fact that machine-made papers are printed 'on the move' can result in a loss of pattern definition, so if you really care about 'sharp' prints, go for hand-mades.) Neither 'pulps' nor 'grounds' are washable unless stated; if you want to give them some degree of wipeable protection with one of the special, proprietary wallpapers sealers, check for color fastness first. Machine-produced papers in Britain are normally sold ready for hanging in pre-trimmed rolls 11yd (10.05m) long by 21in (533mm) wide. American papers are usually the same width, but supplied in rolls either 7yd (6.4m) or 14yd (12.8m) long.

Hand-printed

These papers are now mostly printed through a silk-screen, although some may be hand-stencilled or block-printed, and although some modern designs are produced, their emphasis and their strength lies in classic or traditional designs, in some cases using the original blocks made by masters such as William Morris and the Victorian architect Augustus Pugin. If you're prepared to pay the price, you may prefer these papers, not only for the quality and sharpness of their printing and the cachet of having a highly individual paper made by skilled craftsmen in limited quantities, it will also probably be the only way you'll get wallpaper custom-made to any particular

coloring or design and this is always a bonus — more scope for individual taste. Despite the price they are rather special coverings.

Hand-prints are usually made in 11yd (10.05m) rolls, but both lengths and widths can vary. Some are also still supplied with selvages, in which case you'll need to trim the edges yourself. In most cases, trim the paper dry with a proprietary pocket trimmer or a very sharp-bladed craft knife and straight-edge. For really top-quality papers (or if you're a perfectionist), you'll get a cleaner cut if you trim the paper wet, either with a straight-edge and knife (but blades must be really sharp) or with a patent trimmer, designed specially for this job, which will also cut through several dry layers of paper at once. Always trim on a totally flat, stable, rigid surface and trim both sides, one side at a time, off the whole length of each roll before you start cutting it up. Hand-print pattern repeats can also be more difficult to match on the wall; one professional told me pessimistically — with a life-time's experience behind him — that you can't hope to get an accurate match over more than a 3ft (90cm) span of each join, so aim for an eye-level match based on some of the more dominant features and colors in the paper and let happen what will above and below this point. In this way at least the part that attracts the eye immediately will seem to match up fluently, and the rest will simply have to be accepted.

Hanging wallpaper

Adhesives

Practically all the professionals I've talked to say that, for most wallpapers, there is still nothing to beat the 'old-fashioned' flour or starch-based pastes. Either make your own or buy any of the standard pre-prepared, proprietary hot-water or cold-water paste mixtures that come in powder form, and follow the instructions on the packet. Hot-water pastes take a little time to prepare and usually need boiling water; whereas cold-water pastes are made in minutes. Starch-based paste is better than flour-based for fine papers as it's completely transparent. As a general principle, mix and use the paste as thick as it's workable — you're better off with a strong, thin coat than a lot of weak paste which may squeeze out between the joins and onto the face of the paper. When hanging vinyls it is essential to use a paste containing an anti-fungicide, or a semi-liquid PVA adhesive.

Home-made paste Add lukewarm water to a bucket containing about 2lb 3oz (1kg) of *plain* flour and beat the mixture into a creamy paste. Boil about $8\frac{3}{4}$pt (5 liters) of water in a saucepan and pour it straight on to the paste, stirring vigorously until the paste thickens. Let it stand for a minute or two before pouring on a cupful of cold water to prevent it forming a skin on top. Don't use the paste until it's cool, but use it while it's still fresh — it'll go off after a couple of days.

Cutting up

There can be quite marked differences in tone from one roll of wallpaper to another. The first job, therefore, is to 'shade' the rolls by unrolling each one a little and over-lapping the free, top edges in a good light. Group them so that any obvious change in tone does not appear in the middle of a wall. If you're a perfectionist, you can repeat this process once the paper has been cut up, by putting the lengths in a sequence minimizing tone discrepancies.

Most papers come with pre-trimmed edges these days, but some hand-prints may not. Before you start cutting, also check whether the pattern repeat is at the same level on both edges of the paper or whether it drops on one edge. This is quite common on patterns with large repeats and the most economical way to use the paper is to cut the lengths alternately from two different rolls of paper. To save constantly holding a tape or rule to the paper, use the paste-table itself as a measuring tool. You'll either be using one of the older, 6ft tables or newer, 2 meter versions; either way you'll find it helpful to mark the table out down its length at 1in or 300ml intervals. Cut the paper face up on the board, organize the cutting so that you always get one full pattern repeat at the top of the wall where it's most obvious and let whatever happens happen at the bottom.

Cut each length so that there's about 3in (7.5cm) overlap at top and bottom. Use the first full cut length as a measure for all the others and leave cutting any short lengths — over doors, windows — until last when you'll probably be able to use up the left-overs at ends of rolls.

Pasting and folding

Stand the paste table near a window so light reflected off the wet paste will show the evenness of the covering. Dab-handed professionals then lay a sequence of full lengths face down on the table, overlapping an equal amount over each end and pushed well back from the front edge. They then pull the first length forward and to the left until paper and table are flush along front and right-hand edges and lift the far edge of the top length when they paste it. If you

Above There are various methods of cutting paper to size. Here it is being torn across, using a straight-edge. Care must be taken when cutting to get an even match of color, as tones vary from roll to roll.

don't trust yourself not to get splodges of paste on the second length while you paste the first — causing uneven expansion — then only lay one length at a time on the table. Apply the paste by striping a brushful down the middle of the paper first, then brushing out to the sides in herringbone fashion. This ensures that the edges get a good covering and lessens the risk of the paste leaking onto the face of the paper. Some professionals prefer to paste with a roller — saying it gives a more even distribution. Paste the whole area of paper that's on the table, then gently fold the pasted section in half, pasted sides together. Move the rest of the paper over onto the table, paste and fold the second section in to the middle, leaving a couple of inches gap between the two folded-in edges and turn these back by about 1in (2.5cm) to make unfolding easier. If you work methodically, always putting the top of each length on the right and pasting it first, this will save you having to mark the paper 'top' as it will always be the largest fold. Keep clean rags handy and do not hang lengths as soon as they're pasted — most papers need 5-7 minutes to expand — or they may bubble and wrinkle. Once you get into a rhythm, you'll find it works to paste and fold two or three lengths ahead of the one you're hanging, so that there's no break in the work sequence.

Left Paste is applied to paper using either a brush, as here, or a roller (as shown, **below left**). It is useful to work in direct light as the areas of paste will then be reflected.
Below Folding paper in half, pasted sides together, prior to lifting and hanging.

Above Striking a vertical with a plumb-line. This ensures that your first sheet hangs vertically. Care must be taken to allow for any deviation at window edges or architraves.

Hanging

Start papering from a window but aim for your papering to 'meet up' in the least conspicuous corner as the final match is unlikely to be perfect. Don't rely on the edge of the window to be vertical. Use a plumb-line to mark a line down the wall whose distance from the window is about $\frac{1}{2}$in (1.2cm) less than the width of the paper; this will ensure that your first sheet is vertical and allow for any deviation in the window edge.

Keep the paper folded over one arm until you're ready to hang it then, holding the top, folded back edges between fingers and thumbs, allow the folds to fall open gently so that the pasted side is facing the wall. Place one edge of the paper against the marked line a few inches down the wall, letting the top overlap fall towards you and, with the other hand, hold the rest of the paper away from the wall while you swing the length into position. Once the whole of the edge is flush with the line, the paper will fall quite naturally into position against the wall; brush straight down the center with the papering brush first, then cut towards each edge. Apply firm, even pressure to push out any air bubbles and if any wrinkles appear, ease the paper away from the wall and brush it smoothly back. For paper with very delicate finishes, use a paper-hangers' felt-covered roller instead of a brush to prevent marking or damaging the surface.

The most common way of finishing top and bottom edges is to mark the paper by running the back edge of the scissors along the angle between wall and ceiling or base board, pulling the paper away, cutting along the crease and brushing it back into position. Some prefer the old-style method of straight-edge and *very* sharp-bladed craft knife; this ensures a straight edge every time, but you must be prepared to waste blades because if they're not really sharp the damp paper may tear. This method is often more highly recommended as some claim that if you use the scissors to score a line, it may be false, and also be peeling the paper away, you end up with less paste just where you need it most. The choice is up to you in the end.

Joins should preferably not be butted, as they may open as the paper dries; overlap them by the merest fraction, about 1/16in (1.5mm), and towards the light. Seams should be rolled but not until you've papered a whole wall, otherwise you risk squeezing adhesive out onto the face of the paper. Once you've completed a wall, roll seams in the same sequence as the paper was hung and use the edge of the roller, not the face, to avoid 'tracks'.

It's worth checking every hung length with a plumb-line to make sure it's vertical, and check angles, too. You can usually take paper round external angles, but never risk it round internal angles, as plasterers are not required to get these true. When you've hung the last full length before reaching the corner, measure at top, center and bottom the distance from the corner to the edge of this last sheet. Add $\frac{1}{2}$in (1.2cm) to the widest measurement, cut the next length of paper to this width and hang it, brushing the 'turn' wall into the corner and trimming off top and bottom. Hang the remainder of the cut sheet so that it overlaps the turn, but check that it's vertical and adjust, if necessary, before finally smoothing it down. You really can't hope to get a perfect match in an internal corner, so the best thing is simply to aim for neatness instead.

To paper round a door or window, hang the top few inches of the pasted length, brushing it into position, but let the rest hang loosely over the obstruction. Cut the paper roughly to the shape of the frame, allowing about 1in (2.5cm) overlap and make a diagonal cut to $\frac{1}{2}$in (1.2cm) beyond the corner of the frame. Brush the cut edges well into the angles between wall and frame and trim off the overlaps as above.

Papering awkward places

Round sockets and switches If the switch-plate can be removed (turn off mains first), paper straight over the recess, make diagonal cuts to the corners, trim the surplus paper and replace the switch. Alternatively, for a fixed switch or socket, let the paper fall loosely across it and, from the center of the switch, make diagonal cuts in the paper to extend about $\frac{1}{2}$in (1.2cm) beyond the corners. Brush the paper gently into position round the switch, then trim the edges.

A recessed window If the window from which you're starting is recessed, mark a vertical line on the wall at a point which allows the width of the paper to turn the corner and fill the recess with a $\frac{1}{2}$in (1.2cm) overlap next to the frame. Hang the paper to this line, make horizontal cuts just above and below the recess and brush the paper into position on the returns. Leave overlaps on top and bottom internal angles as 'turns', but trim overlap down the edge of the window frame. Cut the next length $\frac{1}{2}$in (1.2cm) too long so that it turns into the recess and overlaps the frame, hang and trim. To fill the remaining gap, cut a piece of paper to the exact width but about 2in (5cm) longer than the depth of the recess. Hang this so that it overlaps both frame and recess equally; trim at window frame but turn the front overlap up and over the trimmed horizontal edge of the first length and tear carefully, rather than trimming, to hide the join.

A chimney breast If the paper has a very dominant or large pattern, it may be better to start papering from this point rather than the window. Using a plumb-line, hang either one or two lengths centrally — whether it's one or two depends on the pattern (center large patterns) and the width of the chimney breast, but you need at least 2in (5cm) overlap to turn the corners each side. To paper the side of the chimney breast, mark a vertical line 1in (2.5cm)

back from the external corner. Measure from this line to the internal angle between chimney breast and wall, add ½in (1.2cm) and cut the length to this width. Hang this length so that it's flush with the marked line and brush the turn into the corner as usual.

A ceiling The ceiling should be papered before the walls and in addition to the normal equipment you will need two step-ladders and a scaffold board so that you can walk the full width of the room at a comfortable height.

Start papering from the window. To position the first length accurately, on the two opposite walls next to the window wall, measure and mark a point about 1in (2.5cm) less than the width of the paper from each internal angle. Snap a chalked line between these two points to mark the ceiling. Paste the paper as for walls but fold it concertina-fashion in roughly 18in (45cm) folds and use a spare roll of wallpaper to support the pasted and folded length as you hang it. Gently pull open the first fold and brush it onto the ceiling, positioning it along the chalked line and leaving the usual 1in (2.5cm) overlap against the wall. Open and brush on one fold at a time until you reach the other side, then trim all three overlaps as for walls. Hang the first length right to left (the other way if you're left-handed) and facing the window, but you'll find it easier to hang the remaining lengths in the opposite direction, with your back to the window, overlapping joins by a fraction towards the light and rolling seams as for walls.

To paper round *ceiling roses*, pierce through the paper at the center point of the rose, make star-shaped cuts to about ½in (1.2cm) beyond its circumference, fit paper over ceiling rose, brush smooth and trim edges.

Above, left to **right** Hanging wallpaper. It is important to remember to leave enough on the top and bottom of a drop to allow for trimming. With the back of a craft knife or pair of scissors, score the line to trim. Then peel the paper back and make the cut. It is sometimes possible to cut straight through with a sharp craft knife without peeling back.
Upper left The same procedure is used for fitting to architraves and window frames.
Lower left Cutting around light switch. Two diagonal cuts are made from the center of the light switch. The paper is then attached to the wall and the excess paper trimmed around the switch. Here shown using a scraper as a straight-edge.

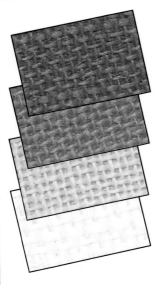

Above Paper-backed burlaps are now made in many 'real' colors as well as the more obvious earth tones and neutrals. A generally available broad width is about 51in (130cm), ideal for facing the standard 4ft (120cm) wide panels of chipboard, blockboard or ply.
Below Fake suedes on a non-woven fiber backing can be stuck straight to sound, flat walls. Clean with vacuum or brush, use detergent or dry cleaner for stains.

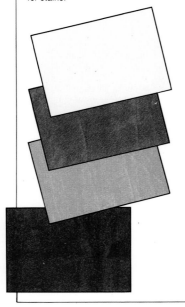

Washables

These can almost be described as cheap vinyls. This is because these papers, which are usually printed, are coated with a thin, transparent plastic film to give them some protection which means that they can be washed or even gently scrubbed with soapy water; they will not withstand detergents or abrasives. In addition, however, they come in a variety of surface finishes from matt to glossy, whereas vinyls generally have a distinct plastic-type sheen, which you may not like. The water-resistant surface of washables obviously suits them for use in kitchens and bathrooms, or in any room that gets grubby enough to merit frequent wiping over, although they will not stand up to as much wear as vinyls. Like vinyls, it is better to hang washables with a paste containing anti-fungicide because of their impervious surface (see below). Another characteristic of washables is that they can be harder to remove than standard papers, but if you score through the plastic film first they should then come off using the normal stripping process and in some types the surface film will simply peel off.

Vinyls

These printed and/or textured wallcoverings are made from paper that's coated or laminated with PVC and printed with special inks or dyes which fuse with the surface. They're not only waterproof but also generally tougher than standard wallpapers or washables, they can withstand scrubbing with detergents and abrasives (although don't attack them with something too vicious, like steel wool) and take general wear and tear with better grace. Because of their impervious coating, ordinary water-based pastes cannot dry out through the surface; the paste has to dry out through the wall and will therefore remain wet for some considerable time and may start to form mold. When hanging vinyls it's therefore essential to use a paste containing an anti-fungicide. A good, if more expensive, alternative is to use a PVA adhesive — a chemical polymer containing no water at all. These adhesives come in various strengths, denoted by color coding on the canister, for different weights of material, but consult either the manufacturer or supplier if you're in any doubt about which one is most suitable. PVA adhesives are normally applied to the wall rather than the covering. If you're using paste, hang vinyls almost immediately (they don't expand to the same degree as ordinary papers) and butt-join rather than overlapping as vinyl will not stick to itself. (When an overlap can't be avoided — for example, on an external angle — use adhesive to stick edges down.) Use a papering brush or damp sponge to smooth the paper down firmly and be especially careful about brushing out any crinkles, paste splotches or air bubbles, and wipe off immediately any excess paste

appearing through the joins. If the surface coating and backing separate at any point — this sometimes happens when you're trying to cut the paper in round awkward shapes — simply insert a small amount of paste or adhesive between coating and backing paper and press it firmly back into position.

Apart from the obvious sheen, the other disadvantage of vinyls is that light tints in particular are affected by fumes from things like cigarettes or gas fires; these react with the PVC coating and permanently discolor it, so that they cannot simply be washed clean. But stripping is easy; the top printed or textured PVC layer simply peels off leaving the paper backing, which can then either be stripped in the normal way or left as lining for the next wallcovering.

Pre-pasteds and non-pasteds

Pre-pasted papers were designed with the DIY market in mind, although they're still more popular in the US than Britain. Backed with an adhesive coating and supplied with a plastic trough, they need only to be dipped in water, to activate the adhesive, and applied to the wall. Once they're wet, you've usually got about 15 to 20 minutes working time to allow the paper to expand and to get the positioning right before the adhesive sets. Pre-pasteds are more expensive than standard papers, but if this time, trouble and mess-saving gimmick is what persuades you to do it yourself rather than hire an expert, you'll save more than the extra money you spend. These papers, too, are made for easy, peel-off stripping. I call the other variety 'non-pasteds' because, in this case, you apply the special adhesive supplied by the manufacturer to the wall, not the 'paper', which is actually a lightweight foam film, suitable again for kitchens and bathrooms because of its steam- and water-resistance.

Relief papers

Many standard wallpapers have a texture, sometimes to imitate a fabric such as burlap or linen, or a slight emboss-ment where the surface is raised to form all or part of the pattern. But there are two distinct types where the relief surface is more pronounced and is there for its function as much as its form.

Ingrain papers you will probably recognize more easily under their familiar name of 'wood-chip' — paper of various thicknesses where the wood pulp has been mixed with wood-chips, sliced straw and other fibers during production to give it a textured surface with considerable 'body'. Ingrains are most commonly used to disguise uneven or rough walls in older houses and although they are available in patterns and broken-color effect, they generally look best if they're bought in their raw gray or white state and then painted. A modern version with the same ability to disguise flawed walls comes in glass fiber, in several different textures; it's supplied with a special adhesive for hanging and can also be painted over.

Anaglypta and Lincrusta are almost universally recognized trade names for those distinctive wallcoverings whose various patterns and textures are formed entirely by surface embossing to various depths of relief. *Anaglypta* is made from heavy white paper backed with another layer of ordinary wood pulp and embossed while damp so that the pronounced relief patterns remain in the paper when it is hung. It is thick, strong stuff, so particularly good for covering old, cracked or uneven plaster, and as well as rolls or panels, it's also made to resemble decorative plaster mouldings such as those found on ceiling roses or cornices — although it doesn't take an expert eye to distinguish these from the real thing.

Anaglypta is best hung with the special paste recommended by the manufacturer; if you use an ordinary starch or flour-based paste, make it fairly stiff and dry. Paste two lengths before you hang the first, paste the third before you hang the second and continue in this sequence so that each length has a good time to expand and become flexible. But don't leave them too long, and brush out any excess paste that has settled in the recesses or the paper may expand unevenly, or over-expand, so that it becomes limp and may distort as you hang it. Fold it carefully to avoid creasing; don't stretch it too much over the wall or it will shrink back as it dries and the joins will open; and instead of brushing across the face of the paper, use the brush tips of the paper-hanging brush, as if you were stippling, to beat the paper firmly into position.

Lincrusta is a more rigid material made from a solid paper backing, coated with a putty-like mixture of linseed oil and filler. This is pressed while still soft into relief patterns and textures and other effects resembling tiles and wood panelling. While it can do a great cover-up job, it should be stuck to smooth, properly prepared walls over a heavy lining paper if it is to adhere well and look its best. Although you can use a very stiff flour-paste to hang it, it's far better and safer to use the special glue supplied by the manufacturer. Before hanging, lie each length of material face down, sponge it with warm water and leave this to soak in for about 30 minutes to make it pliable and allow for expansion, before blotting up any excess water and applying the glue. Lincrusta should be butt-joined and, once each length is in position, gone over first with a pad of rolled or bunched-up cloth to press it against the wall, then over the whole surface again with a clean paint roller. Make sure you work firmly and evenly from the center outwards to push out any surplus glue, which should be wiped off at once with a damp cloth. This material can be stained, painted or glazed; it is best prepared for the glazing with a coat of sharp paint, well thinned.

Lincrusta and Anaglypta are the two most familiar relief wallcoverings, but further developments have been made by the same manufacturer, including a higher-relief version of Anaglypta, based on a 'web' of cotton and clay, and a washable, vinylized version of Lincrusta, which is supplied pre-finished, but can also be painted.

It is useful to note that although lining paper improves the quality of most finishes, it is not strictly necessary to line walls for the lighter-weight ingrain papers. But the other relief papers mentioned are all quite heavy and walls must be cross-lined first to provide a surface which is sufficiently, uniformly porous for good adhesion.

Fakes and fantasies

Wallcoverings are made from, and made to look like, many materials other than paper. Fake fabric is a favorite and many modern ranges include hessian and linen-look papers, which have a clean-textured, rather Scandinavian feeling to them. Flock is another and much older favorite, designed to look like the alternate raised and flat pile patterning of cut velvet. Some flocks are still hand-made by dusting or blowing minute particles of wool, silk or synthetic fibers onto an adhesive backing, but most are now machine-made, and these include washable, vinylized versions. Even these, however, are generally produced in traditional patterns which, with their heavy texture and generally rather rich coloring will only really suit older, somewhat formal settings. Rather more rarified and elegant are moirés, in which the paper is subtly shaded to look like watered silk or 'shot' taffeta; there are also, of course, fake leathers and suedes and some very sophisticated reptile skin effects.

Among the 'hard finish' look-alikes, foil papers are probably the most dramatic of the newcomers, although after more than a decade of development they can no longer really be called new. The gold or silver reflective finish is made by applying sprayed polyester to a paper backing and whereas this type of paper used to be made only by a few, specialist firms, it is now produced in many, more widely available ranges and the foil is over-printed with a variety of designs. It's essential to line walls first when hanging foils and check on the method of hanging; PVA adhesive should be used for all foils, but in some types it is applied to the paper backing rather than the wall.

At a more mundane level, wood grain papers are photographically printed to resemble a variety of wood-types and you can also get 'marble' papers produced by the same method. Some firms still make marbled papers by hand and, although usually made to order with a custom-made price to match, the individuality of color and absence of pattern repeats put them into a completely different class.

All sorts of natural materials are also applied in very thin or fine form to paper-backing material to make wall-

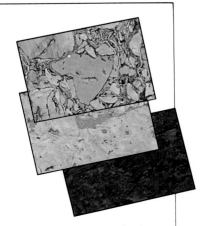

Above Wafer-thin sheets of cork laminated to a colored paper backing create almost marble-like veins and swirls.
Below Grass, hemp and cane are also paper-backed for easy hanging, but it's still wise to get the more delicate materials professionally hung.

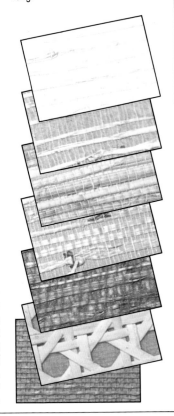

Wallpapers can make it easy to be grand with, for example, eye-deceiving murals or marbled opulence. Most home-decorators shy away from using their brushes and paints to create the real, three-dimensional effects of trompe l'oeil pictures, but this neo-Palladian entrance (**above**) is a fake of a fake: with the exception of drapes and balustrades, it's all made from a 'collage' of cut-up wallpaper — something anyone can do. Similarly, you may lack sufficient confidence to tackle hand-marbling your own walls, or sufficient funds to get this done for you, or even to buy hand-marbled paper.
Above right Although the pattern repeats on commercial paper will fool no-one, this bathroom proves that a good quality print can still lend considerable luxury to large expanses of plain wall.

coverings: tiny granules or slim strips of cork, fine films of wood veneer, slivers of wood woven together with cotton. Some of these can be stained and varnished or polished after hanging. One of the most expensive and exclusive of these types — or, indeed, of any wallcovering — is Japanese grasscloth, for which dried grasses are woven together before being stuck to a paper backing. Grasscloth is a luxury material in more ways than price: it's extremely fragile and difficult to clean; it requires a felt-covered rubber roller rather than a brush for hanging; and unless the joins between lengths are protected with beading or braid, creating a series of panels (which is aesthetically wise, too, as you can never hope to achieve a 'match' between lengths of this horizontally woven material), the edges can start to lift, curl and fray, so that it all too quickly begins to look like a badly thatched roof. It's only sensible to line walls before you hang any of these very specialized papers but, before you do, consider whether it's sensible for *you* to be hanging them at all. Unless you've acquired a near-professional degree of expertise and have absolute confidence in your own ability to carry out the job well, don't risk spoiling the material for lack of a little professional help.

LINING PAPER

Whether you're painting or papering, there are two main reasons for using lining paper: to improve uneven or cracked plasterwork and/or to provide a surface with even, all-over porosity, without 'hot spots' — the trade jargon for isolated and exceptionally porous areas of plaster, which will drink up all the paste or paint and leave you

with unstuck or bare patches.

Lining is absolutely essential under foils, grasscloths and delicate or fine fabrics, and highly recommended under any of the more expensive wallpapers, especially hand-prints, if you want a first-class finish. Even with standard wallpapers, lining paper can be a help to adhesion on smooth, hard surfaces and useful if you're changing the color of the surface dramatically, particularly from dark to light; it provides a good clean surface as well as a neutral background for any new wallpaper, and flattens out bad surfaces.

Lining paper comes in a variety of different qualities and types for different purposes. The lighter papers are fine for ordinary walls and general purpose work, but use the heavier, brown lining papers for rough walls and under heavy, relief coverings. If the wall is prone to damp, tar- or pitch-coated papers (hung coated-side to the wall) will provide some protection, but these can never be regarded as more than a temporary solution to a real damp problem and you will always find you need to get to the root of the problem for a long-term, satisfactory finish. You can sometimes find calico or muslin-faced papers for lining plaster that is badly cracked, or for making a sound, smooth surface when papering over tongue-and-groove boards. The alternative for boards is paper-hanger's scrim — a thin, strong muslin. On old woodwork, either soak the muslin in flour-paste first and spread it across the surface, or paste the wood, lay the dry scrim on it and roll it flat and smooth with a wide clean paint roller. In either case, use tacks around the edges to hold the scrim taut while it dries. On newer wood, which is still drying out and may unsettle the scrim, one decorator suggests stretching and tacking the dry scrim over the surface, then giving it a superficial coat of size. In each case, the scrim will tighten as it dries and should then be lined before painting or papering to give a really sound-looking finish.

If you're hanging a wallcovering, the wall should always be cross-lined: the lining paper is hung horizontally so that there is no risk of vertical joins meeting up (on ceilings, the joins should always run away from the main light source). Opinions vary so much about which way you hang lining paper if you're intending to paint it that I simply have to say, it's a matter of preference. Whichever way you hang it, lining paper should be butt-joined and the joins left fractionally open — just the smallest possible gap — then filled and sanded when the paper is dry. Lining paper is normally hung using standard starch or flour-based paste, but if you are using another type of adhesive for the wallcovering, use the same for the lining to avoid any possible chemical reaction between the two pastes, leaving you with an adhesive which refuses to stick at all. That is just a waste of time, effort and money.

FABRICS

Fabric wall-hangings pre-date wallpaper not just by centuries but by civilizations. Draft exclusion, at least on walls, is now a thing of the past but there's still something extraordinarily luxurious about fabric-covered walls. Although using the more expensive fabrics in any great quantity is beyond most people's budgets, using a lot of even a very inexpensive fabric can feel just as sumptuous as a smaller amount of a luxury fabric like silk or velvet. In theory, any fabric can be hung on the wall, one way or another. In practice, it's usually cost, which proves the restricting factor.

Paper-backed fabrics, made especially for the purpose, are easiest of all to manage, although some are more straightforward than others. Ranges include paper-backed burlap, linen, jute, wool, chenille, velour, silk, felt and PVC. Most paper-backed fabrics can be applied exactly like wallpaper, although silk is especially delicate and difficult to apply as it can be easily marked during hanging. In some cases the supplier may recommend using adhesive rather than paste and applying it to the wall rather than the paper

Below When hanging unbacked fabric on a wall, always work from the center out to the corners. This applies whether you're using frames or stapling the fabric directly on to the wall and will ensure that, since it's unlikely that the wall will accommodate exact, full widths of fabric, cut pieces are of equal measurement at corners. If you're stapling, back flimsier fabrics with cotton or polyester wadding for body. You'll also find it easier to get it hanging right if you staple the bottom edge and one side first, then pull and staple the other side to get the correct width-ways tension before stapling the top edge last.

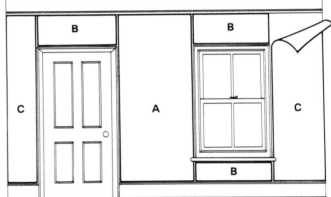

Far left This bedroom relies entirely on a delicate, blue-on-white print for decoration and although it does all the obvious things it's neat, pretty and, above all, quick.
Left If all-over pattern is too much for your eye, use braided borders to edge plain fabrics. There can be a cost advantage, too, in that really quite inexpensive fabrics like calico and jute are lifted out of their class by a few meters of fancy braiding.

backing of the fabric; the deciding factor is generally whether or not the material needs time to expand (if it does, you use paste), but it's essential to check this out before you proceed. Some manufacturers supply the fabric pre-prepared with a self-adhesive backing, in which case you simply cut it to length, line it up and then, starting from the top, peel away the backing gradually as you smooth the fabric over the wall.

Unbacked fabrics should normally have been made or pre-treated to make them suitable for sticking to the wall and there are specialist firms who will prepare fabrics for you in this way. To hang unbacked fabrics of this type, you roll PVA adhesive onto the wall and overlap each length by 1-1½in (2.5-3.5cm). Leave the adhesive to go off for about 10 minutes before cutting straight through both layers down the middle of the overlap, using a steel straight-edge and a sharp craft knife, to leave a clean butt-join.

It is generally unwise to attempt sticking any untreated fabric directly to a wall. The only types I would risk hanging like this are cheap burlap and canvas or calico — perhaps in a room which needs a quick and budget-minded facelift. In this case, brush a stiff paste onto the wall and unroll the dry fabric over it, brushing it out well to flatten it and eliminate crinkles and creases. But try to avoid over-stretching or it may shrink and distort as it dries. Either overlap and cut joins as above or neaten butt—joins by covering them with beading, webbing or braid.

The proper method for hanging good quality, unbacked and untreated fabrics is to make rectangular frames out of battens. Stretch the fabric tightly over the frame and fix it to the back with tacks or staples (using a mechanical or electrically-powered staple gun), then mount the frames on the wall. The size of the panels will be dictated by the width of both fabric and wall. It's very unlikely that a series of identical panels will fit the wall exactly, so treat each wall as a separate entity and work out from a central panel so that any smaller, corner panels will be of equal width.

An alternative method is to fix the battens to the walls first and then tack the fabric to them, although it's hard to get the fabric evenly taut, avoid wrinkles and make neat joins. There is also a commercially manufactured fabric-hanging system, which needs to be professionally installed but enables fabrics to be taken down for cleaning or use elsewhere. If you don't mind having the fabric gathered rather than flat, a demountable DIY version can be achieved by stretching the fabric between chrome, brass or even wooden rods (hemming the fabric or stitching channels in it to take the rods), mounted at top and bottom of the wall on the appropriate brackets.

However you hang the fabric, bear in mind that if there is a gap between fabric and wall and you want to hang pictures or mirrors, you will need to decide their exact position first and fix battens behind the fabric as support.

HARD CASES

After researching this section I begin to believe that there is nothing you could imagine having on your walls that you would not be able to find and put up — and that what is available and possible these days is virtually beyond imagination. For there are not only all the more familiar natural materials such as stone, brick, marble, ceramic, mirror and metal, wood and cork — and these can be real or fake — but all the man-mades like vinyl, glass fiber and plastic laminate, some of which set out to imitate other materials, others which pretend to be nothing but themselves and have their own appeal.

Most of these rigid and semi-rigid materials are applied in one of two ways, either stuck straight onto the wall or fixed to wall-mounted battens. If the wall surface is flat, even some of the heavier-weight claddings can often be glued on directly, but in most cases it's better to nail or glue them to a pre-fixed framework of battens.

Whatever the fixing method, and even though you may be using the covering to hide rough or cracked walls, they

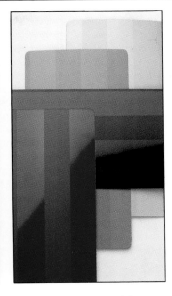

Above and above left The design of plastic laminates has taken something like a quantum leap over the last few years, making them now among the most exciting interior surfaces available. Here, a range of broad satin-and-matt stripes looks innocent enough in sample form but resembles sand-blasted mirror when in situ and cleverly lit.

Left In complete contrast, natural brick remains one of the most sympathetic facings for interior walls and is equally flattering to modern or traditional furniture.

should obviously be sufficiently flat and/or sound for you to obtain a good fixing or good adhesion and to bear the weight of any material you put up. If you're intending to clad all the walls in a room, especially with any timber material (including hardboard), it's important to check fire regulations first. Depending on the size of the room, you may only be allowed to cover a proportion of the wall area with untreated timber. But you can obtain both wood and hardboard pre-treated to resist fire and in some cases, coat untreated material with a fire-resistant paint

Plasterboard
This functional cladding is actually a 'sandwich' of plaster between sheets of strong paper. Some kinds of plasterboard are finished ready for decoration, others with a base for a skim coat of plaster; dual-faced plasterboards combine the two finishes, one on each side.

Fiberboard
This covers a variety of high, medium and low density materials made from processed wood, minerals and other fibers, and depending on the density, fiberboard is sometimes also called wallboard or insulating board, the latter being a lightweight, low density board with heat and/or sound insulating properties. All types of board come in a very wide range of finishes from plain and ready-for-painting to paper, fabric, foil, plastic sheet, cork and wood veneer.

Hardboard
Although this is basically a high-density fiberboard, it still deserves a slot to itself because it is versatile, generally quite inexpensive and comes in such a variety of types and finishes. There are three main types, the standard hardboard, which is lightweight and fairly rigid, a 'medium' version, which is softer and generally used for surfacing stud partitions, and a tempered hardboard, impregnated with oil to make it tougher and more resistant to water. It comes in a range of decorative finishes. Plain hardboard can be stained and varnished, or painted if it's sealed with a proprietary hardboard primer first; it will then also need a coat of size before papering.

Decorative panelling
Chipboard, blockboard and plywood are all types of fabricated timber, more commonly used for construction than for decoration. But they can be stained and varnished, or primed and painted, but it seems a waste to paint good timber cladding.
TONGUE-AND-GROOVE BOARDING This type of panelling is one of the classics and a naturally good insulating material. These interlocking boards are today generally made of either cedar or pine and given a chamfered edge to emphasize the join. Mounted on battens fixed to the wall, tongue-and-groove can be hung vertically, horizontally or diagonally.

Wall tiles
Brick-shaped and textured tiles, which can be stuck to most surfaces, come in several realistic shades and can also be painted. Wallboard with a molded surface that resembles brickwork is also available in several colors, it wouldn't survive too close an examination in its natural state, but looks quite realistic once it's painted. You can also get thin facings of real stone or slate to apply to walls, or cheaper composites that simulate these materials.
Cork is obtainable in panels of varying thicknesses — and in the form of tiles. Both are usually stuck to the wall with a specified adhesive but some are backed with a self-adhesive coating. The color of cork varies from honey to dark chocolate; texture from a single-tone granular appearance to small-squared, checkerboard effects, and strips and chips of various different tones. And although it's nicer left unsealed, it is vulnerable and can stain, so choose versions pre-sealed with PVC or polyurethane.
Ceramic tiles offer the widest choice of color and design within any single category of wallcovering. Machine- or hand-made they can be found in dozens of different shapes, sizes and thicknesses — from chunky, platter-size to tiny, thin mosaics — and glazed or unglazed in plain colors, textures and patterns.
Vinyl tiles can be used on walls as well as floors for an integrated scheme, but beware of using them too near sources of direct heat. Some manufacturers make a flexible vinyl wall sheet to match their flooring.

Plastic laminates

These are made by bonding resin-impregnated layers of paper together with heat and pressure to form a thin, near-rigid sheet of material. The top paper layer is colored, textured or printed and protected with a clear, hard film of plastic such as melamine. This makes a tough, waterproof surface, which is why laminates became so popular for kitchen units and worktops. But designs and colors in laminates have come a long, long way since the early days when, as I remember it, you could find only rather hard, crude colors, nasty woodgrain replicas and bland, safe, characterless patterns. Today, although not cheap, they are one of the most exciting, modern decorative materials with literlly hundreds of colors, designs and textures; for example, one company makes a very sophisticated, co-ordinated, single-color trio of raised dots, satin/matt stripe and similar graph check; another uses natural materials, instead of printed paper replicas, under the clear plastic coating — materials such as wood veneer, linen, burlap, cane and cork.

You can get laminates cut to size, but on large jobs, such as whole walls, it's cheaper to buy complete sheets, usually about 8 ft (2.4 m) or 10 ft (3 m) by 4 ft (1.2 m). The standard thickness is $\frac{1}{16}$in (1.5 mm), but you can also get flame-retarding types, versions which can be heat-softened and molded and extra-thin sheets, around $\frac{1}{32}$in (1 mm), which are usually used for lining shelves or balancing the insides of panels or cupboard doors. 'Balancing', covering the other side of a laminated wood panel with a thin, cheap backing of laminate, is done to prevent the panel warping. If you don't use a balancing laminate, you should at least give the other side a sealing coat of paint which will help prevent warping. Laminates can be stuck directly onto walls, but they do need an absolutely smooth, clean surface. There are several alternatives: you can glue the laminate to wall-mounted battens or to panels of hardboard, ply or chipboard, which are then stuck or screwed to battens (pre-bonded panels are also available, but in a limited range of finishes). The simplest method for large areas is probably to use the custom-made, plastic edging strips, which include extrusions for raw edges, butt-joins, internal and external angles. These are stuck to the wall with adhesive, the last strip being stuck in place *after* its panel has been inserted. One word of caution: plastic laminates are generally stain-resistant, but some household cleaners, like bleach, may cause stains and very hot objects may also leave a mark.

MATERIALS You can use a variety of tools to cut laminates: a craft knife with a laminate-cutting blade; a special, tungsten-tipped laminate cutter (particularly useful for cutting narrow edging strips); or a fine-toothed veneer, panel or tenon saw — but you'll blunt saw teeth quite quickly if you're doing a lot of cutting, and a tenon saw needs to be used at a very low angle or the broader back edge may hit and damage the laminate. In fact, whatever saw you use should be kept at an angle of not more than 20 degrees to the surface to save edges flaking. For cutting shapes or circles, the easiest tool is a power jig saw. Make templates out of card to mark and cut awkward shapes, use a straight-edge for marking and cutting straight lines, use a pencil or felt-tip pens as marking tools and, when the laminate is to be applied to a backing panel, allow a little extra all round (about $\frac{1}{8}$in/3mm) for subsequent trimming.

METHOD When cutting laminate with a knife, mark the cutting line, then hold a straight-edge firmly along the line as a guide for the knife. Score gently down the whole length of the cutting line, drawing the knife towards you and keeping the blade firmly against the straight-edge to prevent wobbles. Repeat complete cutting strokes, lightly at first, but increasing the pressure as you cut deeper into the laminate. Either continue until you cut right through the laminate or, when you are half-way through and can see the backing material as a clean, unbroken line, break the laminate by bending the spare piece upwards.

To saw laminate, mark and initially score the line a couple of times as above. Then, keeping the sheet flat, place it so that it is supported on both sides but with a clear space under the cutting line. Saw gently, working towards you with smooth, even strokes; don't saw too fast or the friction may over-heat the laminate. As you reach the last few inches of the cut, hold the edges together with one hand to prevent the sheet breaking and increase the angle of the saw.

Trim edges with a sharp plane, set at a very fine angle. Work from the outside to the middle of each edge with long, firm strokes. When applying the laminate to a wood panel, trim edges *after* the laminate has been stuck down; for this you can also use a coarse file, a metal scraper or a perforated rasp and finish with fine abrasive paper.

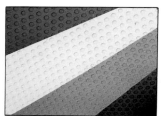

You can stick laminates with synthetic or epoxy resins, which give you time to maneuver the laminates into position before they set. However, the two surfaces need to be held together under pressure while these adhesives go off, which proves an impractical arrangement over large areas. For this reason, contact adhesive is generally recommended. This demands that you get the positioning right first time, because the two surfaces will bond as they touch, although you can get contact adhesives that give you a small amount of maneuvering time before the surfaces are irrevocably joined.

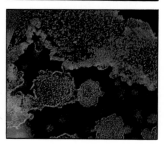

To fix laminates with contact adhesive, coat both surfaces evenly using a notched spreader and wait until they are touch dry, making sure there are no damp patches. If you're using an instant-bond type, place slim wooden battens or a sheet of siliconized paper between the

Above Plastic laminate provides a hard-wearing and easily cleaned surface on kitchen units and work-tops. But whereas it used to be a rather prosaic, almost cheap-and-nasty material, applied for its practical properties rather than its elegance, the best designs now have real glamor. This kitchen combines two of the single-color, matt/satin finish check designs (**top left**) which co-ordinate with two other motifs — the small, raised dot (**center left**) and the textured strip on the previous page — to form a beautifully integrated trio.

Below left Hard to believe that this, too, is a plastic laminate. Looking more like a section of exotic, polished stone, studded with minerals, this abstract metallic laminate is hand colored and finished to a high shine.

Right Although this bathroom has some striking architectural features which have been well emphasized and matched with the treatment of bath and basin, the room itself is actually quite small. But large panels of mirror, smoked and plain, play glorious havoc with perspective and the sense of space.

two surfaces while you position the laminate and withdraw them before pressing the two surfaces together. Rolling the surface with a clean paint roller — better still a paper-hanger's felt roller — will help get a good bond. If you're using edging strips, you'll get a neater edge with less of the backing material showing by applying these first. Trim both laminate strip and facing edges as above. If you try and follow these instructions fairly closely, you should end up with a neat job.

Mirror

Mirror is quite simply magic. Panels of mirror can often more than double the perceived space and, placed opposite or at right angles to a window, increase the amount of light, too. Even a small amount of mirror can earn its keep: a strip filling the space between top and base units in a kitchen, or two at ceiling and baseboard level, flanking shallow shelves or cupboards in a narrow hall can reduce that shut-in feeling, by suggesting something beyond.

It's only sensible to get large, single panels of mirror professionally hung. They need absolutely flat, smooth walls and also to be sufficiently thick (the larger the thicker) if there's not to be a risk of shattering. Always check a mirror for distortion — by looking at it from various angles and distances — before accepting it, and make sure that the back is sealed to avoid scratching and that any exposed edges are polished. Whether you hang mirror yourself or get it hung for you, check what adhesive is being used and how. I know someone who had a whole wall of mirror 'professionally' hung only to find that the adhesive had reacted with both the seal and the silvering, resulting in ugly patches on the face. The safest method I've found is to use a purpose-made, self-adhesive foil (there's also a plastic version), which acts as a buffer between adhesive and mirror back; it's expensive, but you don't necessarily need to apply either foil or adhesive right over the mirror back — sometimes several broad strips will do, but check with a reputable supplier. If weight is a problem, it's also worth checking out the newer plastic mirrors, which are also fractionally cheaper than glass although, to my eye at least, they don't have quite the same dazzling reflective quality as the real thing.

The alternative to large panels is mirror tiles, and although these break up the reflected image to some extent and will distort it if you don't get all the tiles flat, they're a much more manageable proposition for the home decorator and often come backed with self-adhesive tabs for easy fixing. The smallest of mirror 'tiles' come in mosaic form — tiny squares on a cloth backing which enables them to be bent around curves and corners. All these mirror types are usually also available in colors other than clear.

Stainless steel and aluminum

Tiles made of these materials are not strictly reflective, but they do have that hard, pure metallic sheen beloved of purists. Probably too expensive to use other than in limited areas, they'd nevertheless make a very smart splashback — between upper and lower units, for example, complementing the other stainless steel and chrome bits and pieces often found around a kitchen. They're lightweight, cut quite easily with scissors, they can be bent to a right angle to go around corners, they're simple to fix and do not need grouting.

Above A bad ceiling disguised with heavy relief panels which, painted in white gloss, somehow flatter this unusual mixture of expensive and cheap chic.
Top Curving the angle between ceiling and wall automatically makes this area more interesting.
Above right Beams 'lower' a sky-lit ceiling but are made from new wood and clean-painted so that there is just the suggestion of a country kitchen.

Ceilings

Just as the bathroom used once to be the most neglected room in the house, from the point of view of decoration, ceilings still tend to be the most neglected surface in any room. In many, many cases — perhaps even most cases, although this is a personal view — this is the best way to treat them. By 'neglect', I don't mean letting them fall into disrepair, but simply leaving them as a plain, undemanding surface which is properly integrated with the rest of the room's scheme, but does not play an active decorative role. A fussy ceiling in the average interior can very easily weigh down both the room and its occupants. I have come to the conclusion that, where ceilings are concerned, the natural order of things outdoors has a lot to do with our comfort or discomfort with spatial and surface relationships indoors. When you're out in the open, whatever's going on around you and however 'busy' the immediate environment, the sky remains clear and uncluttered, giving us a remedial sense of space, light and air. I think that's the much-needed balance a ceiling can bring to a room — it can be the one place where *nothing* is happening and *nothing* need happen.

Plain and simple
That said, a ceiling is nevertheless part of any room's proportions and you may need to involve it in a little subtle, decorative trickery if those proportions are not ideal. Low-ceilinged rooms benefit enormously from having both ceiling and floor in a lighter color than the walls (but make the floor darker than the ceiling) and a smooth, flat ceiling could even be varnished to a high gloss to give the surface both depth and reflection. High ceilings seem lower when painted a darker color than the walls, but it's somehow visually awkward if the darker color stops at the angle where walls and ceiling meet. The trick is to take the ceiling color down onto the first 12-18in (30-45cm) of the wall itself, either as solid color or, say, graduated horizontal stripes, and finish it neatly with a picture rail, a shallow strip of plain molding, a thin, painted line of a darker tone or the slimmest band of the same stripe color. Don't paint ceilings too dark, however, or you'll find that at night, and especially if all the lighting is at low level, they'll simply 'disappear'. In cases where the ceiling is structurally broken up — for example, in a large room that has been opened up from several smaller ones with the resultant network of plaster-covered steel joists — you may find that, rather than trying to 'hide' the extrusions with a one-color treatment, the best way out is to display what you can't disguise and emphasize them in a contrasting color; but try to link them through color with other elements in the room and perhaps by taking the color down on the walls at one or more appropriate points. In this way you can both highlight and blend the extrusions into the rest of the room successfully without making them too overpowering.

New dimensions

If a plain surface above your head is just not good enough, there are, of course, plenty of other ways of making ceilings more interesting. You might choose to take any pattern or texture on the walls across the ceiling too, but be aware that pattern, in particular, given this treatment will tend to bring both walls and ceiling in and make the room feel smaller. We tend to think of ceilings as being essentially flat, but they can be given other dimensions: a tented ceiling can be particularly pretty in a bedroom; undulating loops of an inexpensive fabric such as canvas or calico, supported by horizontal poles spanning the walls, can often soften the lines of a plain, uncomfortably angular living room; tongue-and-groove boards can be mounted on joists, fixed diagonally from a little way down one wall to the top of another to make a sloping ceiling. For old properties, you can even get 'Tudor' beams pre-fabricated out of rigid polyurethane foam — although before buying you should be sure that they're appropriate to the setting and that existing ceiling can take even their light weight. It would be a disaster if you were either to ruin the style of the room by imposing an unsuitable feature onto it, or, having decided on the feature, you went ahead with it without testing whether the existing ceiling could take it. It is obviously helpful to consider these aspects before diving head first in and then regretting it later.

You may, anyway, have some very good, practically-based reasons for wanting to cover up the existing ceiling with something other than paper or paint. Ceilings are particulary prone to stains and cracks. Aluminum primer over stains and strong lining paper right across a surface scattered with hair-line cracks will do a good cosmetic job on ceilings which are otherwise in good condition. For more serious cases, the cheapest solution will probably be to fix new plasterboard over the existing plaster by locating the joists and pinning the plasterboard to them with galvanized nails. (Locate joists from above by lines of nails on floorboards, from below by knocking the ceiling with your knuckles — the gaps between joists will sound hollow — and make test holes in the ceiling with a drill until you're sure of the direction and spacing of the joists.) Either finish the plasterboard with a skim coat of plaster or, on the pre-finished side, fill joins and nail holes and line before painting or papering. This should ultimately ensure that you have a pretty tidy finish.

Insulation

If you want to insulate the ceiling against heat loss or noise transmission, resist the easy, cheap way out of lining it with polystyrene tiles. On ceilings, even the flameproof types are a serious fire hazard because they exude poisonous and asphyxiating fumes and, as they melt, hot droplets will fall and may set fire to the furnishings and floor beneath. There are so many alternatives which, although more expensive, are also infinitely more attractive. Even the most basic, grooved insulating board can look remarkably smart, fixed in large square panels with the grooves alternating in direction, like large, geometric tiles. You can get mineral insulating board and acoustic board in a variety of interesting textures — including various fabric finishes — but other materials not necessarily designed to insulate, nevertheless perform this practical role as well as a decorative one: materials such as corkboard, chipboard, plywood or tongue-and-groove.

In a room where you want both to lower and insulate a high ceiling, the answer may be to suspend a new, false ceiling from the old one. As long as the existing ceiling can bear the weight and the new, lower height does not contravene the building regulations, this is generally an absolutely practicable job and not that expensive. But it's quite difficult and I'd therefore recommend getting a builder both to design and install it. In a room where you need it to do a visual job only, it can be quite effective if you don't take the new ceiling right to the walls, but leave a 6-12in (15-30cm) gap all round and conceal lighting above the gap.

Below In a dark, almost window-less room you can either woo what light there is with pale shades and masses of mirror — or decide virtually to do without it. Here the 'lacquered' blue-black ceiling and walls are dramatically lit and combined with other reflective surfaces to make the most of a room with little natural light.

Windows

Windows are the eyes of a room. They let light in and they frame a view. While they are not strictly surfaces or finishes in themselves, they inevitably need to be integrated with the surfaces and finishes around them. There is such variety of window treatments possible and available now that they deserve a book to themselves, but here are a few ideas — traditional and modern, plain and extravagantly pretty — to get you started. The way you treat windows will depend on a number of factors quite apart from the style of the room around them: how much light you want or need to let in, whether the view is worth looking at or better hidden, whether you are overlooked yourself and whether you care about it. There are also proportions to be considered. Windows can not only be generous or mean; they can be tall and thin, long and low, high and small — and each shape and size demands careful co-ordination with the wall in which it is set. So whether you want your windows to be plain or pretty, to stand out or stand back or blend in, treat their treatment with the same degree of care as the rest of the room so that they represent forethought, not afterthought.

Far left Traditional yet original treatment of a bay window. A dressing-table is set in the bay to take full advantage of day-light with simple roller blinds for night-time privacy. But the whole bay is framed by full-length curtains which can be released to fall across it, making an enclosed dressing area and changing the proportions of the bedroom behind.

Center The view is marvelous, the room is not overlooked and there's a stiffened voile blind to shade the sun, so these curtains are for decoration only. But for a tall, single window in one corner, it is essential that the treatment is in harmony with the rest of the room. Long, simple swathes of cream sateen, held back by silk tassles, add exactly the right note of understated elegance.

Above left When the view from a window is less than lovely, the focus needs to be inside rather than out. This bay goes over the top with generous, scalloped headings, swathes and drapes and encircles a fully-clothed dining-table and chairs in such a stagey way that the whole atmosphere becomes intimate and introspective, setting the area apart from the rest of the room as well as the world outside.

Below left Crocheted cotton curtains provide all the privacy that's needed during the daytime and let sunshine filter through to transfer a dapple of pattern on to the walls. At night, pale pink Roman blinds pull down to shield the bay beyond.

Below right In this case the 'curtain' is the picture rather than the frame — a ruched festoon blind in a chintz with a grainy ground to complement the texture of the hand-grained window-frame and panelling that surround it.

Right A plain Roman blind that tones with the walls best suits a well-proportioned window in a room already made busy enough by its contents.

Far right A wall of windows by day becomes wall by night, too, with this austere yet elegant treatment using simple and relatively inexpensive silver-gray, pleated-paper blinds.

Below left Another window which proves that treatments need be neither fussy nor costly to be effective. The tortoise-shell coloring of split-cane blinds works perfectly against the mellowed pine frame, panelling and pale honey-colored walls in this country-inspired kitchen.

Below center If you can leave beautiful windows unadorned and unadulterated, do. Any kind of blind or curtain would only have made less of these and their aspect leaves privacy unthreatened.

Below right If you have shutters, use them. They're the treatment for and with which the windows were designed and therefore usually the one which best suits the room's architectural style, too. This window needs nothing more.

Floors

Choosing a floor type or covering is one of the most important and far-reaching decisions in the interior design of a home. It's not just the high level of visual contribution it makes to the overall setting, it's also usually one of the most costly items, so mistakes are expensive and correcting them, sooner or later, means double the upheaval (unlike simply repainting a wall or two), as well as more than double the outlay. More than double because the most common error is to spend too little in the first place. Floors get more wear than any other interior surface and yet, because even the cheaper floorings represent a substantial hole in the budget, we expect them to last. They won't — at least, not if they're given a harder job to do than befits their quality. In flooring, you really do get what you pay for and there's no other ingredient, decorative or practical, for which it's so well worth paying for the very best you can afford and, if necessary, sacrificing other things for its sake.

Of course it matters what the floor looks like, as much as it does any other decorative surface, but because most floors take such a beating, practicality just has to come first. These are some of the things you should consider before making a choice.

Above In older properties, floorboards which are in reasonable condition can be transformed with a couple of coats of paint. Make the most of this by choosing a more unusual shade. In this room full of soft blues, none of the tones are obvious and the old floor becomes remarkably expensive-looking in its new guise of glossy duck-egg blue. But paint for floors must be durable or protected with several coats of varnish.

Right One of the most welcome assets of natural materials is their tendency to age more gracefully than man-mades. Here, the woven rush squares make no demands of perfection from a mellowed wood-strip floor and complete a set of natural materials — unvarnished wood, stone, cane, calico and fur — in which rich textural variety makes colour superfluous.

Far right But these cleverly chosen, ultra-modern vinyl tiles prove that easy-care man-mades don't need to masquerade as naturals to work in traditional interiors.

Wear and tear

Halls, and any other areas leading directly from an external door, are especially vulnerable to traffic. All the door-mats and scrapers in the world won't collect every bit of dirt and grit from shoe soles. Anyway, people get absent-minded — although you can defend yourself against this by having as large a doormat as possible, for example, laid like carpet right across the first few feet of hall. Stairs not only get a lot of through traffic but a particularly abrasive type of wear. Playrooms are weak spots, too, not just

because of children's generally high mobility and mostly innocent but nevertheless effective carelessness, but because for almost all activities they seem to gravitate towards the floor. Whichever room you are choosing floors for, bear in mind that although most of the floor may only get light to medium wear, there may be isolated areas of heavier traffic that will quickly erode worn patches or 'pathways' in poorer quality flooring. A prime candidate is the floor area along a line of kitchen units and especially just in front of sink or stove.

Maintenance

How dirty will the floor get and will it be easy to clean? Keeping a floor clean is pure self-interest because nothing wears it down more quickly than traffic over dirt. It's also absolutely pointless making a stick to beat your own back by laying, for example, a light, plain-colored, delicate-surfaced floor covering in a place where it's going to need cleaning twice a day to keep it in anything like good shape; similarly, think twice about laying a heavily embossed flooring somewhere where keeping it clean means constantly digging dirt, grease or grit out of its crevices. If you have a house full of children, animals and coal fires, with the resultant dirty boots, hairs, ashes and soot, it's crazy not to have a floor you can wash, because however scrupulous you are about vacuuming carpets, some dirt

will still get ingrained in the pile. On the other hand, in a less accident-prone household, it's wonderful to be able to whizz a vacuum-cleaner round a totally carpeted home without stopping to change tools and wash or sweep areas of hard floor. Carpet also disguises some kinds of 'dirt' better than hard floors: I once lived in a house with a lot of fabrics around and noticed that they continuously shed their own kind of dust in the form of microscopic fibers which showed up less on the carpet than against the tongue-and-groove boards. In general, on both hard and soft floors, pattern shows dirt less than plain, mid-tone neutrals less than very dark, light or positive colors.

Safety

Any floor that gets wet or just wet feet walking on it, needs a relatively non-slip surface. For example, high-glaze ceramic tiles in the bathroom can be dangerous. Kitchens can obviously be even more precarious because of what you may be carrying if and when you slip. Loose rugs also need non-slip underlay on hard floors.

Warmth, comfort and noise

Floors get walked on, stood on and sat upon. Warmth and comfort levels vary both on carpets and hard floorings. Noise is something we tend to consider less, but its presence or absence can make a considerable difference to the quality of life in a house. Obviously carpet, especially with a good underlay, absorbs footfalls and cuts down noise transmission between floor levels more than hard floorings, but even these vary as much in 'noisiness' as they do in comfort.

The existing floor

While almost any type of flooring can be laid on a solid floor that's in good condition and incorporates a sound damp-proof membrane, suspended floors pose some limitations. Some hard floorings need to be set into a bed of cement mortar and may, anyway, either be simply too heavy for a suspended floor (seek expert advice on loading) or, once laid, may crack if the floor is very flexible. In small, upper rooms, such as the bathroom, laying ceramic tiles should be feasible if the floor is levelled with hardboard or chipboard first and this is also a sensible precaution when laying any semi-hard or soft flooring over boards. Tongue-and-groove boards cause fewer problems than the butt-joined type, but coverings laid straight over noticeable gaps between boards will tend to wear unevenly and may eventually crack or tear. You should also, of course, consider whether anything can be done with the floor as it is: sanding boards clean and smooth, laying hardboard or chipboard as floors in themselves and painting, stencilling, staining, any of these before varnishing.

Laying costs

Although some cut-rate carpet dealers include a 'free' laying service within the cost, this service is more often than not an extra, especially (and perversely) when you're buying better quality. As an amateur, you'd have to be brave and almost certainly foolish to risk ruining top-class carpeting by laying it yourself — it is a skilled job. But carpet tiles are manageable, as are many of the flexible, semi-hard sheet floorings and tiles. I would also lay ceramic tiles myself, but I'd draw the line at quarry tiles or anything heavier which needs laying in a bed of cement mortar. As a general principle, unless you are exceptionally skilled, experienced or confident, I'd advise that the more expensive the flooring and the longer you want it to last, the less sensible it is to lay it yourself.

VISUAL CONSIDERATIONS

Although the practical issues are crucial and should lead the way in any decision-making about floors, they cannot, of course, be considered in isolation. As well as knowing that the floor will serve its purpose, it's a distinct advantage if you like it, especially as it's likely to be around for a while. But in some ways, particularly if you're starting from scratch, practicality can be a positive limitation — too much choice can be as bad as too little and across the whole range of flooring types there are an awful lot to choose from. When there's a big task to be tackled, the way to pull oneself back from the brink of 'overwhelm' is to divide it up into manageable sections. In visual planning, it's simplest to go back to color, pattern and texture.

Color

If all the options are open and you have neither a clue what colors to go for, nor any particular preference, choose neutrals or earth colours. It's not that these are safe, bland choices — there's a whole world of wonderful shades from oatmeal, sand, ginger, terracotta and coffee to all the shades of gray from oyster to charcoal — but they're good companions, easy on the eye, you won't tire of them too quickly and, most important, they're adaptable. You can build up a lot of different color schemes around them and they'll change their character accordingly. Decisions about light versus dark colors involves other considerations apart from the practical ones. Wall color will probably have the most say in the choice as floors that are a lot paler than their surrounding walls seem to 'float', so that the room doesn't feel properly grounded. It is also at floor level that rooms most obviously meet, so you need to decide how you're going to make that meeting work. Nothing unifies a collection of small and/or oddly shaped rooms more than carrying the same floor treatment throughout, or at least the same color, and in this case even quite a dark color will still make the space feel larger.

If, in small groups of rooms, a series of dramatically changing identities is disquieting, larger areas and larger rooms present a different problem. You could find one floor treatment throughout very tiresome, or at least unstimulating, on a grander scale. The eye needs variety, but the change from area to area needs to be accomplished either by harmonious tonal transition, subtle blending or clever contrast, but not with a jarring juxtaposition of mutually uncomplementary colors. If you want to organize a satisfactory sequence of floor treatments, these are the options open to you, in ascending levels of contrast: retain the same tone of one color, but vary kinds and textures of surface; progress through varying tones of the same color, with or without changes of texture; blend severl harmonious colors (those adjacent to each other on the color wheel), keeping them of the same tonal value — that is, the same level of lightness or darkness; blend harmonious colors of different tonal values. These are all reasonably safe bets, but beyond this you get into real contrasts. These can work, but this is where the eye has to replace mere words — just remember that each open doorway makes a picture frame for the room beyond. The task is to make each picture work in its frame.

Pattern

Pattern can be a blessing but, on floors especially, it can also be a banana skin. A blessing when you can simply take the colors someone else has worked out on a patterned floor covering and work a complete color scheme around them; a blessing when pattern adds a little sharp or soft variety, interest, emphasis or impact to a room with a lot of plain surfaces; but pattern can also be the banana skin on which a whole room can slide if scale and quantity are not kept tightly under control. Put too much or too dominating a pattern on the floor and the eye will see nothing else; use too large a pattern and both furniture and people will look as though they belong in a doll's house. Small rooms, especially, need small patterns to suit them. The alternative to the all-over treatment is to use isolated areas of pattern and this can very often be much more effective: a painted or stencilled border or a single beautiful rug on an otherwise plain wood floor. These can serve a purpose, too, on a plain tiled floor you might, for example, inset a bordered or patterned area to outline the dining or seating section in a combined living/dining room. Pattern on floors can be many things: it can be boards painted in different colors, hardboard or chipboard checkers, different-colored vinyl or different-textured cork tiles laid straight or diamond-style, and pattern that is made rather than bought is very often more satisfying. Whatever you do with pattern, just remember that, on a floor, it's likely to be with you for a long, long time.

Above Sometimes a floor is best left soft and simple. The surfaces in this unusually-shaped studio are given the plainest treatment so that architectural details stand out and the room as a whole becomes a pale gray shell to show off some marvelous modern furniture. But a hard floor would have been just too severe.
Right Butter yellow, studden rubber flooring completes a masterly scheme, containing an extraordinarily disparate collection of surfaces, finishes and colors, which only talent and extreme confidence could have imagined as room-mates. The floor is a very practical choice, too: its embossed surface is good at disguising dirt but it's easy to clean, when necessary, and exceptionally hard-wearing.
Far right Ceramic tiles make a classic floor which, properly laid, will quite simply last for ever.

Texture

I've already said that I consider texture one of the most neglected aspects of decoration generally. Where floors, especially, are concerned you should not — indeed you cannot — ignore it, since these are surfaces with which we're in physical contact more than any other. From the point of view of comfort, the texture of a floor should obviously be appropriate to the room's usage, but encountering a variety of floor textures as you move about the house gives you the same kind of relief as changing shoes at the end of a day. Texture is visual, too — half-way between plain and pattern.

Texture can be used to change the character of a series of interlinking rooms without changing floor color; all the floors might be blue, for example, but one is stained wood, one ceramic tiles, one linoleum, one has a densely woven, short, loop pile carpet and another a shaggier carpet in longer, cut pile. Or you might choose a series of natural floorings in harmoniously toning neutrals — wood, quarry tiles, cork and sisal. Texture can also be used to provide the link, rather than the contrast, between areas. Imagine the same tongue-and-groove boards through all rooms but each given a separate identity by different-colored rugs or different types of stencilled or painted pattern; or ceramic tiles in a hall becoming a deep, tiled border to an inset area of carpet in an adjoining room. Texture is under-rated and under-used, yet it's one of the most versatile and effective tools in the decorator's kit.

HARD FLOORINGS

One way of classifying hard and semi-hard floors is by their relative porosity — and therefore the degree to which they're vulnerable to spills and stains. The stone-type floors like slate, ceramic, quarry, brick and quartzite are non-porous and therefore highly resistant to almost all kinds of domestic spills; it's pointless sealing them, and any seal would also probably peel or chip off. The most porous include wood, cork, chipboard, hardboard, some of the older types of linoleum and, strangely enough, concrete, but these can all be sealed to make them non-porous. Check with the manufacturer/supplier which type of seal is most suitable, but the choice is generally between the oil/resin versions that sink into the surface, and the one- or two-pack polyurethanes (two-pack usually gives a tougher finish) that form a protective skin on top and may therefore crack on very new wood, which is liable to shrink as it adjusts to room atmosphere. In the middle are a variety of semi-porous floorings — vinyl, vinyl asbestos and thermoplastic tiles, rubber, most of the newer linoleums and all marbles or marble aggregate floors like terrazzo tiles. These are generally waterproof, but only resistant, not impervious to oil and grease. They can't be sealed, as this may damage the surface, and are also vulnerable to household solvents such as kerosene, gasoline or mineral spirits.

While this method of classification gives you some clue about suitability and treatment, it's by no means all you need to know as you will, or should, be asking all the other aforementioned questions concerning durability, warmth, noise, safety and comfort — by which I mean the 'feel' of a floor, usually allied to its resilience. Unfortunately, none of these qualities follows exactly the same formula as the one above. It would be wonderful, for example, to be able to say that all non-porous floors are more durable than all semi-porous types, but rubber is actually very hard-wearing. Or that all porous or semi-porous floors are warmer than non-porous varieties, but marble and concrete can feel very cold to the touch; how cold a floor feels is also determined by the temperature of the air at floor level — stone or brick with underfloor heating will almost certainly feel warmer than cork without. So, to save giving you five or six different charts from which you'd then have to collate the characteristics of each different floor type, I've indicated all these different areas of performance in the captions accompanying their illustrations, as well as any particular considerations concerning laying or maintenance. As a general principle, the more wear a floor gets, the fewer choices there are and you may have to sacrifice warmth or quietness for the sake of safety or durability, unless you are prepared to re-finish the floor every few years, because if they really do receive a great deal of wear they will not survive for long.

LAYING FLOORS
Sheet flooring

Flexible sheet-flooring materials such as vinyl and linoleum are usually sold in rolls up to about 7ft (210cm) wide. When measuring up, decide first which way the flooring is to be laid and add about 6in (15cm) extra to the total width and length of the room (including alcoves and doorways) to allow for fitting and the fact that vinyl shrinks a little when laid. Plan the laying, so that you avoid joins in doorways and if the room is a complicated shape, draw the plan out on paper first. The floor on which you're laying the material should be clean, smooth and level, and the flooring should be left, preferably unrolled, in the room for which it's intended for about 48 hours before laying so that it can adjust to the atmospheric conditions. If there are only a few minor irregularities in the floor surface and you're not going to stick the flooring down, lay a paper felt underlay first. Otherwise use the adhesive recommended by the manufacturer, but allow the flooring to settle (see below) before sticking it down permanently.

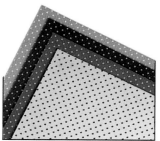

Linoleum is a warm, practical, durable floor but was long overdue for a design re-think — until two clever designers produced a series of marvelous, modern tiles (**top**) based on Venetian marble or mosaic originals. In a different mood, but still a nice idea, polka dots (**above**) on hard-wearing, matt synthetic rubber, available in tiles or rolls.

METHOD You will find a marking tool helpful in adjusting the flooring to any irregularities in the baseboards and fitting it around extrusions such as door posts and architraves. Either use a 2in(5cm) square, softwood block and a pencil or make a marker by banging a nail through a short batten, 2in (5cm) from one end, so that the tip of the nail protrudes by about in (3mm) — just enough to score the flooring lightly. To lay the first sheet, cut from the roll a piece that is 2in (5cm) longer than the room and lay it parallel to the wall and about 1in (2.5cm) away from it, so that the ends turn up by an equal amount against the adjacent walls. Hold the marker at right angles to and against the wall and run it along the length of the sheet so that it transfers any undulations in the baseboards. To cut the flooring, first score along the line you've marked with a craft knife con-

taining a straight blade, then bend the sheet upwards along the scored line and, with a hooked blade in the knife, cut along it from underneath.

If the wall has a doorway in it, use a combination square to mark on the flooring the distance from the door stop to the edge of the baseboard. Cut a wood block the width of this line. Butt the edge of the sheet of flooring as close to the baseboard as possible and parallel to it, and run the block and pencil along the baseboard as before, then round the door frame to transfer its main features, filling in any minor ones by hand. Score and cut as above. Use a similar method to transfer any major extrusions or indentations such as alcoves and chimney breasts. In this instance, cut a block the depth of the extrusion (if there are several unequal ones, cut to whichever is the deepest) plus 1in (2.5cm), butt the edge of the flooring against the wall that projects furthest into the room and use block, pencil and knife as above. Set the first, cut sheet flush against the wall and lay the second sheet so that it overlaps the first by about 1in (2.5cm). Allowing for the retention of that overlap, make preliminary marks and cuts on the edge of the second sheet as above to accommodate any extrusions and so on, but leave about 2in (5cm) extra so that the final, exact trimming can be done when the flooring has settled. Leave a two-week settling period, check that the first laid sheet of flooring is still flush with the wall and trim the second sheet to an exact fit. Trim the central join by placing a straight-edge squarely down the middle of the overlap and scoring and cutting straight through both layers with a craft knife.

To trim the remaining, turned-up edges make a pencil mark 12in (30cm) from the wall on the edge of the sheet, pull the sheet back until it's flat on the floor and then, from the first mark, measure and mark a second point on the sheet 12in (30cm) back towards the wall. Keeping the central join butted, position the sheet so that the edge or tip of your marking tool is on the second point when the marker is held flush and at right angles to the wall. Run the marker along the wall, then score and cut as before. To stick sheets down, pull each one back to half its length, apply the adhesive to the floor and roll the sheet firmly back over it; repeat at the opposite end. Use a serrated spreader to apply the adhesive (they're often supplied with it), but don't use too much or it will bubble up round joins and edges. Alternatively, use heavy-duty, double-sided sticky tape to secure just joins and edges.

Flexible tiles

The method of marking out described applies to all flexible tiles that are laid edge to edge (that is, without grouting). The fixing method applies specifically to vinyl tiles. Some other flexible tiles are stuck down in a slightly different way. See captions for exact information.

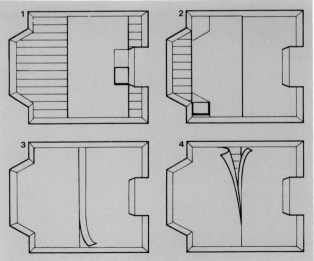

Above More innovation from a company whose speciality has always been cork flooring. They're now making rectangular, wood-veneered cork tiles, vinylized for protection, which can be stuck down, just like ordinary cork tiles, on to a dry, flat, sub-floor with the recommended adhesive. They also make a wider, rigid version of this tile, backed with fiberboard and tongued-and-grooved. These can be laid over virtually any kind of existing floor, even over old carpeting, to provide a new, almost-instant, 'floating' floor.

Left Laying flexible sheet flooring is well within the range of skills of most home decorators. The stages are illustrated here, with instructions also on this page.

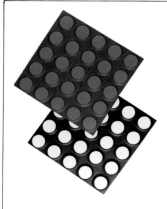

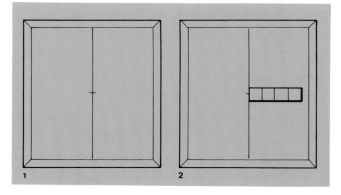

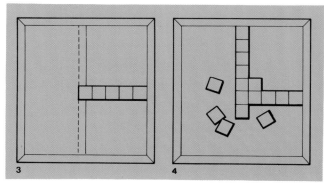

1 2

3 4

Above Studded real or synthetic rubber flooring has become a modern classic — good looking, hard-wearing, burn-resistant and easily maintained. It's a matter of opinion whether this two-tone version, intended as a decorative update, is an improvement on the original.

Right To lay flexible floor tiles, find the center point of the room (as explained by the instructions on this page), lay tiles loose first to check that borders will be even and make any necessary adjustments before sticking tiles down from the center outwards, leaving border tiles until last.

Far right You may think you've seen this type of floor before — and indeed it is one of the classic Western European designs, found in Renaissance churches as much as 18th-century town houses. But this is neither the original marble nor the modern 'Fake' in vinyl, but a hand-marbled version on wood panels ½in (1·2cm) thick and about 16in (40cm) square.

In order to lay flexible tiles evenly and symmetrically, always start from the center of the room. To find the center, hammer a panel pin at an angle into the baseboard, just above the floor, at the mid-point of two opposite walls; stretch and tie a chalked line so that it's held taut between the two pins, then snap the line so that the chalk marks the floor. Untie the line, but leave the panel pins in place. Mark the mid-point of the chalk line on the floor, then mark the mid-point on one tile edge; set the edge of the tile against the line so that the two mid-points meet and lay a row of *loose* tiles (without adhesive) at right angles to the line. If the gap between the last full tile and the wall is less than 3in (7.5cm), move panel pins, chalk line and row of tiles away from the wall by the width of half a tile, to ensure that the borders will be even. Lay a second row of tiles at right angles to the first and along the chalk line. If the gap between the last full tile and wall, in this direction, is less than 3in (7.5cm), move the whole L-shape of tiles back as above and snap another chalk line at right angles to the first to mark the position. With both chalked lines retied and taut between the panel pins, remove the tiles and spread tile-width bands of adhesive centrally over the full length of both chalk marks. Wait until the adhesive has become tacky and then you want to snap both chalk lines so that you have marked the adhesive.

Place two tiles next to each other at the point where the chalk lines intersect — that is, so that together they make a rectangle which spans one line and rests on the other. Lay the remaining tiles, working outwards from the first two towards the walls in pyramid fashion, spreading more adhesive as necessary and placing the tiles straight down on the adhesive rather than sliding them, which will push adhesive up between the tiles. If this does happen, wipe the adhesive off with a wet rag before it sets or with wire wool and warm soapy water afterwards, but don't attempt to use any type of solvent.

After you've laid the last full tile round all the walls, mark, cut and insert the border tiles. To cut a border tile, place one loose tile squarely on top of the last laid one. Hold another tile on top of this one so that the sides line up but one edge is flush to the wall. The other edge of this top tile is your guide for marking, scoring and cutting the middle one and the exposed portion of this tile will then fit the gap between the last laid tile and the wall. Use the same method for cutting corner tiles, moving them around external angles without turning them and making both marks (which will be at right angles to each other) before cutting out the L-shape.

1 The simple set of ingredients needed to provide an almost-instant new floor: a sheet of building plastic, felt floor underlay, the cork-faced tongue-and-groove planks and woodwork adhesive to make the joins secure. This flooring can be laid over virtually any existing floor.
2 An insulating sheet of building plastic is laid straight over the existing floor.
3 Thermal padding is loose-laid the building plastic.   padding is a useful buffer on cold or uneven floors.
4 The planks slot quickly and neatly into place, with a thin ribbon of adhesive to make joins secure. The overlapping edges of plastic sheeting are slipped behind the baseboard and neatened off just below their top edge.
Left Hardwood strips still make one of the most elegant and practical timber floors. They're hard-wearing and resilient and, once sealed, need only to be swept, mopped and polished although, like any wood floor, they should not be doused with water.

Ceramic tiles

Unlike flexible tiles, the placing of ceramic tiles is determined from the doorway of the room, mainly because the grouted spaces between them make the grid pattern much more obvious to the eye and it is from the doorway that the floor is generally first seen as a whole.

First make up a measuring stick from a long piece of battening, marking it off in tile lengths and leaving $\frac{1}{8}$in (3mm) between these to allow for the spacing of the tiles. If you're using rectangular rather than square tiles, you'll need a second measuring stick, marked up in the same way for tile widths. Mark a line across the doorway, between the doorposts, and from the center point mark another line which is at right angles to it and stretches to the far wall. Use the measuring stick to mark off tile widths and spacings along the second line. At a right angle to this line and at the point where the last full tile finishes, fix a wooden batten right across the room. From the right angle where line and batten meet, mark out tile widths and spacing along the batten; whether this is to left or right will depend on the position of the doorway, but work towards the furthest corner of the room. From the point at which the last full tile is marked on the batten, fix another batten the full depth of the room and at right angles to the first. The accuracy of this angle really matters, as it is from this point that you start to lay the tiles. Using whichever adhesive is recommended by the tile manufacturer, spread it over about the first 1sq yd (90cm²) in the corner where the battens meet. Inserting a couple of $\frac{1}{8}$in (3mm) wide pegs to space the tiles evenly (you'll need to leave these in place until the adhesive has hardened, so cut enough to start with), set the tiles firmly down into the adhesive, pressing with your palms to get them level. When you've laid the first 1sq yd (90cm²), scrape out any surplus adhesive between the tiles — being careful not to disturb them or the pegs — and apply adhesive to the next area. Work roughly in 1sq yd (90cm²) sections and diagonally across the room towards the door. Leave the tiles for a day or so to let the adhesive harden before removing pegs and battens.

Next, lay the border tiles. To mark tiles for cutting, use the method described for flexible tiles but mark the edges of the ceramic tile first, allowing for the $\frac{1}{8}$in (3mm) spacing, before marking and scoring across the face of the tile with a tile-cutter. To cut the tile cleanly, clamp a spare tile in a vice (or between your knees) and, holding the tile you're cutting on either side of the scored line and face upwards, strike it down on the edge of the clamped tile along the underside of the scored line. You should get a clean break with this method, but you can clean edges up with Carborundum stone. Coat the underside of the tile with adhesive, press it firmly into position, lay the other border tiles in the same way, using spacer pegs, and leave them to set for 24 hours.

Right Terrazzo, made from marble/mineral chips set in cement, comes in many colors and effects. Sold in precast tiles or slabs, it can also be laid on site and molded into almost any shape. Lay tiles like ceramics, get slab and on-site laying done professionally.

Far right The real thing: marble slabs are expensive and must be set in cement on a solid floor. It's cheaper and more versatile in the newer ¼in (6mm) thick 'tiles' which can be laid like ceramics over a strong, rigid, suspended floor, levelled with either chipboard or blockboard.

Below For laying ceramic tiles, follow this diagram with the instructions, which begin on page 127.

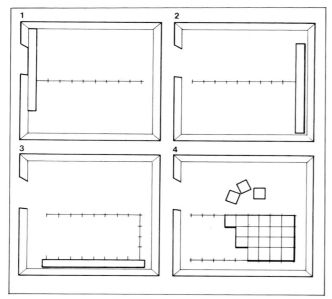

The last task is to grout the gaps between the tiles. Use a proprietary grouting compound and, working in the same sequence as that in which the tiles were laid, grout about 1sq yd (90cm²) at a time. Use a damp cloth or one of those slim, kitchen sponges to spread the grouting and press it down firmly so that it fills in the gaps evenly. Although you can finish each gap at this stage by running the edge of the sponge along it, or your finger (preferably protected by a rubber glove), this isn't strictly necessary. If you grout the gaps flush with the face of the tiles and allow the grouting to dry, the whole area can be cleaned off and the gaps smoothed by polishing with a clean, dry cloth.

CARPET

Both carpet-manufacturing methods and carpet-buying habits have changed greatly in the last decade or so. Several things, including synthetic fibers, the American influence and, probably most of all, the world recession, have contributed to this. In the US it's estimated that people now buy new carpets every four years, in Britain just over every five years. It started as a result of the property boom, when people were moving house more frequently; more recently, once the recession bit, they couldn't afford to move at all, so they redecorated and bought new carpets instead. A greater public awareness of fashions in home furnishing has also affected carpet colors and textures, — people get bored more quickly with what they've got and have a lower life-expectancy of their carpets.

Although the recession hit the carpet industry hard it

has, in general, done the consumer nothing but good. New methods and new materials had to be found and the quality of tufteds, in particular, has improved immeasurably. These days, tufteds can be every bit as hard-wearing as woven carpets, the variety is enormous and, if you compare prices, carpets are actually better value than they were. If color is what matters most to you, there's no doubt that carpet now beats hard flooring hands down.

Fiber types

Wool remains the leading fiber — it's warm, it's soft and it's resilient, so that it wears well and long without much loss of appearance along the way. One of the newer types of carpeting is made with 'felted' wool which has been compressed under heat to make the fibers even more resistant to dirt and wear and the experts say it will outlast anything else. If you get any pilling on a 'wool' carpet, it's more

Above Whoever put this room together really understood and loved texture and was prepared to sacrifice the comfort and status of a wood carpet for the sake of the granular, honey-colored surface of sisal. This unexpected choice, combined with the rough-plastered walls, underlines the theme of this room in which simple, natural materials have been used in a very sophisticated way.

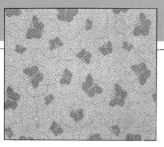

likely to be the nylon content that's causing it, as wool carpeting these days is often a wool/nylon mix. This makes a lot of sense, since of all the synthetic fibers now used for carpeting, nylon is still the most hard-wearing. Where nylon scores over wool is in the way it takes color; wool is naturally a 'dirty' fiber and, however it's dyed, it cannot come up with the 'clean', pure and often brilliant colors available in nylon yarns — and the range, colors and designs now available in nylon carpeting are actually astounding. Nylon, like other synthetics, also lends itself better to the various anti-static, anti-soil methods with which many carpets are pre-treated, although these won't last as long as the carpet itself, renewing them is generally either impractical or expensive and the carpet is more likely to deteriorate faster after they've worn off.

Nylon is inevitably harder to the touch than wool, a disadvantage that it shares with most other synthetics. Of the others, the acrylics probably feel most like wool, are relatively hard-wearing, but soil more easily and are comparatively expensive. A less expensive alternative fiber to nylon is polyester, which still takes color well but is correspondingly less hard-wearing. Polypropylene is used most for the cheaper types of carpeting; it's hard-wearing and stain-resistant, but generally has a rather brittle texture and a slight sheen to it, which cheapens both the feel and the look. These are the main fiber components of carpets today, but others that may be found, usually as part of a fiber blend rather than on their own, are jute, viscose rayon — used mostly to add bulk to other blends and sometimes mixed with jute in cheaper, cord-type carpets — and animal hair, which is used for carpet tiles and good quality hair-cords for its hard-wearing, qualities.

One relative newcomer at the top end of the market is cotton — not the twisted, long-pile rug type, but dense, short-cut pile. It feels like silk to walk on and wears well, so afford it if you can. At the other extreme, scratchy rush, coir and sisal, while not strictly carpet, are still used as carpeting. These, too, are all natural materials; rush is made from rushes, woven into squares (sold loose or made up) or continuous lengths, although the traditional craft of making top-quality, thick rush matting is almost extinct and even if you can find someone to make it for you, you may have a long wait before you get it. Sisal and coir are also both plant fibers (coir comes from the coconut) and are made up either into mats and runners or in carpet widths. The better quality varieties are often backed with foam to give the rather stretchy weaves some stability and make them easier to lay, and for this reason, too, they're usually stuck down to a level, or levelled, floor. Rush matting is usually laid loose and lifted for cleaning, as the dust falls through it to the floor below; some people also recommmend watering it in very dry conditions to keep it supple. Loose coir and sisal can both be vacuumed and then

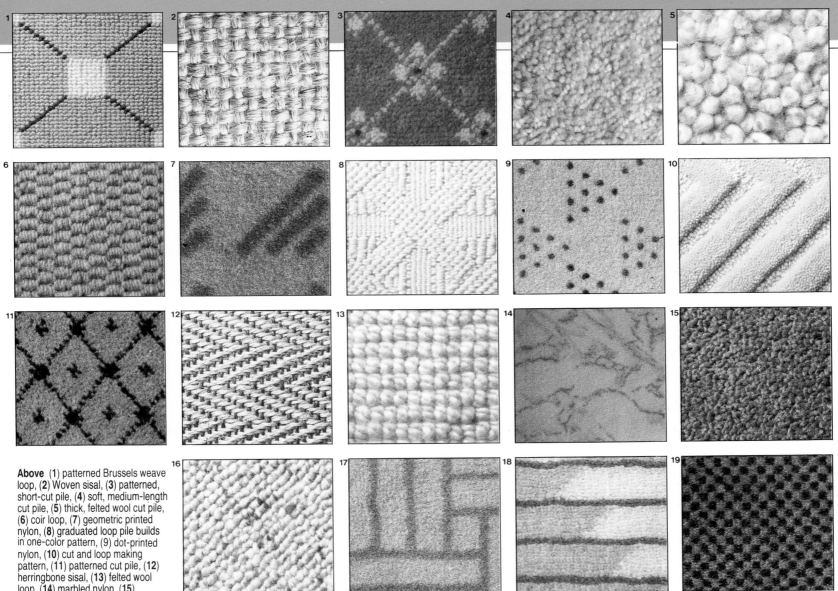

Above (1) patterned Brussels weave loop, (2) Woven sisal, (3) patterned, short-cut pile, (4) soft, medium-length cut pile, (5) thick, felted wool cut pile, (6) coir loop, (7) geometric printed nylon, (8) graduated loop pile builds in one-color pattern, (9) dot-printed nylon, (10) cut and loop making pattern, (11) patterned cut pile, (12) herringbone sisal, (13) felted wool loop, (14) marbled nylon, (15) Hard-twist cut pile, (16) Berber loop, (17) bonded nylon, (18) loop stripes cut pile, (19) duo-tone nylon
Left An imaginative choice of coloring of coconut matting.
Top left Afia carpets' country-inspired collection of designs executed in the fine loop of a Brussels weave.

scrubbed with soapless detergent when they get very dirty. Rush squares are cheap enough to discard when they deteriorate, but coir and sisal — especially the backed versions — are more expensive and although relatively hard-wearing, generally very difficult to keep clean. So buy them with your eyes open and because you like their unusual texture rather than for any practi-cal reasons.

Pile types

There are still basically only two types of pile, cut or loop, but they can each look and feel very different depending on the length of pile and the way in which they're fixed to the backing material. What most affects wear, apart from the fiber used, is the length and density of the pile. The shorter and denser, the better it will wear (which is how Wilton acquired and retains its reputation). This is also one of the main reasons for the decrease in popularity and manufacture of the long-pile, 'shag' carpets. The amount of material used makes long-pile just too expensive — nor does it lie well unless it is fairly openly woven or tufted, and although everyone bought them when they first came out, they performed badly — matting and flattening fast — and the consumer learned to steer clear of them.

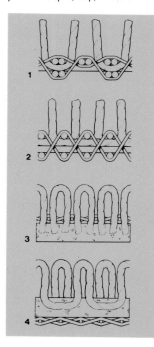

Below The four main forms of carpet construction: (1) Axminster — cut pile woven with the backing; (2) Wilton — all colors being woven as continuous strands into the backing limits the number which can be used; (3) Tufted — cut or loop pile is stitched into an already woven jute backing and secured underneath with a latex coating; (4) Bonded — a sheet of fibers or yarns is bonded to an adhesive backing in various ways to produce cut pile, loop, cord etc.

Both cut and loop pile may be woven or tufted. In woven carpets the yarn and the backing material are woven together simultaneously; for tufteds, separate lengths of yarn are inserted mechanically into a pre-woven backing, and, although this may sound a less secure way of attaching the yarn, manufacturing methods are now so sophisticated that 'woven or tufted' is no longer really a sensible criterion for choice and the design versatility of tufteds give them added advantages.

Both types of pile can provide a range of textures. Cut pile ranges from the close-cut, velvety, bowling-green type to the more granular effect when the pile is slightly longer and has a hard twist or kink built into it, loop pile from the fine, almost tapestry-like stitches of a Brussels weave to tightly curled and distinctly nubby. Some manufacturers also build in sculptured patterns, either by shaving the pile at an angle or combining cut and loop pile; these are both very effective, but whether they're visually pleasing is another matter.

As for relative performance, cut pile is generally softer but is more likely to show pressure marks and 'shading'. Shading is that peculiar, watermark-like phenomenon when tufts lie in different directions and show light and dark patches, which look like moire taffeta or velvet stroked the wrong way. This occurs even on the best carpets and apparently no one, despite all the sophisticated, modern, wear-testing machinery, has yet discovered either cause or cure. Loop pile is harder for both walking and sitting on, it will show dirt more than cut pile, but on the plus side it doesn't shade and is exceptionally hardwearing. In fact, one highly experienced carpet dealer went out on a limb and told me that a good quality loop pile could wear better than cut pile at twice its price.

There is one other method of carpet manufacture worth mentioning, although it is very much in the minority, and becoming increasingly so. Fiber-bonded carpeting — sometimes called 'needleloom', 'needlepunch' or 'needlefelt' — is made by punching layers of fiber into an adhesive-coated backing. This method is used mainly for carpet tiles and one or two of the better quality cord carpets which tend to be partially or exclusively animal hair — hard to the touch but very hard-wearing. But fiber-bonding is generally considered an inefficient and therefore uneconomical way of making carpeting and cannot ordinarily be used to produce cut pile.

CHOOSING YOUR CARPET

There is now an established grading and labelling scheme for carpets — in Britain it has six wear categories from A (extra heavy) to F (light)— which makes it easy to select the most suitable quality of carpet for each area of the house. As a rough guide, the areas that generally get most wear are halls and stairways, next come studies, TV rooms and playrooms, then dining room and, last living rooms and bedrooms. But since everyone uses their home differently, it's sensible to assess the kind of wear each room gets yourself and tell the salesman. It's in his interest to advise you properly, since you do have legal redress if you're sold a carpet that proves unfit for its stated purpose. It's also worth remembering that any grading system can only be an approximation, so you should still inquire about any carpet's resistance to soiling and flatting, as well as any other questions you need answered to ensure that you're buying with your eyes open.

The highest quality the domestic consumer is likely to

Above Graduated cut pile mixed with pile uses texture as well as color to make patterns three-dimensional in this mixture of plain and fancy border designs.
Above left The full potential of carpet exploited in a multi-tiered, living-space where, with the help of a few, loose, calico-covered cushions, sitting is made comfortable at any level. Extravagent, perhaps, but also exceptionally practical since, for cleaning, a single vacuum attachment will suit all the surfaces.

need is the B (very heavy) category — A is mostly for contract use — which you can expect to last for up to 15 years, even on stairs. And whereas you used to be able to get the same carpet in different qualities, this is not an economic method of manufacture, particularly for tufteds, so if you want the same type of carpet throughout the house you may have no option but to choose top quality. One alternative is to buy a slightly lower quality which is generally suitable for the rest of the house, but buy extra initially so that you can replace worn stair treads, even the hall; any initial difference in color will even out after a couple of months. But don't deliberately buy low quality carpet, buy the best you can afford or borrow for; it's a decision you'll never regret once the pain of paying for it is past. And don't attempt to 'patch' worn areas of carpet in other rooms — it simply doesn't work, aesthetically or practically. Either put a rug over the worn bit or resign yourself to replacing the carpet — and this time, get a better one.

Padding

What will substantially increase the life of your carpet is a good padding (*not* old carpet or newspapers), which will also improve its 'feel'. This applies even to foam-backed carpets unless, of course, you are going to stick them down, in which case it's advisable to level boards with hardboard or chipboard first. However, a thick, good quality padding will generally cushion the carpet against minor unevennesses in the floor. Foam rubber is widely used, but even the best quality, which feels superbly springy when first laid, will rapidly loose its 'bounce'. Foam also tends to raise any seams, so that they get worn first. The combination paddings — felt impregnated with foam — don't cause this problem, keep their resilience longer than foam alone, but are still not as good as the best felt pads. These, also, of course, vary in quality from cheap-and-nasty jute and slightly-less-so, man-made fiber versions to top-quality waste-wool and animal hair. Once again, I'm afraid, the advice is to buy the very best you can possibly afford and to check what the felt is made of before you buy.

Width

Broadloom carpet comes in widths from around 6ft (1.8m) up to 19ft (5.7m), but the commonest width currently is around 12-13ft (3.6-3.9m) and it is in this width that there is therefore the greatest choice. The traditional 27in (67.5cm) strip carpeting — either woven to that width or broadloom cut in slices — is now very seldom seen, predominantly because people prefer to close-carpet their stairs. (If you do use strip carpet here, the old advice about buying extra length so you can move it to distribute wear from treads to risers still holds good.) Carpet tiles, which were popular at one stage and then largely disappeared

except for contract/industrial use, seem to be making something of a comeback and the designs, particularly in the US, are becoming more interesting.

Fitting

Tiles are one of the few types of carpeting it's even remotely sensible to lay yourself — use the adhesive recommended by the manufacturer and follow the method described for laying flexible tiles. You can also lay foam-backed carpets and nylons in the same way as flexible sheet flooring, but more easily if the width of the carpet is greater than the width of the room. Seams can be difficult to deal with, and dangerous if you don't stick them down properly. Cutting is another problem — the professionals tend to use proper carpet shears but your best bet is a craft knife with a very sharp blade. (Be prepared to waste blades after a little usage and you'll make the job easier on yourself.) For all other types of carpet, it's sheer folly to throw bad money after good by trying to lay it yourself, or even getting an odd job man or a 'cowboy' to do it. It's a skilled job, requiring specialist tools, so get an expert fitter or firm and check their reputation. You may get the job done more cheaply if you ask a fitter employed full time by a professional firm if he's prepared to do a bit of 'moonlighting' in the evening or on weekends, but it would be courteous to clear this with his employer, too.

Maintenance

All carpets tend to shed fluff during the first few weeks of their laid life and during this period should be vacuumed very lightly or, better still, cleaned by hand with a brush. Don't pull any stray tufts standing clear of the pile — cut them off flush with a pair of curved-blade nail scissors. It also makes sense to put protective furniture cups under any very heavy items and move them a few inches from time to time to save wearing dents in the pile. Once the carpet has settled in, vacuum it normally twice a week. On cut pile carpets, use the kind of machine that 'beats-as-it-sweeps-as-it-cleans' and vacuum in a different direction each time. On loop pile carpets, where there's a risk of snagging a loop if you use a cleaner with a beater bar, use only a suction cleaner or attachment. It will also prolong the carpet's life if you shampoo it occasionally. Professional cleaning is the safest and most thorough method, but if you do it yourself, use only a proper carpet shampoo, observe the proportions recommended and don't get the carpet too wet — this may cause it to shrink or, with some backings, to stain. With most home shampoos, you rub the liquid in with a specially made applicator, leave it to dry and then vacuum up the residue. Tackle intermittent spills quickly, before they sink in and dry, and you'll probably avoid stains. It's definitely worth keeping a stain-removal kit handy for this kind of eventuality.

Preparation is — if we let it be — the least satisfying and most tedious part of decoration. Yet without sound, clean, smooth foundations, not only will the new finish take less well to the old, it just won't look as good as it could. This section takes you through the preparatory stages for all types of old and new surfaces and I can guarantee that if you follow them faithfully you will never regret the time and trouble spent. But you may well have cause for regret if you don't.

STRIP FOR ACTION Take down curtains, pictures and any other easily removable fixtures or fittings that are not to be decorated along with the room. Group furniture in the middle of the room, well away from the wall. For thorough protection, cover both furniture and floor first with plastic sheeting, and then with dust-sheets. The plastic will prevent water or paint penetrating through to whatever is underneath, the dustsheet will absorb spills and stop steps or ladders slipping.

Start cleaning by dusting off dry, loose material with either a soft brush or vacuum cleaner attachment, working across the ceiling, down the walls and around and over paintwork, paying special attention to cracks and crevices. Then vacuum the floor so the dust is not tracked back up the walls or into other rooms.

Ceilings, walls and woodwork that are basically in good condition may only need a thorough cleaning before repainting. Wash off dirt and grime with an old, clean cloth and a bucket containing a solution of warm water and either sugar soap or household detergent. Finish with one or more thorough rinses using clean, warm water and a sponge. Start with the ceiling and work in areas of about 3 sq ft (90 cm²), taking in the top 6-12 in (15-30 cm) of the walls as you go or, if the room has a picture rail, take in the wall area down to that level. Wash one wall at a time. Don't work from top to bottom: if you start at the bottom and wash up in bands of about 3 ft (90 cm), the water will flow down freely over the wet areas instead of drying out in lines. Catch any remaining dirt by rinsing thoroughly from top to bottom with clean, warm water while the wall is still wet — and rinse twice if necessary. Wipe off excess water with a clean sponge or chamois leather and allow walls and ceiling to dry completely before starting redecoration.

Painted or varnished woodwork in sound condition should be washed with warm water and detergent, or mineral spirits, to remove dirt and grease, then rubbed down with fine, wet-and-dry abrasive paper to give a tooth to the next coat. (An easy way is to wrap the abrasive paper around a small block of wood such as a child's building brick.) Wipe over with clean, warm water and a rag to remove all traces of detergent and, when thoroughly dry, use a soft, clean, dry brush to dust off any remaining loose material — clean, dry paintbrushes are often useful for this, especially small ones for awkward places. There is no substitute for good preparation, it is time consuming work but pays dividends in a clean, professional, finished job.

Below To close gaps between floorboards leave one board under each baseboard and lift the rest, remove old nails and clean edges of boards and joists. Re-lay 4 or 5 boards loose, set pairs of wedges across the joists next to the last board and half-nail a spare board tightly against the wedges. Hammer the wedges together to tighten boards, then nail them down. Work across the room like this and fill the last gap with a strip of wood.

Below Plastering over a brick-filled gap in an old fireplace. When doing the brickwork make sure there's about a ½in (1-2cm) gap left between mortar and front face of bricks to provide a tooth for the plaster. Remove all loose material with a wire brush, make up a 1:3 mixture of plaster and clean, coarse sand in a bucket and add enough water for a dough-like consistency. Wet brickwork and float and apply the rendering to fill the gap to about ¼in (6mm) below the surrounding area. Roughen this coat by going over the surface with a wooden float then, just before it sets, lightly scoring it (**1**). Leave the rendering to dry for about 12 hours before applying the finishing coat of neat plaster and water, mixed to the same dough-like consistency. This finishing or 'skim' coat should be brought flush with the surrounding plasterwork (**2**). Just before it begins to set, dampen the surface with a wet brush and polish it with the face of a steel float. Before papering (**3**), fill and sand smooth places where old and new plaster meet and give new work a weak, sealing coat of size.

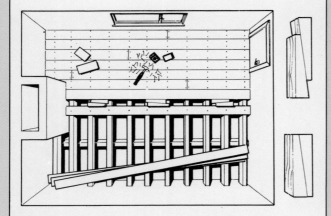

Below To lay a new, square-panelled, chipboard floor, first remove baseboards and lift old boards. Measure the room and draw up a floor-plan so that the first panel is as near the center of the room as joists will allow; panel edges must meet in the center of joists. Fix 3 × 2in (7.5 × 5cm) supports between joists to support panel edges at right angles to them. Fix center panel first, then work clockwise round the room, using 2½in (6.3cm) screws, drilled and screwed about every 8in (20cm) through panel edges into joists and supports. Stagger screw holes on adjacent edges.

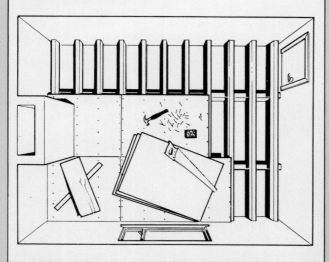

Above and **left** A new room from start to finish. Unless old wallpaper is really well stuck to the wall or the plaster in such poor conditions that you fear it may come away with the paper, old paper should be completely removed before new paint or paper is applied. Strip dry, if possible, by sliding the blade of a stripping knife under loose edges and pulling away. A steam-stripper will remove stubborn cases. If you leave old paper on, sand away or stick down loose edges, fill all other defects and cross-line with lining-paper to hide old joins and make a sound, uniformly-porous surface for the new paint or paper. This will make all the difference to whether the result looks like a new room or merely one that's been 're-decorated'.

1 Repairing holes in a lath-and-plaster surface. If laths aren't broken simply scrape away loose material and re-plaster. If they are, fill small to medium holes with screwed-up paper, soaked in plaster, large holes with expanded metal.
2 The first filling should stop about $\frac{1}{16}$in (3mm) below the surface. When this is dry, damp the surface and apply the top coat of filler to finish flush.
3 For holes in solid walls, just remove loose material and fill. In plasterboard, cut a recess in the sound surface around the hole, dab it with filler and patch with scrim-cloth.
4 Build up filler in $\frac{1}{4}$in (6mm) layers, using a wet brush to lightly blend the top coat with the surrounding area.
5 Surfaces which simply can't be got smooth and even can be disguised with textured paint.

Upper right Peeling paint with dirt-filled crevices can make the condition of woodwork look far worse than it is. Strip old paint off by one of the methods described but, if using a chemical paint stripper, rinse off thoroughly afterwards as any residue may affect the new paint finish.
Lower right Woodwork that's to be painted can be filled with all-purpose proprietary filler but if you're intending to use a clear finish, choose clear or tinted wood filler. For nail holes, crevices and gaps around windows, use putty over aluminum primer.
Far right Paint can't disguise a poor surface so there's no magic about this transformation. It's simply the result of time and trouble taken to strip carefully and thoroughly, then fill and sand, fill and sand until a smooth base surface has been regained.

REMOVING OLD FINISHES

Paint

The basic principle about removing paint is — don't, if you can avoid it. Only remove old paint when there is no alternative. Where a painted wall can easily be patched or filled and sanded smooth, do it — extra coats of paint over a good surface can often mean better protection, whether on ceilings, walls or woodwork.

The exceptions are surfaces painted with lime-wash, whiting or distemper. Test the surface, either wet or dry, by rubbing it with your finger. If the paint comes off easily on your finger, it is one of the distemper-type finishes and will have to be completely removed before painting or papering. These are fairly easy to get off: first remove any loose material with a stiff, dry brush, then use a really firm scrubbing brush and plenty of warm water to soak and scrub the whole area. Change the water frequently, as soon as it starts to become cloudy with the distemper, rinse off very thoroughly with clean water and swab down with a cloth or a sponge. Allow to dry completely before applying any form of paint or sealer.

Other paint or varnish finishes need only be completely removed when they show obvious, all-over defects such as extensive blistering, peeling, crazing, wrinkling or cracking. But paint may also have to be removed from all or part of a wall where it has become soft or tacky or is badly stained, due either to dampness or to some chemical reaction between the plaster and subsequent paint finishes. The root cause of these blemishes will need to be established and treated before the bare surface is refinished.

☐ **Do** try and remove any loose material on a distemper-type finish first, using a dry brush and then a dampened scrubbing brush

☐ **Do** try a wallpaper steamer to soften particularly stubborn distemper — a steamer may also be one of the easiest ways to soften latex paint.

If there is no alternative but to remove the paint, try scraping it off dry before resorting to any more drastic measures. With luck, there may be such a build-up of thick coats of old paint that the plaster will have shrunk away from the back of the paint so a stripping knife can be slipped between the two layers. Try an inconspicuous corner first and, as always when stripping, keep the blade of the knife as flat to the wall as possible to avoid scoring or gouging the plaster. Even if all the paint will not come off, you may be able to remove the loose or damaged areas. Fill and sand these until you regain an even surface, but bear in mind that plaster is cheaper than filler over large areas.

If the paint will not come off dry, the two main methods of removing it from plaster, wood or metal are either to burn it off or to dissolve it with a chemical paint remover. Each of these methods has its devotees and detractors, its advantages and disadvantages. Whichever method you use is really a matter of preference and skill, but as a general principle, burn off large areas where possible and use solvent for small areas, detail work and where you intend the surface to have a natural finish.

Method I: Burning off Burning is generally considered a quicker, cheaper, cleaner and therefore more convenient method of removing paint, but it is least effective on latex or other water-based paints because they contain no oil; cellulose paints may catch fire and the heat will make some varnishes and oil-based paints sticky and hard to handle. (If old paint is very soft and sticky, apply a thick coat of lime-wash first and allow it to dry. This will harden the paint so that it comes off more cleanly.) Burning can be a slow job on surfaces like plaster, which conduct heat quickly away from its source, and can also damage the surface beneath the paint unless you are careful. Plaster and cement will crumble if heat is applied too directly; heat can also warp plywood, destroy hardboard and insulating board, or crack glass if care is not taken when working on narrow window-bars. There is also a danger of scorching wood, not especially important if you are planning to repaint, but for a natural finish, removing the marks with wood bleach and sandpaper will prove a laborious job.

TOOLS AND PREPARATION There are several types of burning-off equipment available today, ranging from the old-fashioned blowlamps fuelled by gasoline or kerosene blow-torches powered by butane or propane gas and the relatively new hot-air strippers. The advantages of blow-torches over blow-lamps are considerable. Attached to a gas cylinder, the blow-torch lights and is ready for use immediately, whereas a blow-lamp must be refilled constantly and warmed up before use each time. A blow-torch flame is hotter, meaning work is quicker and, by using a series of nozzles, both its intensity and the shape of the flame can be adjusted to suit different types of work. Nor is there any loss of pressure while working with a blow-torch, and the flame is less likely to be blown out by a sudden gust of wind, for example, as someone opens the front door. Since the job can be done more quickly, cleanly and efficiently, these advantages tend to compensate for the greater expense. The cost can, anyway, be minimized by planning your work ahead so that you make full use of the torch in the period for which it is hired.

The only other burning-off equipment that is, in some circumstances, preferable to a blow-torch is the new hot-air stripper. This is electrically powered and works by blowing air along a flexible hose and over a variably controlled heater in an insulated hand-piece. It is efficient, economical and particularly useful for working where a naked flame might be dangerous, or where it is essential not to scorch wood intended for a clear finish; it is also excellent on detail work on both wood and plaster. However, make sure you use an electrical hot-air stripper, not just an electrical stripper where the head is merely made up of a small electric element within a guard; this only heats up one tiny area of paint at a time and work is therefore agonizingly slow.

Besides burning-off equipment two scrapers will also be required: one flat scraper with the widest blade that the working area will accommodate and a shave-hook for corners, quirks and moldings — a combination shave-hook is useful as it has both straight and curved edges. As there will be hot and sticky strips of paint falling from the work surface, make sure the floor area immediately below is protected with aluminum foil and keep a metal container handy — a bucket or an old paint can will do — to collect the debris (it is also useful for scraping your knife clean). If you are using a blow-torch or blow-lamp, it is advisable to keep a piece of wet sacking nearby, just in case you set anything alight.

METHOD Whichever appliance is used, the most important aspect of the technique is not to concentrate the heat-source in one place for any length of time but to keep it moving. Work from the bottom up, so that the rising heat makes the job easier by softening the paint above, and in areas of about 1 sq ft (30 cm^2) at a time. Play the flame or hot air over the paint surface and then, as the paint starts to soften, move the heat source up and slide your broad knife straight in underneath, keeping the blade as flat as possible to save stabbing the plaster. The whole operation may feel rather awkward at first, but if you get both hands moving together, knife following torch, it will soon become an easy, almost mechanical action. Don't attempt to soften any more than you can immediately remove with the knife, as paint that has heated and cooled is even har-

---

Do tackle detailed areas first, to save heat damaging the surrounding area while you work on the fiddly bits. Give it time to cool off before going back to the flat work.

Don't burn off rotten wood, it's far too easily inflammable.

Do stop 20 minutes before the end of each working day, for safety's sake.

der to get off. Where there are several layers of paint, don't try to remove them all in one go. Take off the first, softened layer and then try again. Once you get near the bare surface, be extra careful how much heat you use in any single area, especially on plaster, which will crumble or 'blow' under concentrated heat.

Method II: Chemical paint and varnish removers Paint removers are proprietary brands of chemical solvents, which soften paint and varnish until they can be scraped away. Chemical solvents will not damage the basic surface of wood or plaster, but they are messy to use and clear up and can be expensive, especially over large areas, since it may take more than one application to remove a build-up of paint layers.

There are two main types of chemical remover, alkaline and spirit, but the alkaline or 'caustic' type is best avoided or at least left to the professionals. The caustic solution is absorbed by porous surfaces such as wood and plaster and is therefore extremely difficult to remove completely; it also raises the grain and darkens the color of wood. Treat it with some caution as it ruins natural bristle brushes and splashes can quickly damage you or your clothes. For home use, therefore, stay with the excellent range of spirit removers now available. These, too, should be handled with care, as many of them are highly inflammable and toxic, although some non-flammable types are available. On the whole, however, the spirit removers are far safer than caustic, they are easy to work with and they do a good job on most surface types — there are even special types that don't damage plastic — so I would generally recommend that you stick to these.

TOOLS AND PREPARATION A broad knife and shave-hook will be required as before, and/or steel wool for delicate woodwork. An old paint can is useful for collecting up the softened paint and for cleaning off your knife. An old paintbrush, rubber gloves, toothbrushes, toothpicks, rags and newspapers will also be needed at various stages during the working process.

METHOD The cheapest and most efficient way to use paint remover is simply to be patient and let it do the job for you. Unlike heat, it needs time to 'take' and it is both pointless and wasteful to try to strip the paint immediately after applying the solvent. Brush on a thin coat and wait for about 30 minutes until it has begun to soften the top film of paint. Then, without removing the first coat, apply another really thick coat on top, leaving it well alone until the paint has softened throughout. This may take several hours — on build-ups it can take days — but it is worth the wait because you should then be able to scrape clean through to the bare surface. When using paste remover, brush it on in one direction only and avoid going back over the area as this would disturb the film and reduce efficiency. Liquid removers work slightly differently and here the surface needs to be kept wet with repeated applications until the paint is soft. In both cases, test the softness of the paint by scraping away a small area first; if it peels away easily, revealing the bare surface beneath, then you're ready to go. You may find that the full selection of implements mentioned above is needed to remove the paint: a broad knife for the wide, flat areas, a shave-hook for quirks and moldings, old toothbrushes and toothpicks for awkward corners. When stripping wood that is going to be polished or varnished, especially softwood, it might be better to use steel wool or rags to save damaging the surface. Keep everything as clean as possible, washing out rags and steel wool in detergent regularly and cleaning off tools with old newspapers to keep their edges sharp and visible. When the surface is clear of paint, clean off thoroughly with either mineral spirit or water, depending on the solvent.

Do read the manufacturer's directions before opening the container. Many instruct you to shake the container first. Open it slowly and carefully, holding it away from you, especially if it's warm or has been stored for a while — the contents could splash out of the container as the build-up of pressure is relieved. To be doubly safe, cover the top of the container with a rag as you open it.

Do be patient and wait for the solvent to take effect before trying to strip off the paint — this can take several hours and even days, depending on the paint. Otherwise you will just be wasting time, effort and money on the whole operation.

Do keep windows open, the fumes can be toxic, and do wear protective clothes, gloves — even goggles.

Don't use your best brushes for paint removing as solvents can damage the stock. Use an old brush, preferably with an unpainted handle.

SPECIAL CASES

Textured paints

Never was there a clearer exception to the rule 'what goes up must come down'. These 'stone effect' paints compound the removal problem of some latexes because they contain various types of fine to coarse grit; this produces a surface that can be both very attractive and an excellent camouflage for irregularities and cracks, but is virtually impossible to get off. Covering over this surface is not a simple solution either, although cross-lining twice — vertically first, then horizontally — or lining once with linen-backed paper will probably do the trick. If you do try this, it will pay to coat the surface first with old-fashioned, glue-based size, and use a flour-based paste to help it stick. It may be worth sanding it first with a mechanical sander, but it would help to know the nature of the grit in the paint finish in order to use an abrasive paper that is tough enough for the job. If you are going to attempt to remove the paint completely, try stripping it dry first. The coating is sometimes so close-textured that it forms a skin over the wall rather than bonding to it completely and it may well peel off in strips if a knife is put behind it. Failing this, the next step is to try using a wallpaper steamer to soften the surface sufficiently for stripping. As with wallpaper, work from the bottom up so that the rising steam starts to soften the paint immediately above the area being worked meaning that it will peel off more easily and ultimately make far less work for you. These can be very successful but it is often best to experiment with a friend's or a kettle first.

The last resort — or perhaps the first if there is only a small area to handle — is a new paint stripping compound specially formulated for the job. It is a petroleum-based gel (therefore inflammable, so take the usual precautions) which softens the surface in about an hour. The paint can then be easily stripped off with a knife and the surface washed down with cold water. This chemical remover will also deal with some of the powder-based textured paints — although it may take two coats and will then need a hot-water wash — and the more stubborn of latex paints. The reason for the *caveat* is that it is expensive, but when there's no other alternative, it's probably worth paying the price.

Lacquer, shellac and old-fashioned varnish

Until fairly recently the only thing that would dissolve lacquer was lacquer thinners, and shellac needed shellac solvent. There is a solvent now available that removes these finishes as well as traditional varnish and wax from fine wood on which you do not want to risk the harsher chemical solvents. Not surprisingly, therefore, it will not strip paint or polyurethene varnish, but it is extremely useful on precious surfaces.

Wax

The method you use to remove wax depends on the surface it's covering, whether you want to get right back to the original material or simply, for example, to a still-sound coat of varnish. If it's only the wax you want to remove, a traditional, very mildly abrasive brass polish will take off the surface film from wood, leaving varnish intact. On flat surfaces you can also use a cabinet-maker's steel scraper. Blunt the corners of the scraper first to save scratching the wood then, exerting just a light pressure you will be able to remove the wax only, with heavier pressure take the varnish off too, although if you want to get the varnish right out of the pores of the wood, you may still need a light application of chemical solvent remover. On large areas of wood, the cheapest and quickest method of removing wax is probably to use mineral spirits and steel wool or abrasive paper. An alternative is to scrub the wood first with wire wool and hot, soapy water to lift off most of the wax, let the surface dry and then remove the residue with steel wool and benzene. Try a small area with each method first to see which works best on the surface. Where there's a build-up of dirt, wax and varnish, and a clean, bare surface is wanted, the most thorough and efficient way will be to use a chemical paint/varnish remover. But this drastic method is not suitable for all other surfaces. Use a proprietary wax remover on delicate pieces of wood, on cork, rubber or thermoplastic sheet flooring and tile, and use either wax remover or mineral spirits on linoleum. In all cases, wash thoroughly after wax-removal with warm, soapy water (not detergent), rinse thoroughly and allow to dry.

Wallpaper

Try to avoid applying either new paint or paper on top of old wallpaper. Painting over old paper makes any subsequent attempt to remove it twice as difficult, and even if the paper is really well attached and the wall in good condition, one coat of paint may be enough to pull it off. The texture of the old paper will show through a new paint finish and its dyes may bleed. In addition, if the paper is in bad condition, it can take as long to get a sound, smooth, all-over surface as it would to strip the paper. Hanging new wallpaper over old is a similarly hazardous business. The old paper could loosen and blister, damaging the new, and the old joins will also show on the new surface. There are only two situations where it is better to leave old paper on: the first is if the original paper was stuck onto unsized gypsum board — it will be impossible to remove this without ruining the surface of the board — the second is when the state of the plaster beneath is dubious. In both cases, try removing the paper from a small area in an inconspicuous corner. Use your own judgement and, if you think you will only cause more trouble, make good, seal and cross-line.

METHOD On rare and lucky occasions, wallpaper will strip dry. It is certainly worth trying this by prizing away a bottom corner with a knife, loosening the lower edge and pulling the paper off from the bottom up. If it does not come away cleanly, you will have to use one of the 'wet' methods. The classic, most basic method involves a bucket of warm water, the hotter the better, a flat, 4 or 6 in (10 or 20 cm) brush, a broad knife and plenty of elbow-grease. It is possible to buy sachets of wallpaper stripping compound which, when added to the water, help it to penetrate the paper by removing the surface tension, but this is an accessory rather than an essential, as it is actually the water that does the job. Working from the top of each wall down, wet the whole room several times until the paper has been thoroughly soaked. When stripping with the broad knife, follow the same sequence as wetting in and strip across, not down, the wall as this is usually easier.

Some paper — or a build-up of old papers — may only respond to a steam stripper. This machine, usually available from rental shops, has a tank in which the water is boiled (generally either by electricity or gas cylinder, but sometimes, in older models, by kerosene) and the steam is sent via a long hose through a perforated plate. Once the steam is up, hold the plate against the paper for about 30 seconds to allow the steam to penetrate the surface and soften the paste; the paper can then be peeled from the wall with a broad knife. Work from the bottom so that the rising steam starts to soften the paste further up, but do not keep the plate too long in any one place as this could buckle and lift the plaster. The steamer should deal with most stubborn papers and one of its advantages is that, because it works quickly and thoroughly, the knife is used less and not as hard, so there is naturally less risk of stabbing the plaster.

Varnished papers These old papers, dating back to early Victorian times, are probably the most troublesome — although you may well find that, because the next generation could not remove them, they papered over them using flour paste. With luck, the paste will have eaten through the varnish and everything will come off quite easily. If not, scoring the surface with coarse abrasive paper or light strokes of the knife will help the steam penetrate. In really stubborn cases, you may have to apply either a proprietary varnish remover or a strong solution of sugar soap to soften the surface, but try a small area first. If it will not move, you can assume the rest will be just as obstinate and it is therefore not worth time or money keeping the steamer (try the test area with the spout of a boiling, electric kettle to save yourself a pointless trip); you will just have to find some other way of covering it up.

Heavy, embossed papers These include Lincrusta and Anaglypta and will very often strip dry, but papers coated with emulsion or other water-based paints will probably need the steam. Again, it helps to break up the surface and at least the raised pattern on these papers gives you something to get at, either with a wire brush or by punching flat across the embossed surface with a broad stripping knife.

Vinyls, washables and pre-pasted papers These modern wallpapers are typical examples of coverings that need a different approach. The pre-pasted papers usually come off quite easily if you prize away the bottom two corners of each panel and pull it steadily upwards away from the wall. If this fails, strip in the normal way with warm water or the steamer. With vinyl papers, the trick is again to lift a lower edge and pull each length away from bottom to top, but in this case it will be the top vinyl layer only that comes away, leaving the backing paper on the wall. For a thorough job, it is better to strip this backing in the normal way, but you can paint or paper over it as long as it is firmly stuck to the wall. When papering straight over it, at least make sure that the joins in the new panels do not correspond with the old and better still, fill, and/or cross-line first. Washable papers are usually the hardest of all modern papers to strip because they are waterproofed and generally quite thin. Scoring the surface will help, but after that it's back to hot water, the steamer and old-fashioned elbow-grease.

Once any paper has been removed from the wall, wash the bare wall thoroughly to remove all traces of old paste and size, leave it to dry, then sand down with fine abrasive paper and dust off before applying a new finish.

FABRICS

The principles for removing a fabric wallcovering are nearly identical to those for wallpaper, although fabric may strip dry more easily because it is less likely to disintegrate. Try to do this anyway, if at all possible, as water or steam may reactivate the adhesive and leave quantities of 'jam' on the wall. If this happens, remove as much as possible with a broad knife, then leave the rest to dry, sanding and dusting off the wall as before.

HARD COVERINGS ON CEILINGS, WALLS AND FLOORS

The main problem with any hard covering is not so much the material itself as the adhesive — the better it sticks, the harder it is to unstick. Even the professionals can find it impossible to decide, simply by looking, just what type of adhesive has been used for the job. In any case, the enormous range and complex make-up of modern adhesives means that it is usually neither time- nor cost-effective to try to find the appropriate solvent. Even if you find it, trying to remove the adhesive with a solvent is a messy job; the solvent will penetrate the surface, which in turn can mean a lengthy cleaning and sealing operation. In most cases, therefore, it is advisable to try removing hard coverings and their adhesives dry and just resign yourself to the fact that it may be a tedious job. The condition of the wall will also have to be taken into account. Some adhesives are so strong that the plaster will also be pulled off and you may have to replaster or at least re-skim. So, before attacking the old surface, do consider whether there is any other acceptable method of covering it up.

The tools that are likely to be needed for dry stripping are a hammer, chisel, broad knife, craft knife, various grades of abrasive paper and a sanding block. Punch ceramic tiles off the wall with a hammer and chisel first, using the stripper to scrape away any remaining adhesive. With more flexible hard coverings rubbery strings of adhesive may be found, connecting wall to covering as you start to pull it away. Use the craft knife to sever these strings as close to the background surface as possible. In all cases, once the covering is off, punch away as much of the remaining adhesive as possible with the stripper, trying not to damage the surface, then sand off the rest and dust down.

Adhesive manufacturers are well aware that, in solving some of the problems, they have created others and are themselves experimenting with various methods of adhesive removal. This is very much at the 'trial and error' stage, but it is worth reporting their findings so far, in case dry stripping does not work and you find yourself, quite literally, stuck. The most successful method to date appears to be the wallpaper steam stripper, particularly in softening the standard, ready mixed PVA adhesives often used to stick ceramic tiles and expanded polystyrene ceiling tiles. They will still need punching off first to allow the steam to reach the adhesive and, with porous surfaces like plaster, be prepared for a thin film of the surface to come away with the adhesive as you scrape it off. If you're proposing, therefore, to re-cover with a heavy cladding, bind the wall first with a PVA bonding agent, diluted according to the covering — for example, 1:5 with water for a heavyish wallpaper, but undiluted for ceramic tiles, and make sure that you put the tiles up with the recommended adhesive while the bonding surface is still tacky, otherwise they may well not stick securely.

The steamer is less successful with the rubbery types of adhesive, particularly if there's a hard, impervious surface behind it. However, good reports have been received about using a hot-air stripper on this type of adhesive. Burning it off is another possibility, provided it is not cellulose-based and therefore likely to catch fire. But test a small and preferably isolated area first to check the behavior of the adhesive and whether it is likely to give off unpleasant and possibly toxic fumes, as this can be dangerous and, anyway, is unpleasant. So be warned and take the extra time to test first.

Good foundations

The treatment of new plaster depends not only on the type of plaster but on the finish intended for it. In new 'wet-built' homes the brickwork and plaster contain a lot of water. This can take many months to dry out and only certain finishes can be applied safely before the process is complete. The risk of damaging both plaster and finish is less on exterior walls, where much of the moisture will evaporate via the cavity, than in prematurely sealed interior partition walls. The basic principle, therefore, is that only finishes that 'breathe' — that are porous — can safely be applied to new walls. In practice, this means you can usually go ahead immediately with latex or other water-based paints, paper wallcovering and natural fabrics, but you would be well advised to wait before using oil-based paints, wallpapers coated with vinyl or other impervious seals and synthetic or synthetic-coated fabrics. However, remember that this applies to entirely new walls, not old walls that have been replastered. As the building industry is constantly working on ways around this problem, there are many different types of plaster and new types are appearing regularly, the best procedure is to find out which kind of plaster you have and follow the manufacturer's advice. In the opposite situation, that is where the plaster is basically new but has been left undecorated for some reason — like lack of time or money — while the room has been in use, it may have absorbed foreign material such as soap or oil, especially in kitchens and bathrooms. In this case, wash the plaster down with an anti-fungicide solution and, when the wall is dry, apply an alkali-resisting primer before further decoration.

Paint on new plaster
Before applying the first coat of paint, go over the surface with a 4 in (10 cm) stripper to remove any nibs left by the plasterer, keeping the blade flat to avoid damaging the plaster. But never, never sand fresh, uncoated plaster before painting. Plaster has a smooth, surface sheen and, although porous, it is not in itself a texture. Even the finest sandpaper will create surface scratches, which will show through a first or second coat of paint, and further filling and painting will only be required.
Water-based paint When painting with latex or any other water-based paint, the first coat should be a 'mist' coat, thinned half and half with water. The idea is not to achieve coverage, but to seal the wall and create a film which is absorbed by the plaster. Most modern paints tend to lie on top of plaster rather than penetrating it, and this mist coat will create a 'bridge' between plaster and paint and ensure better adhesion of subsequent coats. When this first coat is dry, fill any defects, cracks or scratches with an all-purpose vinyl-based filler and allow the filler to dry

before sanding off. Use only very fine sandpaper, to avoid breaking the paint surface, and touch up the filling with whatever first coat you used. If the surface does break, fill any scratches, sand these smooth very carefully, touch up and allow the paint to dry before applying the finishing coats.

Oil-based paints The safest way to prepare new plaster for finishing with flat oil, eggshell or gloss is with an may also be one of the easiest ways to soften latex

dry as it should be before starting, this type of primer will seal off any remaining salts or acids which might otherwise make their way through the wall. These can simply be brushed off dry if they appear through the porous finish of latex or other water-based paints, but when they meet an impervious surface, their only way out is to bubble, craze or crack the finish. Apply the primer before filling and sanding and touch up any fresh work with primer before moving onto the finishing coats.

Wallpaper/fabric on plaster
These coverings should only be applied to plaster that is completely dry and chemically neutral. If you are in any doubt about the chemical content, it is worth testing for alkalinity by moistening a patch of plaster with distilled water and sticking a piece of pink litmus paper to it. If the litmus turns blue, the wall is chemically active and should be given a coat of alkali-resisting primer. Do this after sandpapering to remove any nibs or splashes of plaster and follow up with a weak coat of whatever sealant is appropriate to the adhesive you're using, which will in turn depend on the material that is about to be hung. (Glue-size and flour-based paste are best for most wallpapers; vinyls and washables take longer to dry out and ordinary paste may 'rot' so an anti-fungicidal version should be used instead.) If the wall is dry and chemically neutral, simply sand and size or paste. New plaster usually has a considerable amount of suction and this mildly sealing first coat is to give the wall some 'slip', so that you can adjust the position of the paper while hanging it. But don't make the solution too strong or it will over-seal the wall, making it lose the degree of suction needed to help hold the paper to the wall, although using the same 'base' for both sizing and hanging is a great help to adhesion. The only variations to this process are with an exceptionally 'thirsty' plaster, for example some lightweight aggregates, where you may need to apply two weak coats of size or, alternatively, where the plaster has a hard, highly polished and *less* absorbent finish. In this case, cross-line the walls first, after sizing, to make absolutely sure that your wallcovering will cling tight. In fact, if you are going to hang an expensive wallpaper or fabric, it is best to cross-line anyway to be sure of a smooth finish; it would be very irritating to ruin a good covering.

Do mix size with hot water, but not boiling water, otherwise it won't set properly as it begins to cool.

Don't make too strong a solution of size. 'A bit more for luck' won't be lucky at all — it will seal the wall, the paper will take too long to dry out and may shrink in the process.

Paint on paint
If the wall has been previously painted with latex paint, oil-bound water paint, eggshell or even a flat oil paint, as long as it is in good condition it should only require washing down. Gloss paint will need to be wet-rubbed at the rinsing stage, either with waterproof abrasive paper, pumice stone or steel wool to 'tooth' the surface for new paint. After wet-rubbing, rinse off the whole surface again with clean water, wipe off most of the water with either a sponge or chamois leather, and leave it to dry. If your heart sinks at the idea of rubbing down a whole room — and it is a tedious enough job — a quicker and reasonably effective alternative is to wash the wall with a medium solution of sugar soap which, if left on for just a few minutes so that the paint doesn't have time to soften, will not only help lift the dirt but mildly etch the paint surface. Rinse this off, then rub down with pumice powder on a cloth before a final, thorough rinsing and allow to dry completely before moving on; this should give you a good surface to work on.

The next stage is to make good any cracks, nicks or other defects in the plaster. After filling and sanding flush, the final stage, to 'bring forward' the new work to the same finish as the surrounding area, is touching up. On walls painted with latex or other water-based paints, touch up filled parts with primer, tinted to match the surrounding area. You may need two coats if the filler shows signs of bleeding through or, if working on a very dark color, use paint to mix the filler — this will often give a smoother finish to the filled area anyway. Touching up small patches is only really successful with flat paints. Anything with a slight sheen — even a vinyl latex — will show up the smallest variation in surface so it is best to coat the whole of it. For the same reason, it is difficult to successfully fill or patch a gloss-painted wall, which is why, in this case, the old paint should be removed wherever possible. But if this is not possible for any reason, prime plaster or other filled patches with 'sharp' oil paint, diluted half and half with mineral spirits. Allow this to dry, sand down the surrounding edges of old paint, fill, sand smooth and touch up again before applying the first coat of new finish. It is worth taking enough trouble with this preparation work to ensure a good clean surface and, ultimately, a polished finish.

Paper on paint

Papering over previously painted surfaces can be a tricky business since, depending on the paint finish, the paper may either fail to grip properly or, as the paper shrinks while drying out, it may pull the paint off the wall. It is therefore well worth taking all possible precautions to see that this does not happen.

Distemper must be completely washed off before making good any holes or cracks; sandpaper smooth and then apply a weak coat of appropriate sealer such as size.

Oil-bound water paint is insoluble and therefore cannot be washed off. If the surface is in good condition, it will only need sandpapering and sizing. But if any parts of the surface are loose and/or flaking, thoroughly scrape and wash these sections before making good and, to be on the safe side, give the whole area a thin coat of oil-bound sealer, which will penetrate and help to bind the surface. Allow this to dry before sizing. If the whole surface is suspect, and especially where there is an accumulation of layers of paint, you may have to give in and strip everything back to the plaster with a steamer. Then prepare as for bare plaster.

Latex paint can be a real problem because it does not wash off. Some kinds cannot even be stripped off with a steamer, but because of their composition they generally lie on top of the plaster rather than penetrating it, so tend not to adhere very well to the wall. Play safe and, even if the paint seems in perfect condition, give it a coat of oily primer. Allow this to dry completely before sizing and then, especially when hanging a good paper, cross-line the walls first.

Oil paint is probably the most difficult surface on which to hang paper because of its hard, non-porous quality. A wet rubbing down with coarse, waterproof abrasive paper and a medium sugar soap solution will help kill the gloss and provide a tooth, but rinse the wall thoroughly afterwards, preferably with some vinegar in the water to neutralize any alkalinity. When the surface is completely dry, go over it with fine abrasive paper and dust off before coating with weak size. Again, especially with an expensive paper, you would be well advised to cross-line first; and use flour-based preparations for both sizing and pasting as these will provide better adhesion and will dry through the paper. But take extra care not to get paste on the front of the paper as it can leave a mark.

Paint on paper

You may want to paint over paper for one of two reasons — either because you want to retain it as a texture, or because you fear that the plaster is so old and brittle that half the wall will come off with the paper. Although this is a far from ideal solution, it can work as long as preparation is done properly. Obviously, the paper must be firmly stuck to the wall, so any loose pieces should be pulled off and all gaps, joins and rough edges filled with an all-purpose, vinyl-based filler. Do not be tempted to size old wallpaper as any watery solution is likely to swell it, causing wrinkles and blisters, and, although these may shrink back once the wall is dry, all this movement may be too much for the old paste, causing the paper to come away from the wall.

This is just as likely to happen where a water-based, especially a water-thinned, paint is applied directly onto old paper. The safest method is to give it an all-over coat of either primer or thin oil paint. Some wallpaper colors have a tendency to bleed — reds, pinks, mauves and metallics are the worst offenders. Test for bleeding by painting a small patch with light-colored, oil-based paint and keeping an eye on it for a few days. If the color starts to show through the paint, you can insulate the paper with a thin coat of knotting (diluted with methylated spirits). Unfortunately, the whole area will need coating, not just the patches of suspect color, to keep a uniform degree of suction over the surface, otherwise your paint finish could be patchy, too. For a really proper job you should then cross-line the walls, to give a smooth, clean surface with uniform all-over suction for the paint and to hide the joins in the old paper.

Paint on fabric

It is not generally desirable or possible to paint over expensive fabrics like silk or non-wovens such as felt, but in the case of fabrics of the 'natural' or 'slub' variety — canvas, burlap, jute, linen — you may want to retain the texture but change or brighten a tired color. If you are using a latex-type paint, simply prime the fabric with a liberal coat of well-thinned paint first, and allow this to dry before painting with one or two coats of normal consistency. If you prefer an oil-based paint — either a flat paint, eggshell or gloss — you will need to protect the fabric from the oil, which would otherwise make it go brittle. Although you wouldn't normally use this underneath paint, the best method in this instance is to use a weak, warm solution of size, which will penetrate and protect the fabric without affecting its texture. Let this dry before applying either a flat oil paint or primer and finishing coat.

Paper on paper

Obviously it is better to strip off the old paper wherever possible, but if you cannot avoid hanging new paper over old — often, because you fear for the plaster beneath — follow the same initial procedure for painting: pull off all the loose bits, fill these and all joins and damaged edges, sand smooth and then cross-line to completely lose all the joins in the existing paper. If you simply hang new paper over old, the original joins will inevitably show through, however well you have filled and sanded, and it really is worth the extra work for a perfect finish. If you do hang new paper straight over old, at least stagger the joins.

Cross-lining

Cross-lining is just as it sounds — hanging lining paper across rather than down walls. It is the proper way to line bare or painted walls for hanging good quality wallpaper and to line pre-papered walls for painting or repapering; in the latter case it is used especially to prevent the joins in the old paper showing through on the new finish. Preparation for cross-lining cannot, however, be skimped. You still have to fill and sand defects on a painted surface and, on wallpaper, make sure any loose bits are pulled off and that these areas plus joins and edges filled with an all-purpose vinyl filler and sanded smooth.

Besides the usual wallpapering equipment, the most important accessories are a couple of sound step-ladders and a sturdy scaffold board, for working from one end of the wall to the other. Paste up the paper in the normal way, but fold it like a concertina in fold-widths of about 18 in (45 cm). Start at the top and, setting the top edge of the first fold in the angle between wall and ceiling and leaving a 2 in (5 cm) overlap in the angle between the walls, stick the fold down by brushing from the ceiling edge down. Work across the wall like this, sticking one fold down at a time. Hang subsequent lengths in the same way, butting the horizontal joins. Leave a 2 in (5 cm) overlap on both internal and external angles and, when the paper has been well brushed out, cut directly into internal angles, but trim external angles to leave a $\frac{1}{8}$ in (3 mm) overlap and leave this sticking out. Hang vertically any returns that are narrower by 4 in (10 cm) or more than the width of the paper (the aim is to create as few joins as possible), butting the edges against external angles and cutting into internal angles. When the paper is dry, trim the overlaps on the external angles right back to the corner with a craft knife and rub the corner down with fine abrasive paper so that you get a seamless, slightly rounded edge. Although paint or paper may disguise really good butt joins, these should all be filled and sanded smooth, too, for a perfect finish.

Paint/varnish on wood

When dealing with new or stripped wood with no remaining traces of paint, fine abrasive paper or steel wool should be enough to rub it smooth. If any traces of paint remain on, or in the pores of, stripped wood, give it a wet-rub with water and either pumice stone or waterproof abrasive paper. Let the wood dry and, if the water has raised the grain, go over the surface again with fine abrasive paper. If you need to paint the wood immediately — or if, for any reason, you don't want to risk raising the grain — use a 1:3 mixture of raw linseed oil and mineral spirits with pum-

ice stone, or a self-lubricating abrasive paper. Clean off with mineral spirits and a lint-free rag or a painter's tack rag — a tack rag is a slightly sticky cloth used to pick up every speck of dust from surfaces on which you want a perfect, polished finish and is especially useful for varnish-work. They may be bought from paint shops, although they are no longer used very much, and it is also easy to make your own. Cut about 3 sq ft (90 cm²) out of an old sheet, wring it out in warm water, lay it flat and sprinkle a few drops of turpentine over it. Wring it again to distribute the turpentine evenly, then trickle a generous soup-spoonful of highly water-resistant boat or 'spar' varnish over the flat surface. Wring tightly and shake it out to spread the varnish, and hang the cloth to dry for about 30 minutes. To fold the rag into a pad with no loose edges, fold the four corners into the middle, then fold again in the same way. Always shake the pad out after use, refold it and store in an air-tight container. If it starts to dry out, simply repeat the lubricating process.

Many wood surfaces contain knots which, if left untreated, leak resin into a painted finish and cause staining. One way of treating these is to chisel out the knot and fill with proprietary filler; an aluminum primer will also successfully seal knots, but both of these methods are obviously only satisfactory under a painted finish. The standard 'invisible' method is to seal the knots and up to about $\frac{1}{2}$ in (1.2 cm) around them with two thin coats of good patent knotting, which is a quick-drying sealer and should be made of pure shellac in methylated spirit.

If you are applying varnish, follow the manufacturer's instructions for sealing the wood — it's usually done by thinning the varnish itself with a specified solvent. If you intend to paint the wood, priming will be necessary first. It is worth using an aluminum primer in areas such as window and door frames, which are exposed to the weather or in contact with wet brickwork, or on woods containing a lot of resin and/or highly contrasting areas of soft, plain wood and hard, resinous grain. Otherwise, use a good, lead-free primer for interior work. A dual-purpose primer/undercoat is now available, which cuts out one process, as well as all-purpose primers that are suitable for both metal and wood, useful on areas containing both materials such as window frames. The consistency of the priming coat is dictated by the absorbency of the wood. On highly absorbent woods, such as soft whitewood, mineral spirits may be needed to help the primer penetrate and seal the surface, whereas hardwoods and burnt-off wood are less absorbent and need a primer consistency giving the greatest possible degree of adhesion. If there is any doubt about the surface, follow the manufacturer's recommendations or take the advice of a reliable builder's supplier.

Paint on metal

The interior metal-work home-owners most commonly

have to deal with is on window frames, radiators and the copper piping found in the majority of heating systems. Modern metal window frames are generally made of *galvanized steel*, which has been factory rust-proofed. The bare, clean surface of galvanized steel, whether new or newly stripped, has a greasy surface, which works against good paint adhesion — although some new metal-work is also pre-treated in the factory to remove this greasiness. The traditional decorator's way of dealing with untreated galvanized metal is to remove all superficial grease with a solvent such as mineral spirits or cellulose thinners, then coat with mordant, a chemical etching solution which gives the metal a tooth. Rinse the metal thoroughly with water after applying a mordant solution to remove any loose material, and allow it to dry before priming. This process can be omitted by using one of the specially formulated calcium plumbate or zinc chromate primers, which also protect metal against rust as long as all traces of dirt, grease and rust are removed first. But not all undercoats adhere well to these primers — one of the rare cases where primer is relevant to the finish, as well as the surface — so follow the manufacturer's recommendations.

Over a period of time, of course, even a galvanized finish can become vulnerable to rust, especially if the paintwork has been neglected until it is badly and extensively flaked, if the surface has been chipped in use or by careless paint-stripping. In these instances the rust can get through to the metal and even work its way along under the galvanized finish. It is absolutely essential to remove all rust before refinishing. There is no doubt that this is a tedious job, but, nevertheless, it must be done thoroughly. The chemical rust-removing solutions are only really adequate for lightly rusted areas and, unless cleaned off carefully, can leave a surface residue that affects paint adhesion. There is still no real alternative to chipping, scraping, brushing and scouring the rust away with any effective combination of knives, scrapers, wire brushes, abrasive paper and steel wool that will reveal a clean, bare, smooth metal.

Should you ever want to paint *aluminum*, you will need to remove dirt and grease by scrubbing it with mineral spirits and a stiff brush. You can obtain a key on it by rubbing with an emery cloth, but it may be quicker to use a proprietary etching primer before coating it with a sealing primer like zinc chromate.

Paint does not stick at all well to *copper* and most purists recommend leaving it unpainted. The least unsatisfactory method (rather than the 'most satisfactory', as hot pipes are always liable to flake) is to tooth and degrease the copper in one operation by rubbing it down with mineral spirits and an emery cloth. Do not rub it dry, for the copper dust will eventually cause grey-green spots wherever it lands. Prime with zinc chromate or calcium plumbate and, when

this is dry, apply an oil-based paint such as gloss directly, without undercoat. Some manufacturers' gloss paints can even be applied without primer, but check the label or ask first.

Some new radiators are pre-finished with stove-enamel, others simply with a flat, white undercoat; existing radiators tend to be neglected, painted some time in the past, but now dirty, dusty, with paint flaking off and spots of rust. Clean and strip the paint if necessary, deal with the rust as described above and then prime with zinc chromate. If possible, get the radiator hand-hot after it has been cleaned to dry off any moisture, and prime while it is still warm. There are special heat-resistant paints that are applied without primers to clean, dry metal. Otherwise, always use oil-based paint — water-based paint will only encourage any vulnerability to rust. Even though color does not seem to affect radiation (whereas, of course, radiation will always affect color in time, especially pale shades), research suggests that flat paints are better heat conductors than gloss. On bare, hot pipes where color is not important — or, perhaps, where a metallic finish is actually acceptable — aluminum paint is by far the most successful, durable finish.

WOODEN FLOORS

Loose floorboards are a common occurence and if this is all that is wrong with a wooden floor, first try hammering in the existing floorboards more firmly with a nail-punch. If this does not do the trick, buy new brads at least ¾in (1.9cm) longer than the thickness of the boards and hammer in two per board in line with the existing brads and ½in (1.2cm) towards the board's center. Neither the new nor old floorbrad heads should protrude above the surface.

Creaking floorboards may need fixing even more firmly with screws. Using 1½in (3.8cm) screws, drill a narrower pilot hole first then, with one knee on the board for weight, drive the screw in firmly until the head is just below the surface. On hardwoods, it may be easier to countersink then fill the hole for the screw-head. Sometimes the creaking may simply be caused by two boards rubbing together. Try silencing them first either by working talcum powder between the squeaking edges or with an aerosol timber lubricant. Alternatively, especially if the sub-floor is concrete, the squeak may be caused by a loose batten or insufficient battening below. You can buy aerosol cans of expanding foam which may be squirted through a hole drilled in the board. Try not to get too carried away as the foam goes on expanding for quite a while before it sets hard, and you could find one problem replaced with another as the board arches above it neighbors.

Warped floorboards may simply need sanding down. If you lie on the floor and look along and across it with one eye, you will be able to see how serious the undulation is. Do not try sanding by hand — rent a sanding machine. the floor is very uneven, some or all of the joists beneath may have bowed or twisted and may need replacing, but if it is just in a couple of places, you will only need to lift and replace the offending boards.

Lifting floorboards

First find out whether the boards have straight or tongue-and-groove edges by slipping a knife blade between the boards. If the blade won't go through, they have tongue-and-groove edges and it may be necessary to cut one board free, after which the other boards can be levered up with the claw of a hammer. But check first to see if there is a 'key' board — often located near the baseboard or a radiator and looking slightly tatty around the edges — which has been lifted before. This will only be helpful if it is near the board you want to replace or if you are renewing the whole floor, but it is worth a try. Otherwise, cut through the length of one tongue with a floorboard saw. This has a specially curved blade so that you can avoid sawing at an angle and possibly through cables and pipes beneath, although it is wisest also to turn off the power supply before you start.

If it is necessary to replace a whole board, which stretches across the width of the room, and/or you don't want to cut it, you may need to prize one or both baseboards off with a crowbar before lifting the board. If only part of its length needs replacing, cut across the board with a padsaw. Cut near but not over a joist. Draw a pencil line as a guide and drill two or three holes close together and at a slight angle to provide a starting point for the padsaw then saw at the same angle, using the back of the saw blade to feel for pipes and cables and keeping the blade high to avoid severing them. Start lifting the board with a hammer and chisel near this cut edge, or near the natural end of a short board. Tap the chisel gently into the crack between the boards. When it is well wedged, life the board by tapping the chisel handle away from it with the hammer, moving the chisel along gradually until you are able to get the claw of the hammer under as well. Then lever the board up and slip the other end out from under the baseboard. If the board needs to be cut in two places to remove it, slip a batten under the free end and cut across the board directly over another joist with the floorboard saw.

Replacing floorboards

The only real difficulty in replacing boards, particularly with older houses, is that you may not be able to match the thickness. If so, buy thicker boards, cut them to size — allowing the extra lengths if they are to slip under baseboards — and cut grooves out to the underside, with a tenon saw and chisel, to fit over the joists. Where part of a board has been cut away and the remaining edge finishes flush with a joist, cut a block 2×1 in (5×2.5 cm) slightly over the width of the board, cut notches to accommodate any pipes or cables and nail it to the side of the joist, making sure the top edges are flush. Put the board in place, drill two holes through the board into the new support and screw the board down. Fix the board to any other joists either with floorbrads that are longer than the originals or with screws and make sure that the new board is flush with its older neighbors.

Closing gaps in floorboards

Generally caused by shrinking, these not only spoil the look of a polished floor, they cause uneven wear on any covering. With narrow gaps — say, less than $\frac{1}{4}$in (6 mm) — try the 'cosmetic' trick of filling them with papier mâché. Scrape the gaps clear of dirt/varnish/wax first and vacuum thoroughly. Shred unprinted paper — lining paper is ideal — into a bucket, pour on small quantities of boiling water at a time and beat the mixture into a thick paste with a piece of scrap wood. Leave it to cool a little before beating in some adhesive powder to make the paste even thicker. Wait until the paste is cold before pressing it well down between the boards with a scraper. Remove any excess paste from the surface and leave it to dry for several days before sanding down with fine abrasive.

Any occasional wider gaps that are evident should be filled with strips of wood, matched as closely as possible to the wood type of the floor. Cut the strips to size, making each strip slightly wider than the gap (it needs to fit tightly to allow for shrinkage), although the thickness should match that of the boards and any joins should occur over a joist. Use a plane to shave away a very small amount from each side of one long edge, insert the tapered edge into the gap and knock the strip into place with a hammer. Use long panel-pins to fix the strip to each joist, but tap them in gently or the wood may split.

If there are gaps right across the floor, you may feel it's worth re-laying the floor to close them. Start by lifting the second board out from the baseboard, leaving the one under the baseboard in place. As you remove each board, take out any nails and scrape the edges so that they are clean and even. Do the same with the top edges of the joists when all the boards are up except the last one under the baseboard on the opposit side. Re-lay the boards from this side. Lay four or five boards first, without nailing them down. Then cut enough scrapwood wedges to allow one pair for every 3 ft (90 cm) of board. The wedges should be slightly thicker than the boards, long enough to span the joists and about 2 in (5 cm) wide at the broad end. Set each pair of wedges in place across a pair of joists and against the last board to be laid. Push a spare, straight board firmly up against the wedges and half-nail it to the joists, so that the nails can be removed. With a hammer in each hand, knock the wedges towards each other so that they push the boards tightly together. Nail the nearest board to the joist with floorbrads about 1 in (2.5 cm) in from the edge of the board, then nail down the other boards. Work across the room like this until you come to the last loose board. If this has a tongue on the edge nearest the baseboard, plane it off. Lay the board in place and hammer a couple of floorbrads into it, over but not into the joists. If the gap between the board and the board beneath the baseboard is too narrow to use the wedges, make a lever by driving a sharpened chisel at an angle into the joist below the board. To force the loose board tight against the last nailed one, pull the chisel upright and hold it in position while you hammer the floorbrads home. Fill the gap with wood.

Levelling wooden floors

Floors that are worn beyond rescue can be levelled with tempered hardboard, either as a firm, flat base for another covering or as a finished floor that can be stained and/or varnished. Lay the hardboard rough side up for covering, smooth side up for clear finishing. Buy hardboard in the standard 8 × 4 ft (240 × 120 cm) sheets and cut it — or have it cut — into 4 × 2 ft (120 × 60 cm) panels. This is the most manageable size and the one that causes least wastage, although, if the hardboard is to be left bare, you may prefer the look of panels 4 × 4 ft (120 × 120 cm). Use special hardboard nails for fixing — these are circular and have a screw-like head without the groove — but don't buy them too long or you will risk puncturing pipes and cables, 1 in (2.5 cm) is quite long enough. For speed you can also use ½ in (1.2 cm) staples or a power-driven staple-gun, which is simpler to rent than to buy. For a 'belt-and-braces' job and a really solid floor, you could also coat the underside of each panel, just before laying, with an all-purpose adhesive, but not of the 'impact' type.

Prepare the hardboard by standing it on its edge for a couple of days in the room where it is to be laid, so that it becomes accustomed to the temperature. The night before laying, dampen it either by dipping it quickly in and out of the bath or by spraying it with a shower-head, then put the panels back in the room, laying them back to back on a flat surface. The dampnesses will help the hardboard mold itself to the contours of the floor. Prepare the floor by filling gaps, sanding any gross unevenness and punching all nailheads below the surface.

Before you begin laying, find the center point of the room by pinning two pieces of string from the middle of opposite walls. The place at which they cross is the center point, so line up your first piece of hardboard squarely under this point. Nail along one edge with ½ in (1.2 cm) nails, 4 in (10 cm) apart, then work your way across the sheet with rows of nails every 4 in (10 cm), starting each row from the middle and working outwards. Lay subsequent sheets in a clockwise direction around this first one, but stagger the joins in one direction only. For looks, you may decide not to stagger them at all, particularly as it is not essential, but it does strengthen the surface. When you reach the edge of the room, shape hardboard to wall contours by placing a complete panel in position against the baseboard, so that it squarely overlaps the nearest nailed panel. To transfer any angle or deviation in the baseboard to the panel, hold a pencil against a rectangular block and move both along the baseboard. Use a similar trick to indent the hardboard at doorways: mark on the panel the distance from the door stop to the edge of the baseboard, cut a rectangular block the width of this measurement and use block and pencil to outline the basic shape of the door frame on the hardboard, filling curves in by hand. In both cases, cut along the pencil line with a tenon saw, put the panel in place against skirting and/or door frame, mark on it the edge of the nearest nailed panel, cut off the excess and nail the panel down. This should ensure that you end up with a pretty neat job.

Levelling or replacing with chipboard

If the boards are badly damaged as well as worn, you may need a sturdier covering of ½ in (1.2 cm) thick, floor-grade chipboard to level them. Follow the same procedure as levelling with hardboard, but cut the standard 8 × 4 ft (240 × 120 cm) sheets in half: 4 × 4 ft (120 × 120 cm) is a size which combines manageability (your needs) with stability (the floor's) and is the best looking option if the floor is to be clear-finished. Use 1½ in (3.8 cm) wide nails all over — about every 8 in (20 cm) will do with chipboard. To prevent this number of nail-heads showing, either punch them below the surface and fill the holes or choose/cut the panels so that they meet over a joist. In this case you can simply fix the panels around the edges, but drill and screw 2½ in (6.3 cm) screws right through into the joists so that they are quite secure.

The measurement of the panels will also be dictated by joist positions if you intend to replace the floorboards with a new chipboard floor since, in this case, it is essential that the panels meet on the center line of a joist. Measure carefully before starting, allowing for the fact that the skirting will have to be removed. Also, although the existing lines of floorbrads will tell you roughly where the joists are, it is safer to take a board up to obtain a really accurate measurement of the distance between the center of each joist. If you are intending to carpet over the chipboard, or lay sheet flooring or tiles, use the largest panel-size the joists will accommodate; if the floor is to be clear-finished, square panels will be more pleasing. Again, the joist will dictate the optimum size of these panels and you may have to sacrifice a degree of economy to aesthetics and be prepared for some wastage. In both cases, you will also need a quantity of 3×2 in (76×63 mm) softwood to fix between the joists and support the panel edges at right angles to them.

With square panels, put the first panel as near to the center of the room as the joists will permit and work in clockwise sequence from that panel, but without staggering the joins. With large, rectangular panels, the distribution of panels will vary with the size and shape of the room. As a general principle, set the long edges on the joists, work from the center of one wall, aim to use as many full-size panels as possible and cut into the panels for extrusions such as chimney-breasts rather than adding bits on for alcoves. The aim is to have as few joins as possible and again you should match rather than stagger joins.

METHOD Remove baseboard and lift floorboards, then remove any nails from joists, scraping and brushing the top edges clean and even. Go around the walls at baseboard level and, if necessary, clean up the bare surface of the plaster with a hammer and chisel so that the chipboard can easily be laid flush to the wall with no lumps or bumps behind. Next, cut softwood supports to fit between the joist at the point where the edge of a panel falls, cutting these accurately.

Lay the first panel in place so that each long edge falls on the center line of a joist and one short edge is against the wall. Mark and cut this edge to follow the contour of the wall and indent for any extrusions. With the cut edge against the wall, mark the position of the other short edge on the joists. Lift the panel away and hammer the softwood supports in position, so that the center of the top edges are in line with the pencil marks on the joist and the top edges of joists and supports are flush. Fix alternate supports by hammering 3in (7.5cm) nails straight through the joist into the softwood supports. Fix the supports in between by partly hammering a nail at an angle into each side of the softwood near both ends, holding the support in position and driving the nails into the joist. Fix supports next to a wall by partly hammering two nails in at an angle near each end of one side of the support, hold the support against the wall and hammer the nails quite firmly into the joists so that they are well held; it is no good if they are likely to fall out easily.

Lay the chipboard panel in place. Round the edges, drill undersize pilot holes for the 2in (5cm) screws, drilling through into joist or supports every 12in (30cm) and countersinking each hole. Insert screws all the way round, driving them half-way home, then go round again and tighten them up. Lay the other panels in the same way, staggering the position of the screws on neighboring ening up the screws afterwards.

Filling, stopping and making good

All these terms are concerned with achieving a firm, smooth surface on either plaster or wood, but they do also have straightforward, specific meanings. 'Making good' usually refers to the repair of plaster or cement surfaces with the same or similar materials; 'filling', or spackling, is just that, usually with one of the proprietary filling compounds. In theory, the different terms arose to provide a demarcation line between work done by plasterer and painter, but in practice, when you are both these, the difference relates largely to the size of the gap to be filled: you 'fill' any defect up to about 4in (10cm) in diameter, you 'make good' larger defects with plaster. 'Stopping' is just another form of filling, usually on woodwork and with a hard material like putty.

MAKING GOOD WITH PLASTER

Unless you really are a dab hand with a laying-on trowel, leave large areas of plasterwork to a professional — it is a skilled job and what you lose on money will be saved on time and temper. But small areas can certainly be tackled with confidence. In almost any plastering job, except superficial dents and deformations, two coats will be needed: the first is the undercoat or rendering, which makes a bond with the wall and is usually a 1:3 mixture of plaster and clean, coarse sand. The top or 'skim' coat gives the smooth, finished surface and is neat plaster. Mix both coats with water to the consistency of dough. There are many different types of plaster to suit different surfaces and finishes, so it may help to describe the job to your local builder's supplier and take some advice. The most suitable all-purpose plaster for the amateur is a moderately burnt anhydrous plaster — it dries slowly, so is good for larger areas and can still be wetted when it is three-quarters set to give it a smooth finish. For a finishing coat on plaster-board use a retarded hemi-hydrate (on top of a rendering layer of rough-textured bonding plaster laid on with a trowel); this can also be used as an undercoat on brick or concrete, but it sets very quickly so it is tricky to use over larger areas. Anhydrous, hard-burnt plasters have an extra-hard, extra-smooth finish — useful for vulnerable external angles. Use plaster of Paris solely for repairing moldings, cornices and other decorative areas of plaster; only mix small quantities at a time and build up defects in stages, as it sets very quickly.

METHOD Remove all loose material with a hammer and cold chisel, roughen smooth surfaces with the same tools to provide a tooth for the plaster (on any parts of exposed or open brickwork you will find that you will have to dig out

½in (1.2 cm) of plaster between the bricks) and clean the whole area with a wire brush. Mix plaster and sand dry in a bucket, then add just enough water to attain the dough-like consistency. Make it slightly too wet if there is likely to be any time-lag before using it, but never mix more than you can use in about 30 minutes. Transfer the rendering to a hawk with a trowel. Wet the area to be worked with a large brush just before applying the plaster and keep the float wet so that it slides easily over the plaster. Hold the hawk squarely against the wall, just below the area to be plastered. Use the edge of the metal float to push the plaster firmly off the hawk and onto the wall, take the hawk away and spread the plaster up the wall with the float. To get plaster onto ceilings, push the plaster to the edge of the hawk and, with the float upside down, slide the edge of the blade between hawk and plaster; or use a large trowel in the same way. When spreading the plaster, hold the blade of the float at an angle of about 30° to the surface — kept too flat and it will stick to the plaster — and fill with this first coat to about ¼in (6 mm) below the surrounding surface to allow for expansion or contraction. To tooth this undercoat, dip the blade of the wooden float in water so that it will slide over the surface giving it a texture; then do the same with the nailed float to score a pattern of deep lines just before the plaster begins to set. Leave this coat to dry for about 12 hours or overnight before applying the final skim coat of neat plaster.

When you apply this finishing coat, follow the same basic procedure but, as you spread the plaster, lighten the pressure and flatten the blade to smooth it flush to the surrounding surface. Polish the plaster before it begins to set by damping it with a wet brush and smoothing over with the float held flat against the surface, but do not over-polish or the plaster will lose the porosity it needs for paint or paper to cling.

FILLING PLASTER AND WOOD-WORK

There are also many different types of filler although the variety is not quite so confusing as plasters, and the choice is more often simply a matter of convenience versus expense. The ready-mixed fillers, usually sold in sealed, plastic tubs, are fine for the occasional small job, but totally uneconomical for major projects. With the traditional, powdery, plaster-based fillers that need mixing with water, the surface must be 'wetted-in' first to help adhesion, whereas the beauty of the newer vinyl-based fillers is that no initial wetting-in is necessary as they have a built-in adhesive quality. They are slightly harder to rub down but still probably the best choice for all-round versatility as they are suitable for most jobs, including any woodwork that is to have a painted finish. One other, rather specialist filler worth considering for fine work is the alabaster-based type. It has a very fine texture and, unlike most other fillers that tend to shrink as they set, this expands and so sits more securely in its niche. It is, however, very porous and therefore needs extra careful sealing when dry.

MIXING Put a small quantity of dry filler onto the palette, make a hole in the middle, load a paintbrush with water and allow it to drip into the hole, mixing the filler into it with a knife until you get the right, smooth consistency. The consistency will depend on the work: you will need a heavy, dough-like consistency for deep, first filling; a medium, spreadable consistency for second filling and for small cracks and holes, like nail or knot holes, and joins in woodwork or between woodwork and plaster. The lightest filling is almost a liquid, but not quite running off the palette and is used for scratches, scores and hairline-cracks on plaster and wood. The less water you add, the quicker the filling will set. As a general principle, mix only the quantity you can use within about 30 minutes but, if there is much filling to do, mix up a larger amount and keep it in a container with a lid to prevent it drying out. It can be reconstituted by adding water, but only up to a point. When it begins to get crumbly and won't blend back into a smooth texture, throw it away and start again with fresh.

METHOD To save time and labor and achieve a smooth finish, use the broadest filling knife the work area will accommodate. The broader the knife, the fewer 'lines' of filler will be left on the surface to rub down — and this will save on filler, too. The simplest way to transfer filler cleanly onto the knife is to scoop it up, wipe it off on the edge of the palette, then take the amount you need from that edge. Use the edge of the palette too, for keeping a clean surface on the knife; you cannot expect to get a smooth finish with bits of filler drying rapidly on the blade. When using a plaster-based filler, dampen the work area with a wet paintbrush just before filling. Then simply pick up the required amount of filler with the knife and press it firmly down into the hole or crack. Do not try to fill deep holes in one operation. Build up the surface with one or more layers of heavy filling, allowing each one to dry before adding the next. Then, depending on how much it has sunk, finish off with a layer of medium and/or fine filling to bring to just above the surface. Finally, using the leading edge of the knife, sweep the blade across the filled area, removing surplus filler and leaving a smooth, finished surface that is flush with the surrounding area.

One trick that will minimize rubbing down is to very lightly go over the surface with a damp paintbrush just before the filler starts to set, but this works best on small areas, in angles or over cracks; on large areas there is a risk of creating 'tracks' or indenting the surface. In some instances, filler can be applied with a brush, particularly on fine joins where timber and plaster meet and also to achieve a really good surface on a new flush door. A sponge is another useful aid for filling awkward cracks or down the sides of a door; sometimes a finger is the best tool, especially for smoothing on filler in internal angles or rounding the edge on external angles, but preferably protected by a rubber glove (use fine hairdressers' gloves for a sensitive touch). This type of filler should always be sealed or primed before painting to prevent a dull spot showing on the finished coat. Perfectionist professional painters will tell you that the art of building up a surface is to fill, sand and coat each layer of filling. It depends on your standards and your patience.

Filling woodwork for a clear finish
Woodwork There is a variety of fillers that can be used on wood intended for staining, varnishing or polishing. Both clear and tinted wood fillers are available, usually in the form of an oil-based paste, and they can be applied either with a knife or thinned about half and half with mineral spirits and brushed on: apply a generous coat, leave it to set about 10 minutes until the surface has dulled and follow this by rubbing first across the grain, then with the grain with a ball of lint-free rag. But don't sand smooth until the filler is dry. If you have difficulty matching the color of filler to wood, tint the filled patches carefully, when dry, with scumble or artists' oil colors, diluted with mineral spirits to the right tone. On prominent, filled areas where color matching is difficult or unsuccessful, try faking a knot.

Wood that's to be stained can also be filled with a proprietary, plaster-based filler, but to prevent the filled patches absorbing more stain than the wood and appearing darker, rub down with fine abrasive paper and apply one thin coat of knotting before staining. This darkening effect can actually be quite effective when used on hardwoods with open grain or pores (it may even be tinted first to get a greater contrast) as long as the surface is well rubbed down so that the filler remains only in these parts of the wood.

STOPPING
Putty is the most common material used for stopping nail holes, cracks and gaps, especially on and around windows and external doors, since it is oil-based and water-resistant. Clear cracks and crevices of all loose material before stopping. Always use putty *after* priming bare woodwork with aluminum primer to protect it from condensation and the elements, and to prevent it from absorbing the oil from the stopping, which would then dry out and crack. The stopping must also be pressed very firmly into any cavity — if you leave air underneath it may move as the air expands or contracts. As with filler, do not attempt to fill large holes in one go; fill half-way to allow for shrinkage while it is drying. When dry, fill again, remove any excess from the surface and leave to dry completely before sanding and painting.

SANDING CEILINGS, WALLS AND WOODWORK
The three main purposes of sanding are to make rough surfaces smooth, to tooth very smooth surfaces for paint or varnish and to remove unwanted surface finishes. Although most of us still tend to refer to all types of abrasive paper as 'sandpaper', this paper no longer exists in the true sense of the word. Even the ubiquitous pale brown paper is coated with silica, not sand, and beyond this there is now a considerable variety of different grit coatings, including glass, garnet, emery, silicon carbide and aluminium oxide. Some are general purpose and some have a limited, more specialist use. The choice depends on the work surface and, as with other tools, it helps considerably to have the right abrasive for the job.

Coated papers
The basic and most inexpensive, silica-coated and glass-coated papers are only used for dry-rubbing on plaster and bare or primed wood. They clog very quickly — which makes them less suitable for 'sticky' surfaces like paint and varnish — and consequently have a very limited life. Painted surfaces are, in fact, the most difficult to rub down successfully without scratching. Fine garnet paper is the traditional choice for 'flatting down' between coats of gloss paint and varnish, but this is rapidly being superseded by aluminum oxide paper and especially by the 'wet and dry' waterproof papers, usually coated with silicon carbide. The great advantage of these is that they can be rinsed clean without the backing paper softening or the grit coming away, so that the higher cost is more than offset by greater efficiency and a much longer life. A further advance on these is the new type of self-lubricating paper, impregnated with an anti-clogging ingredient. All you need do is tap the grit surface from time to time to free any clogging particles, and without water there is less mess and no waiting around for the surface to dry before carrying on with the next stage of the job. Bare metal is best sanded — to degrease it and give it tooth — by either aluminum oxide paper, emery paper or an emery cloth, the latter being used either dry or with a spirit-based lubricant for best effect.

There are a great many grades of abrasives and different manufacturers use different methods of coding. The basic, silica-coated papers tend only to come in about six or seven grades, which may be coded from 'No 3' for coarse to '00' or '000' for very fine, the finest sometimes being called 'flour' paper. Some manufacturers code with letters — F for fine, M for medium, C for coarse and S for strong. The grading of other papers is generally coded by the number of holes per square inch of mesh through which the grit will pass. Thus 16 to 40 are generally designated coarse, 50 to 100 are medium, 120 to 240 are fine, 280 to 320 are very fine and 360 to 600 are usually described as 'polishing' papers. Some manufacturers will also code the grit number on the back of the paper, and in this case, the higher

---

☐ **Don't** use coarser abrasive paper than is necessary, it won't do the job faster and may damage the surface.

☐ **Always** sand wood, including plywood, with the grain and other materials in one direction only. The only exception is where you're trying to roughen a very hard, smooth surface.

☐ **Only** hold sandpaper in your hand for rough work. Otherwise, to sand evenly, wrap it round a block — flat for flat surfaces (ideally padded with a $\frac{1}{4}$in (6mm) thick strip of foam or rubber) and round for round surfaces. Keep the pressure even if you want a flat surface and be extra careful not to sand edges harder than the middle, it's easily done. If you're sanding by hand, fold the torn strip in three again so that you get the most even pressure and economy of wear. Don't sand too hard in any one spot, especially on painted/varnished surfaces — this will generate heat, the finish will soften and come off and the abrasive paper will clog.

☐ **Sanding dry** has the fastest cutting action, but **wet sanding** with waterproof or self-lubricating paper lessens the likelihood of scratching the surface, especially important on high-quality painted or varnished finishes. For smooth sanding with waterproof papers, either dip the paper in soapy water or sprinkle the surface with it.

---

that number, the coarser the grit. The backing paper, too, is occasionally coded — grade A for hand rubbing to grade D for hand or mechanical sanding. This is helpful when choosing which paper to buy.

If you would rather not stock up on a large range of abrasive papers, a good, all-purpose selection could include grades 30, 60, 100 and 150, buying especially fine papers when they are needed. Buy abrasive papers in the standard 9 × 11in (23 × 28cm) sheets and for economical use fold and tear in three on the long edge.

Other abrasives
Most of these are the traditional craftsman's methods which have largely gone out of use, but they are still worth knowing about for special finishes.
Steel wool is the exception as it is still in general use and in various grades for rubbing down paintwork, toothing smooth surfaces for paint, such as galvanized steel or alumimum, or removing rust. The fine grades are especially useful for obtaining an unscratched, smooth surface on clear-finished wood. Use it wet or dry, but, when removing rust, use kerosene or mineral spirits as a lubricant rather than water. Wear gloves to prevent particles from getting into your hands and don't use steel wool on surfaces regularly exposed to water or coated with a water-based finish such as latex paint or water-based stains, as some of the particles are bound to get embedded in the surface and will rust and stain the finish. In these cases it is worth using the more expensive bronze wool instead to prevent this problem.
Pumice stone is usually used today only at the washing-down stage on shiny surfaces, like gloss-painted walls, to provide a tooth for subsequent coats of paint. Buy it in a round lump, usually about 5in (13cm) across, saw the lump in half with an old saw and rub it on a wet flagstone to prepare it for use. Rub the two halves together from time to time to prevent them clogging with hard particles and scratching the surface — the noise they make will tell you whether the grinding surface is clean.
Powdered pumice is just what it says. The traditional way of using it for wet-rubbing is to blend it with oil (vegetable oil is adequate) and apply it with a piece of 1in (2.5cm) thick felt to get a smooth finish between coats on high quality paint and varnish work; you end up with a lustrous gleam rather than gloss. Any surface on which it is used must be wiped over thoroughly afterwards with a lint-free rag, then washed with turpentine to remove the grit — which is why waterproof and self-lubricating abrasive papers are now generally used instead.
Rotten-stone is the perfectionist's finishing process after 'felting down' with powdered pumice or sanding with waterproof abrasive paper. Using a lint-free rag and linseed oil as a lubricant, the surface is flattened with powdered rotten-stone and then polished with dry flour. to give a smooth finish.

Power-assisted sanding
Sanding machines take much of the sweat out of one of the more exhausting decorating jobs. The main drawback is that no one machine will do all types of work, so that it is often better to rent rather than buy.
A rotary disc-sander, frequently sold as an attachment to an electric drill, is one of the least satisfactory machines. Anyone who's ever used one — especially for the first time

— has had circles scored in some surface or other to prove it. It is almost impossible to achieve a smooth, flat surface with them, so they should only be used for rough work like scoring previously painted hard surfaces or first-cutting on new woodwork.

A belt sander is similarly not suitable for finishing work. This has a continuous belt of abrasive paper which rotates like the 'wheel' of a caterpillar truck and it cuts very fast. However, the heavy duty models can be very useful for removing tough finishes or taking an initial layer off flat, wood surfaces.

An oribital sander has a flat, rectangular pad that moves in a circle and is undoubtedly the best general purpose machine for painting and decorating as it can be used to rub down bare woodwork, metal and plaster as well as painted surfaces. The job it won't do satisfactorily is the fine finishing of wood surfaces that are to be stained or clear-varnished — the small, circular scratches will show through the finish.

A straight-line sander, on the other hand, is just what's needed for fine sanding, so that you can work only in the direction of the grain. These are ideal for finishing and can be used for rough work, too, although they are a bit slow. **Dual-action sanders** have both an orbital and straight-line facility, and if you are intending to buy, this would be the best choice. One other consideration is how much wet work you expect to be doing. Sanding machines are powered either electrically or by compressed air; the pneumatic models are safer where there is water present.

FLOORS

Floor-sanding is in a different category from other work, if only because of the size of the job. There is no doubt that sanding is by far the most practical way of resurfacing a wooden floor as it will cut through paint and varnish, remove most stains (really stubborn ones can be lifted with wood bleach) and leave the floor clean, smooth and ready for finishing. The only real disadvantage is the dust, and although most sanders come equipped with a dust-bag, much of it still escapes. Close doors, open windows and cover everything in the room with dustsheets before starting, wear a mask yourself and first sweep, then vacuum thoroughly — which means — walls and ceiling as well as the floor.

Two types of machine are needed: a *drum-sander* for the main bulk of the work and a small *rotary edger*. Any areas that cannot be reached by these two will have to be done by hand with a scraper, *abrasive paper* and/or *steel wool*. When using the drum-sander, as with any other type of sanding machine, start the motor before lowering the abrasive surface onto the floor and keep the machine moving as long as this is in contact with the surface. If the machine is kept still while the motor is turning, it will very quickly cut

a depression. Work from coarse to medium to fine abrasive sheets with both drum-sander and edger. Always make finishing cuts with the grain, although exceptionally rough and uneven floors can be sanded against the grain first. Block floors are harder to sand than boards because the grain runs in two directions. It may be wiser to call in a professional firm to do this type of job, but if you're set on doing it yourself, go over it twice only, using medium paper on the drum-sander and then fine paper on a rotary sander. It will probably still be necessary to finish some individual blocks by hand.

Abrasive papers for sanding machines
Similar types of abrasive paper to those used for hand-rubbing are either made for or adapted to machines. The most versatile — and therefore most commonly used — is the aluminum oxide paper, which, when used on a machine, is suitable for bare, primed and painted wood as well as bare and painted metal. Self-lubricating sheets are also available for machines, particularly effective on varnished wood and painted metal surfaces. As a general principle, you can usually use abrasive papers a few grades coarser on machines than you would use when rubbing down by hand.

Moldings

CLEANING The delicately detailed plaster-work of a cornice or ceiling rose may be totally obscured by a build-up of layers of old paint, and although removing it is one of the decorating jobs most demanding of patience, it is also one of the most rewarding as you start to uncover its original beauty. If there is molding work to be done, tackle it before anything else in the room, as it can create quite a mess. Try cleaning it with water first by sponging a small test area. If the paint comes off easily on the sponge, thoroughly wet the molding by spraying it with a plant-spray. Leave it to soak for about 30 minutes, then gently scrape away the paint with whatever selection of tools will fit into the crevices without damaging the plaster — combination shave-hook, putty knife, kitchen knives, toothpicks, screwdrivers. Keep brushing the cornice clean of loose material as you work, so you can see exactly how you're doing; again, use whatever brushes will reach into the cracks — an old, part-worn artists' paintbrush, an old toothbrush, even one of those soft wire brushes used for cleaning suede. If the paint refuses to come off with water, use either a chemical solvent paint remover or a hot-air stripper. If you must use a blow-torch, to save 'blowing' the plaster, too, concentrate on the detail work first, doing a little at a time, and return to the straighter, plainer areas once the plaster has cooled.

APPLICABILITY OF ABRASIVES

	Glass Paper	Garnet Paper	Aluminum Oxide Paper	Lubrisil Paper	Emery Cloth	Waterproof Silicon Carbide
HAND — USE on these surfaces						
Plaster	Excellent		Good			
Bare wood	Excellent	Excellent	Acceptable			
Primed wood	Excellent	Good				
Painted wood	Good		Acceptable	Acceptable		Acceptable
Bare metal			Excellent		Excellent	
Painted metal	Acceptable		Excellent	Acceptable		Good
Varnished wood		Acceptable	Acceptable			Excellent
MACHINE — USE on these surfaces						
Bare wood			Excellent			
Primed wood			Excellent			
Painted wood			Good	Good		Good
Bare metal			Excellent			
Painted metal			Excellent			Excellent
Varnished wood			Good	Excellent		

Excellent (☐☐☐)   Good (☐☐)   Acceptable (☐)

Restoring

To what degree you attempt to restore a damaged molding yourself depends largely on confidence and the will to experiment. The material to use is plaster of Paris, because it sets in a matter of minutes so you can build up layers quite quickly. It is also just about possible to carve it with a spatula (artists' trowel) when it has set. If there are areas of 'enrichment' missing (these are the detailed bits on a molding), build up the depth in layers of about $\frac{1}{4}$in (6 mm) at a time allowing them to harden before applying the next layer. The trick is to overfill with the last layer, let it harden, then carve the shape into it — and although you can sand the shape with fine abrasivepaper, it is better to use a knife at this stage. If you over-carve, it is always possible to fill and start again. Once you are happy with the basic shape, 'set' it with a coat of sealer or thinned latex paint. Then, if necessary, fill any remaining defects with ordinary filler, and make sure that you let this set, then sand smooth before continuing.

If you are feeling adventurous but unsure of your artistic ability, try taking an impression of the molding with papier mâché and then using this as a mold for the plaster of Paris, greasing the mold lightly to stop it sticking. If there is a whole piece of cornice missing, there are two possible restoration methods, which may be tried separately or together. Make up an L-shaped hardboard frame, rough side inwards, so that its length fills the gap exactly and the width of each arm of the 'L' is about $\frac{1}{4}$in (6mm) less than the height and depth of the cornice respectively. Support the frame with battens at each end. Build up layers of plaster of Paris within the frame until it is filled and the ends are flush with the hardboard frame, leaving a smooth, flat plaster surface bridging the two long edges and standing proud of them by about $\frac{1}{4}$in (6mm). Take a profile of the cornice with a piece of card and a pencil and from this cut a zinc template. Draw the template along the face of the new block of plaster to carve in the profile and then add the enrichments by hand. When the block is complete it can be drilled and screwed into place, hardboard and all. The alternative to making a frame is to build up the missing chunk straight into the angle between wall and ceiling, using the template to profile it *in situ*, but this can be an awkward angle to work at, especially if there is any complicated detail.

If the mere prospect of restoring fills you with foreboding there are, of course, other ways out. You may be able to buy some of the more classic designs of plaster detail from a plaster-work company. The cornice itself may be a classic, in which case the company will be able to provide you with replacement sections. And if it isn't, they will come and take impressions themselves and make up a new section: more money but, I can assure you, a lot less time and trouble.

INDEX

ACKNOWLEDGMENTS

The majority of pictures in this book were specially commissioned by Quill Publishing Limited and shot by John Heseltine, Ian Howes and John Wyand. However, there were other contributors as follows: Karen Bussolini; Michael Dunne; Christine Hanscomb; Ken Kirkwood; Tom Leighton; Mark Ross Photography Inc; Spurgeon Walker Associates; John Vaughan; Elizabeth Whiting & Associates.

Author's Acknowledgments

The author wishes to thank the following individuals and companies without whose invaluable advice, assistance and, in some cases, extreme patience, this book would simply not have been possible. Top of the list must come J. Martin Brooks for moral support and exceptional tolerance while this fascinating but totally time- and attention-consuming project took six months out of both our lives. Very special mention to David Afia, Keith Hoy, Tony Jenkins, Lindy Rose, Len Woodard and Fred Woodhams for being prepared to pass on, in some instances, a lifetime's knowledge of their respective subjects. And sincere thanks to all the others who have contributed their time and expertise, including: Abis & Co (Birmingham) Ltd; Afia Carpets Ltd; J. W. Bollom & Co Ltd; British Adhesive Manufacturers Association; The Building Centre; Carson Hadfields; Copley Mouldings; Crittal Windows Ltd; Crown Decorative Products Ltd; Derek Eddowes/Polymers Paint Colour Journal; English Abrasives Ltd; Evode Limited; Peter Farlow; Hamilton & Co (London) Ltd; Imperial Chemical Industries plc; Lyn le Grice; Marrable & Co Ltd; F. T. Morrell & Co Ltd; W. H. Newson & Sons Ltd; Paint Manufacturers Association; Paint Research Association; Pob Savident Ltd; J. H. Ratcliffe & Co (Paints) Ltd; Fred Rich; Sterling Roncraft; Technical Paint Services Ltd; Thomas & Wilson (Plastering) Ltd; Wheatlands Journals Ltd; Wicanders (GB) Ltd; L. G. Wilkinson Ltd; John Windsor; Winsor & Newton.

Quill would also like to extend special thanks to the following: Caroline Clifton Mogg; Sheppard Day Designs Ltd; Dulux; Sheila Fitzjones, PR Consultancy; Formica Ltd; Carl Freudenberg; Daphne Graham of The Rug Shop; Home Improvements Guide; Martex, West Point Pepperell; Muraspec; Osborne and Little; Polycel Ltd; Brian Rose; Rounton Design; Michael Ryan; Leonie Seely; Smallbone of Devizes — specialists in design and handicraft kitchens; TV AM Studios.

Further reading

For those who want to 'read on', here are some of the books I have found particularly useful.

Bishop, A. and Lord, C. *The Art of Decorative Stencilling* (Viking Press, New York; Thames & Hudson, London, 1976)
Cobb, Hubbard H. *How to Paint Anything* (Macmillan, New York; Collier Macmillan, London, 1974)
Hurst and Goodier *Painting and Decorating* (Charles Griffin, 9th Edition, 1980)
Johnson, L. *The Decorator's Directory* (Michael Joseph, London, 1981)
O'Neil, I. *The Art of the Painted Finish* (Morrow, New York, 1971)
The Practical Painter and Decorator (Odhams, London)
(NB This book is out of print, but try libraries or second-hand book shops as it's a comprehensive, although rather wordy and confusing, volume full of traditional techniques.)